For all colleagues in the probation service, whose
work with offenders, though constantly under
threat from political forces, has done much to give
hope for the future and keep the heart of the
criminal justice system alive.

WORKING WITH OFFENDERS

New Directions in Social Work

Series Editor: Antony A. Vass

Recent changes in the training requirements for social workers and allied professionals have prompted the need for a set of textbooks to address issues of knowledge, skills and practice as well as contemporary social debates. *New Directions in Social Work* is designed to cater for students' academic and professional needs, and, in the context of new course guidelines, will address specific areas of practice such as working with offenders; social problems and social policy; children and young people; families; people with specific needs; and working within the community.

WORKING WITH OFFENDERS

Issues, Contexts and Outcomes

edited by
Tim May and Antony A. Vass

SAGE Publications
London • Thousand Oaks • New Delhi

First published 1996

 SAGE Publications Ltd
6 Bonhill Street
London EC2A 4PU

SAGE Publications Inc
2455 Teller Road
Thousand Oaks, California 91320

SAGE Publications India Pvt Ltd
32, M-Block Market
Greater Kailash – I
New Delhi 110 048

British Library Cataloguing in Publication data

A catalogue record for this book is
available from the British Library

ISBN 0 8039 7621 6
ISBN 0 8039 7622 4 (pbk)

Library of Congress catalog card number is available

Typeset by Mayhew Typesetting, Rhayader, Powys
Printed in Great Britain by Redwood Books, Trowbridge, Wiltshire

Contents

Notes on Contributors

Gwyneth Boswell is a former probation officer and senior probation officer responsible for student training in Merseyside where she worked for 19 years. Since 1990 she has been a Lecturer in Probation Practice at the University of East Anglia. She has researched and published in the field of violent young offenders and is the co-author of *Contemporary Probation Practice* (1993) and the author of *Young and Dangerous* (in press), both published by Avebury.

Bob Broad is Senior Research Fellow at De Montfort University. Before that he was Development Manager (Research, Training and Policy) with the Royal Philanthropic Society, a voluntary organisation helping young people at risk in London and the South East. Prior to that he worked in probation in London and as a Social Work Lecturer at the London School of Economics and the University of Central London. His most recent books include *Punishment Under Pressure: The Probation Service in the Inner City* (1991), Jessica Kingsley; *Practitioner Social Work Research in Action* (co-edited with Colin Fletcher, 1993), Whiting and Birch; and *Leaving Care in the 1990s* (1994), Royal Philanthropic Society.

Karen Buckley has been a Senior Probation Officer in Nottinghamshire for 20 years. She gained a BA Economics, an MA in Women's Studies and an MPhil in Social Administration. She writes, lectures and occasionally publishes on gender, sexuality, and masculinity. Her current research interest is on the needs of women clients of probation and working in partnership.

David Denney is Reader in Social Policy at the Roehampton Institute, London. He has written extensively about the probation service and discrimination within social work. He has also worked in London and Birmingham as a probation officer. His publications include *Racism and Antiracism in Probation* (1992), Routledge.

Ellis Finkelstein is currently Lecturer in Criminal Justice at the University of Central England. He previously was a Lecturer in Probation Studies at the University of East Anglia. Before the late start of an academic career he worked as a probation officer for 16 years during which time he earned a PhD from the University of Bristol. His publications include *Prison Culture: An Inside View*, Avebury, among others on the prison and probation services. His research interests are focused on probation and prison management; other research is currently being undertaken on probation hostels.

Daniel Gilling is Lecturer in Social Policy and Criminal Justice at the University of Plymouth. Having completed his PhD research on crime prevention at the University of Manchester, he has written articles and papers on the subject.

Simon Holdaway is Reader in Sociology in the Department of Sociological Studies at Sheffield University. A former police officer, he has researched and published widely on many aspects of policing, especially police and race relations. His book, *The Racialisation of British Policing* will be published in 1996 by Macmillan. His chapter in this book is based on an ESRC-funded project about the work of probation committees.

Tim May is Lecturer in Sociology at the University of Durham. He is the author of *Probation: Politics, Policy and Practice* (1991), Open University Press; *Social Research: Issues, Methods and Process* (1993), Open University Press; and the co-editor (with Dick Hobbs) of *Interpreting the Field: Accounts of Ethnography* (1993), Oxford University Press. He has published articles on such subjects as criminal justice and power, identity and organisational change. He is currently working on a social theory book (Open University Press), a philosophy and social research book (UCL Press) and researching organisational changes in social services.

Mike Nellis is Lecturer in Probation Studies at the University of Birmingham. He was a social worker with young offenders and has written widely on youth justice, probation training and the cultural politics of penal reform. He is currently undertaking ESRC-funded research into probation, penality and the voluntary sector.

Peter Raynor is a former probation officer and is currently Reader in Applied Social Studies at the University of Wales, Swansea where he has particular responsibility for probation training. He has published extensively on probation issues, including the books *Social Work, Justice and Control* (1985 and 1993), *Probation as an Alternative to Custody* (1988) and *Effective Probation Practice* (1994, with David Smith and Maurice Vanstone).

David Smith is Professor of Social Work at Lancaster University, where he has taught since 1976. A former probation officer, he has researched and published widely on criminal justice issues and social work with offenders. His most recent books are *Effective Probation Practice* (1994, Macmillan) with Peter Raynor and Maurice Vanstone; *Understanding Offending Behaviour* (1994, Longman) with John Stewart and Gill Stewart, and *Criminology for Social Work* (1995, Macmillan). He is the co-editor of *The British Journal of Social Work*.

Antony A. Vass is Professor of Social and Penal Studies and Head of the School of Social Work and Health Sciences at Middlesex University. He is professionally qualified in social work (probation studies) and has worked in various fields of social work as research officer, community worker, probationer psychologist and probation officer. He has published numerous articles on penal policy, criminology, probation and social work policy and practice. He is the author of a number of books including *Alternatives to Prison* (1990), Sage; editor of *Social Work Competences: Core Knowledge, Values and Skills* (1996), Sage; and is currently co-writing a book with Geoffrey Pearson on *Social Problems and Social Policy*, Sage.

Brian Williams is Lecturer in the Department of Applied Social Studies at Keele University. He has researched and published widely on probation work in prisons and the community. His most recent book was on probation values and he is currently working on research into victims of crime and anti-racist probation practice.

Acknowledgements

Every life event goes through a 'career'. It has its developmental stages and its ups and downs. The same with writing a book. For the authors or editors its completion normally heralds a sigh of relief that it is all over. For readers, they remain oblivious of the book's career and all they are interested in is whether the book has something to offer to them. Its background and stages of development are of no consequence to them – and rightly so.

However, because of its nature and the complexity of negotiating diverse areas of interest and bringing together material from diverse sources for the purpose of producing a book which readers (academics or practitioners) would find directly relevant to their interests and needs, this life event was beset with considerable difficulties. The finished product belies the amount of time spent in discussing, amending, formulating and reformulating and correcting drafts.

We believe that the book will generate readers' interest and will be considered informative and relevant to their requirements. However, we could not have reached this stage had it not been for a number of people who have helped us over a period of two years.

First, we would like to thank our colleagues and contributors, who have had to cope with our constant demands for improvements to the text. Their staying power was impressive (and on occasion we thought, putting it modestly, *our* staying power, in the face of repeated troubles, verged on the 'superhuman' (if not 'supernatural')). Secondly, we would like to thank Gillian Stern, Commissioning Editor at Sage, whose patience with us and her support throughout the project proved to be a major contributory factor for the satisfactory completion of the book. We are grateful to her for her help and advice. She is more than just an editor, she is a friend. Thirdly, we need to express our appreciation to two other friends and colleagues at the School of Social Work and Health Sciences at Middlesex University. We thank Jenny Bonfield, in the School Office, for the many drafts she had to translate onto Wordperfect, the many hours spent retyping drafts, correcting and redrafting, printing and reprinting. And never once did she say, at least to our face, 'enough is enough!' But it is all over now and thanks to her the book is together as it should be. And we thank Kate Jarvis, the School Secretary, for advising on the 'technical' aspects of the operation, allowing and making time available (in an extraordinarily busy office), and for her overall support.

Finally, we are grateful to Rosemary Campbell, Jane Evans, Karen Phillips and copyeditors at Sage for their support and advice.

Introduction: The Shifting Sands of Working with Offenders

Tim May and Antony A. Vass

In times of rapid change there is a tendency to return, with an air of nostalgia, to past times where certainty and predictability were thought to reign supreme. When it comes to work with offenders, the form of this nostalgia is a yearning for the age of rehabilitation. At that time casework with individual offenders in the community was offered on the basis that psychological maladjustment was a prime cause of offending behaviour. This approach was enabled by a series of post-war Criminal Justice Acts and an organisational culture into which new recruits were socialised.

When the above view is placed under the critical scrutiny of a historical context (McWilliams, 1986), it is not so clearcut. Slowly, but surely, more overt elements of control entered this relationship. Under political, economic and social pressures, successive governments modified approaches to offending behaviour, with implications for the professional status of practitioners. Empirical studies and working parties began to question the efficacy of the therapy approach as a means of reducing the levels of crime in general and recidivism in particular. In addition, the levels of discretion afforded to individual workers were often found to lead to injustices (Bean, 1976), though other authors argued that without discretion structural and organisational anomalies surface which turn the administration and enforcement of laws and regulations into an intractable problem (Vass, 1982; Wilkins, 1980). Concerns then focused not just on the outcomes of working practice, but also on the actual mode of working with offenders. Local discretion, whether organisational, at team or individual level, found itself under scrutiny. Criticisms from the right and the left of the political spectrum, coupled with social and economic change and with 'law and order' high on the political agenda, led to an age of rapid and chaotic changes in legislation. With this came uncertainty for the practitioner.

New ideas on working with offenders emerged in this climate, with the elements of control, a push towards community penalties and their costs relative to prison brought to the forefront of debates (see, for instance, Haxby, 1978; McWilliams and Pease, 1990; May, 1991a; Spencer and Edwards, 1986; Vass, 1990). In the 1970s the innovation was community service, and in the 1980s it was day centres. In the 1990s, with a plethora of penalties, it is 'tagging' which comes to mind as a new innovation. It combines elements so dear to the modern penal climate, claiming a relative low cost with punishment taking place in the community (in practice, however, it is problematic – see Vass, 1989).

Pressure groups and professional associations have also offered their own solutions. A whole new nomenclature has arisen which has not only involved 'cost' but also the idea of 'tough' and 'demanding' regimes. In these changes we witness the undermining of the professional–therapeutic movement in working with offenders and the beginning of the punishment–administrative phase (Lacey et al., 1983; May, 1991a, 1991b, 1994; Vass, 1982).

A new breed of management has arisen in response to these changes who are keen to demonstrate the effectiveness of their working practices. This requires an anticipation of the political agenda. This shift was epitomised by the Association of Chief Officers of Probation (ACOP) document *More Demanding than Prison* (1980). A new sentence known as the 'community restitution order' was offered which emphasised both its demands on offenders and its relative low cost in comparison to prison. This, surely, was attractive to a government concerned to appear both 'tough' on offenders and cost-conscious when it came to the public purse. This gesture proved to be inadequate, however, and was not enough to satisfy the search for tougher regimes. As a result, a gradual but determined official effort to shift policy and practice away from the 'social work' base of probation work to an ethos more conducive to administering surveillance and control was evident. Thus the discretionary element in working with offenders, which permitted an expression of tolerance (Downes, 1988; Vass, 1990: 115–31), needed to be curtailed. This required more centralised government control over the local services, as epitomised by the *Statement of National Objectives and Priorities* (Home Office, 1984; Lloyd, 1986) and attempts to alter the face of probation training to suit the prevailing ideology (CCETSW, 1995; Dews and Watts, 1994; Doherty et al., 1994; Home Office, 1995a, 1995b).

With the legislative and organisational props being slowly removed, the individual practitioner felt lost and confused. The search for a new set of values to inform practice was on (McWilliams and Pease, 1990; Mathieson, 1987). Recruits entered who trained in new methods and brought with them different ideas and working philosophies. Whilst different methods of working with offenders always existed, they now did so with very different causes and consequences. Groupwork was compared to individual work and innovative projects arose to deal with specific issues, for example motor theft and drug and alcohol addiction. This creative energy of practitioners cannot be underestimated, even if it is not tapped as often as it should be, but it never seems to be enough to satisfy the political masters. To compound this further, law and order has, as always, been used as a convenient instrument for political expediency. The only problem is that the goalposts keep moving and the rules of conduct are never explicit, or if they are, they do not last long enough – as new rules are introduced to supersede them – to be properly learned and accommodated. As a result, it all takes place on shifting sands. Just witness the sharp changes from the Criminal Justice Act 1991 to the Criminal Justice and Public Order Act 1994 specifically in terms of the push towards community sentences in the 1991 Act and now the policy of 'prison works'. Similarly, proposals always seem to raise their heads for more punishment in the community in order to tackle the latest target of moral condemnation.

In order to perform their job effectively and competently all of this means that individual practitioners can now assume even less and yet have to know even more. For instance, they now have to understand some or all of the following: the values which both inform and are built into their daily practice; the nature of their accountability and to whom they are accountable; the agendas of the people with whom they deal in different organisations; the organisational and team objectives which they are meant to pursue in their everyday working practice; the means by which their work is being assessed and with what effect; and the types of skills and training which they require to execute their duties, to say nothing of attempting to help people in difficult and demanding situations and dealing with lots of paperwork (see Vass, 1996b).

Notwithstanding the above matters and irrespective of old or new methods of work or ideological niche, the knowledge, skills and context of work requiring appreciation and understanding by practitioners can be grouped under three main headings. These are the *issues* which inform practice; the *contexts* in which working with offenders takes place; and, third, how the *outcomes* of good practice can be built upon, which includes taking lessons from past experience, examining the role of different agencies, as well as understanding the pros and cons of evaluating outcomes. It is these areas of focus which have provided the basis upon which this book has been designed. In so doing, it meets the need of being able to critically evaluate knowledge and its relationship to practice.

In considering these three areas, we assembled a team of authors who are known to possess expertise in matters which we wished to cover. Thus, under the heading of *issues* in working with offenders the following areas are covered: probation training and its future (Mike Nellis); the skills and competences needed in effective working practice (Gwyneth Boswell); the form and role of anti-discriminatory practice (David Denney); the nature and substance of autonomy and accountability (Ellis Finkelstein); and masculinity and perspectives on causes of offending with implications for new ways of working (Karen Buckley).

Under the heading of the *contexts* of work with offenders, we have included chapters on: probation committees, which are often neglected in terms of their role in the management and organisation of the probation service (Simon Holdaway); the practice and presentation of pre-sentence reports (David Smith); the nature, debates, aims, outcomes and implications of community penalties (Antony A. Vass); and working with offenders in transition from prison to the community (Brian Williams).

Finally, in considering the ways in which the *outcomes* of good practice may be built upon, we sought to learn from past initiatives, as well as reflect upon future prospects, together with the ways in which innovative schemes may be evaluated. For those reasons, there are chapters which cover partnerships in working with offenders and the role of non-statutory agencies in dealing with crime (Bob Broad); the practice and effectiveness of crime prevention schemes (Daniel Gilling); as well as how the outcomes of working with offenders, in general, may be evaluated (Peter Raynor).

It must be stressed that whilst chapters have been arranged in an orderly fashion to address the main areas of concern and practice, these areas are inter-linked and should not be seen as separate entities. Thus, for example, although there is a chapter on training issues, the issue of training runs explicitly or implicitly through the rest of the chapters. Similarly, although there is a distinct chapter on evaluating effectiveness (Chapter 12), the concept of effectiveness surfaces in strong and explicit terms in another chapter (Chapter 8) and, in general, is deeply rooted in the content and aims of the book as a whole.

A further qualification must be made. The book does not, nor do we pretend that it does, cover all areas of working with offenders. That is an impossible task in the space available. However, we cover those areas which are of central importance to the altering roles of practitioners and which, in our view, remain the cornerstone of competent knowledge and practice and, at the same time, the source of friction between competing and contrasting theoretical and practice perspectives. It is a question of knowing not only the different methods of working with offenders, but also the conditions under which one does so and the issues which both surround, inform and challenge practice, for these cannot be separated. This book is intended to fulfil part of this function and is designed to be read as a whole, or as a series of individual contributions to a growing knowledge base and practice.

We are confident that the book addresses particular needs in both areas of knowledge and practice and informs current and future debates about the role of the probation service in the criminal justice process and, indeed, the shape and character of criminal justice in general.

We hope you will find it of help, whatever your interests (academic or professional) in the subject of working with offenders may be.

References

ACOP (1988) *More Demanding than Prison*. Wakefield: Association of Chief Officers of Probation.

Bean, P. (1976) *Rehabilitation and Deviance*. London: Routledge and Kegan Paul.

CCETSW (1995) *DipSW: Rules and Requirements for the Diploma in Social Work*. Paper 30 (rev. edn). London: Central Council for Education and Training in Social Work.

Dews, V. and Watts, J. (1995) *Review of Probation Officer Recruitment and Qualifying Training* (The Dews Report). London: Home Office.

Doherty, G., Pierce, R. and Smith, L. (1994) *Review of the Diploma in Social Work* (Part II). London: Central Council for Education and Training in Social Work.

Downes, D. (1988) *Contrasts in Tolerance: Post-war Penal Policy in the Netherlands and England and Wales*. Oxford: Clarendon Press.

Haxby, D. (1978) *Probation: A Changing Service*. London: Constable.

Home Office (1984) *Probation Service in England and Wales: Statement of National Objectives and Priorities*. London: Home Office.

Home Office (1995a) *Review of Probation Officer Recruitment and Qualifying Training: Discussion Paper by the Home Office*. London: Home Office.

Home Office (1995b) *Review of Probation Officer Recruitment and Qualifying Training: Decision Paper by the Home Office*. London: Home Office.

Lacey, M., Pendleton, J. and Read, G. (1983) 'Supervision in the community – the rightings of wrongs'. *Justice of the Peace*, 147 (8): 120–3.

Lloyd, C. (1986) *Response to SNOP: An Analysis of the Home Office Document, 'Probation Service in England and Wales: Statement of National Objectives and Priorities' and the Subsequent Local Responses*. Cambridge: Institute of Criminology.

McWilliams, W. (1986) 'The English probation service and the diagnostic ideal', *Howard Journal of Criminal Justice*, 25: 241–60.

McWilliams, W. and Pease, K. (1990) 'Probation practice and an end to punishment', *Howard Journal of Criminal Justice*, 29: 14–24.

Mathieson, D. (1987) 'This is the heart of probation', *Justice of the Peace*, 151 (29): 458–60.

May, T. (1991a) *Probation: Politics, Policy and Practice*. Milton Keynes: Open University Press.

May, T. (1991b) 'Under seige: the probation service in a changing environment', in R. Reiner and M. Cross (eds), *Beyond Law and Order: Criminal Justice Policy and Politics into the 1990s*. London: Macmillan. pp. 158–85.

May, T. (1994) 'Probation and community sanctions', in M. Maguire, R. Morgan and R. Reiner (eds), *The Oxford Handbook of Criminology*. Oxford: Oxford University Press. pp. 861–88.

Spencer, N. and Edwards, P. (1986) 'The rise and fall of the Kent Control Unit: a local perspective', *Probation Journal*, 33: 91–4.

Vass, A.A. (1982) 'The probation service in a state of turmoil', *Justice of the Peace*, 146: 788–93.

Vass, A.A. (1989) 'Tagging: Spiderman looks at the web of electronic tags', *Social Work Today*, 20: 20–1.

Vass, A.A. (1990) *Alternatives to Prison: Punishment, Custody and the Community*. London: Sage.

Vass, A.A. (1996) *Social Work Competences: Core Knowledge, Values and Skills*. London: Sage.

Wilkins, L.T. (1980) 'Sentencing guidelines to reduce disparity?', *Criminal Law Review*, April: 201–14.

PART I

ISSUES

1

Probation Training: The Links with Social Work

Mike Nellis

In 1971 the newly formed Central Council for Education and Training in Social Work (CCETSW) took over responsibility for the training of probation officers in England and Wales from the Home Office, and incorporated it within the broader context of generic social work training (Younghusband, 1978: 132–44). Such training was undertaken at both universities and polytechnics (via post-graduate and/or graduate and non-graduate routes) and also in further education. Probation students were never more than a small percentage of the students for whom CCETSW was responsible, and (on post-graduate and non-graduate courses) were sponsored directly by the Home Office, rather than being given a grant. Not all such courses had sponsorships allocated to them, and for most of this period the numbers on each course were very small. Non-sponsored students on all courses were in varying degree free to develop interests in probation, and between a third and a quarter of local probation services' annual recruits have always been non-sponsored because the number of sponsorships has never, until recently, matched or exceeded their staffing needs.

Until the commencement of the 'punishment in the community' debate (Allan, 1990; Home Office, 1988, 1990a, 1990b, 1991), there had been no overt questioning of the CCETSW-based arrangements, although a hidden history of criticism from all points on the political spectrum within the probation service can easily be unearthed. The overt questioning, when it began, was seen by many to threaten the so-called 'social work identity' of the probation service at a time when the government was seeking to push the service into a more correctionalist and controlling stance towards offenders, and away from a concern with their welfare and rehabilitation. It was widely assumed within the probation service (and more self-interestedly) by CCETSW and on social work training courses that it was only by reasserting the 'social work identity' of the service that the unwelcome elements of government policy could be resisted.

The critique of 'punishment in the community' which emerged from the National Association of Probation Officers (NAPO) and other social work interest groups, whilst acknowledging the dangers of an untrammelled just deserts philosophy and toughened community penalties, tended to underplay the broad potential of the proposals – a clear government commitment to reducing the use of custody, sentencing restrictions and, possibly, a more central role for the probation service. Conversely, it overplayed the extent to which generic training, based upon proximity to other types of 'social worker', and the dubious premise that a large proportion of knowledge, values and skills was common to them all (CCETSW, 1991: 8), had equipped probation officers to work creatively and effectively in the criminal justice arena (NAPO, 1987). Although CCETSW (1991: 37) has repeatedly paid lip service to 'the encouragement of a thoughtful, critical and analytical approach appropriate to a trained professional', the fact is that it had never in reality fostered a deep understanding of criminal justice policy, or the possibilities of probation practice within it.

'Punishment in the community' also threatened the traditional understanding of social work because, in line with wider government hostility to almost all forms of professional autonomy, it questioned the need for professional training as such, both for some front-line staff and for some managers. It preferred the case management approach, the orchestration of services from a variety of agencies and greater use of ancillary or volunteer staff (Home Office, 1990b). Some service managers were quick to see that such moves away from professionalism and towards managerialism, independently of the shift towards punishment, had, as Matheson (1992) suggested, 'tremendous implications for staff recruitment and training' (see also Fellowes, 1992). In future different types and levels of probation worker may be trained (and retrained) in institutional frameworks quite different from those prevailing now, and employment-based routes, which are already being experimented with (Blumson and Kerr-Rettie, 1993), may assume greater importance. Such routes do not preclude contact with educational institutions, but the insistence that all training should be 'practice-led rather than academic-focused' (Blumson and Kerr-Rettie, 1993) may mean that the intellectual independence and critical spirit once associated (rightly or wrongly) with university-based professional education will steadily be devalued, perhaps even in universities themselves as they succumb to government demands for more narrowly conceived vocational relevance (Jones, C., 1989).

We believe that the collapse of the structures of probation training which were set in place in 1971 was long overdue and, in a sense, inevitable. However, as the chapter will argue, it remains to be seen whether the structures which replace them prove better or worse. While it is far from certain that it will come about, a form of training which fosters intellectual independence in general and criminological sophistication in particular would have much to commend it, and it is with the historical precedents for such a view that we shall begin.

The evolution of criticism

Although the Morison Report (Home Office, 1962) had emphasised the similarity between probation and other forms of social work, misgivings that the move into CCETSW would lead to inadequate representation of probation interests in training were voiced from the outset (Bochel, 1974: 234). It cannot be denied, even without hindsight, that the merging of training courses alongside the continued existence of a separate probation service and a separate professional association, NAPO (when both had had the option of merging with new generic organisations), was more than a little anomalous. The early 1970s saw a number of new developments in probation (for example, community service, day training centres) as well as proposals for a more overtly correctional role for the service (Advisory Council on the Penal System, 1974), all of which raised 'questions of offender behaviour and social workers as agents of social control' which some probation managers (see Fulwood, 1975: 40) felt were not being addressed on the new social work courses. Cohen also wished that social workers and probation officers in this period would 'stop trying to resolve the contradictions between their dual commitment to welfare and control by pretending that the control element does not exist' (1975: 83); and Fulwood himself was prescient enough to recognise that unless attention was paid to such issues, 'we may exacerbate a situation in which the control aspect of our work may either atrophy or *become more akin to the American-style surveillance*' (1975: 40; emphasis added).

CCETSW did not entirely ignore these developments and in the wake of the Criminal Justice Act 1972 it established a working party on probation training. Interestingly, its report tilted away from genericism, listing 15 distinctive features about probation, as opposed to 11 features which it had in common with other areas of social work (CCETSW, 1978). There is, however, no evidence of this report having had much impact on courses, or even for that matter on CCETSW itself.

Thus, although a handful of courses continued to enjoy a reputation for emphasising probation in their curricula, the majority paid little attention to developments in the service and in criminal justice policy, or to criminological theory and its application to practice. Such omissions did not go unnoticed. On the basis of a small survey in the early 1980s, Fielding reported that over and above probation officers' criticisms that their training had not equipped them with an understanding of law relevant to practice, nor of agency procedures, nor to write social inquiry reports (SIRs), their training failed in a much more basic sense: it did not 'provide scope for grounding probation in its place in the criminal justice system' (1982: 11). Blythe and Hugman (1982: 74), two probation officers writing in one of the loosely styled 'radical social work' texts from the same period, reinforced this: 'Probation students', they observed, 'being often in a small minority on a course, may have offered to them material which is of only secondary use or importance, and on the other hand, may have insufficient attention paid to areas of concern specific to their agency', and added:

> It is our impression that penal policy and criminology feature insufficiently for the probation student and that, in the light of the probation service's current disarray with respect to purposes and functions, these are also matters of serious concern; we cannot hope that the service will move intelligently and purposefully forward if its staff are not well informed about the many and complex issues arising from the 'death of rehabilitation' and the now acknowledged failure of almost all measures to reduce or prevent crime.

Given these impressions, it appears that thorough teaching on such basic material as criminology and penal policy, and its relationship to probation practice, was at best discretionary and at worst ignored on the courses for which CCETSW was responsible. The solution to this lack of relevant and critical knowledge was seen to lay primarily with the courses not the agencies. Thus, for instance, Fielding (1982: 18–19) writes:

> The answer is not necessarily to lengthen practice placements but to consider how the college part of the basic qualifying course can better incorporate the material officers see as relevant. . . . Academic institutions should concentrate on helping future officers to achieve an understanding of their place in the criminal justice system, as well as seeking to equip them with practical skills.

Insofar as CCETSW began a major review of training in 1982, driven largely by employer dissatisfaction with the skills and aptitudes of newly qualified social workers (Jones, C., 1989; Parsloe, 1990), it should have been possible to incorporate such criticism. Yet in the course of the next five years, one senior magistrate apart (Ralphs, 1985: 6–7), no distinctive probation voice was to be heard commenting on curriculum issues (except to reinforce genericism and to emphasise the importance of flexible skills at the point of qualification: Scott and Dawes, 1986). Thus, in the initial outcome of the review, *Care for Tomorrow* (CCETSW, 1987), a large number of 'shortcomings' in social work education were acknowledged, but lack of attention to probation matters was not one of them. Worse still, in the débâcle which followed government rejection of the review's key proposals, this omission was hardly noticed.

However, not all of the review proved controversial. CCETSW's attempt to create a new qualification, modelled on the 'academic' virtues of the Certificate of Qualification in Social Work (CQSW) and the 'vocational' virtues of Certificate in Social Service (CSS) (a non-professional qualification introduced in 1975), and to bring about greater employer control by the creation of formal partnerships between agencies and academic institutions was welcomed by government. Its proposal to extend the period of qualifying training from two to three years (with the third year devoted to a specialism) was not, and the government rejected it, ostensibly on cost grounds. Alone among 'social work' interest groups, NAPO had wisely opposed the move to three-year training, believing that the confirmation year for newly qualified probation officers (which had no equivalent in other social work agencies) already constituted a type of third year.

The silence of probation interests in this debate warrants comment, for although it may have been difficult, in a wider political climate hostile to professional social work, to give due consideration to the critique mounted by Fielding, Hugman and Blythe, its neglect points as much to intellectual failure as to defensiveness and prudence. Generic thinking, on courses, in the probation service, as well as in CCETSW itself, had fostered a hubristic confidence in its own infallibility, a trained incapacity to grasp or even see the need for revisions to the knowledge and value base even as the work of the service changed. In 'a climate unfriendly to open and rational discussion' (Timms, 1991: 206), in which even the 'successful revolution' (Jones, D., 1989) in juvenile justice passed it by, CCETSW appeared to have lost whatever critical edge it might once have had, and began to involve itself, again rather uncritically, in new developments in the field of vocational training. As these developments have specific importance to the future of probation training we shall deal with them at some length.

Competence and managerialism

During the 1980s a broadly based coalition of employer and government interests began to develop and standardise new forms of assessment and accreditation in vocational training generally, which shifted attention away from curricular knowledge ('programme content') towards assessable outcomes (Home Office, 1994b; Smithers, 1993). The new approach had started piecemeal in the Manpower Services Commission in the mid-1970s, and had influenced debates about the training of teachers, social workers and youth workers in higher education even before the formation of the National Council of Vocational Qualifications (NCVQ) (De Ville Report, 1986) gave legitimacy and momentum to it. Several commentators have since sought to anticipate the impact of NCVQ's increasingly powerful Care Sector Consortium on social work education (Issit and Woodward, 1992; Jones, C., 1989; Parsloe, 1990). Much less attention has been paid to the fact that within the Care Sector Consortium a Criminal Justices Services Group was formed quite early, recognising from the outset, in a way that CCETSW has not formally done until recently, the distinctive elements of 'social work' with offenders.[1]

NCVQ's model of vocational training (or learning) ostensibly involves little more than the specification of particular competences, the standards of performance required and the devising of means to assess when they have been achieved. Competences themselves are derived from a functional analysis of the tasks required by an organisation or scheme, and for any given occupation they are split into five levels, the uppermost of which denotes a professional or managerial qualification. In its pure form the competence-based approach gives no guidance as to how knowledge and understanding are acquired by learners; it assumes that such knowledge is embedded in the action and that its presence can be inferred (by an approved appraiser) from the performance. In a training context it is claimed that this permits flexibility in the design of curricula, but, more significantly, the approach facilitates workplace learning and employment-based routes to competence, simply by assessing and accrediting what staff learn on the job from their peers and managers, without necessarily experiencing formal or semi-independent training courses. Experienced grassroots practitioners, whose lack of academic credentials may hitherto have limited their career progression, may benefit from this development, and it is largely in terms of equal opportunities that NCVQ has been made to seem anti-élitist and politically progressive.

Notwithstanding these basic claims, there is far more to the story.

The emergence of NCVQ must be seen in the political context of government policy to subordinate education and training in general to the discipline of the market, and to place 'employers in the forefront of any training system' (Issit and Woodward, 1992: 43), including those traditionally rooted in higher education. Definitions of competence are therefore unlikely to be neutral, but will reflect both the increasing ascendancy of employer interests in education and training institutions, and the more managerially defined forms of practice now required in most public sector organisations. The competence movement should in fact be seen not as an autonomous 'vocational' development, but as both the consequence and counterpart of the expansion of corporate management in these organisations (Hood, 1991; Raine and Wilson, 1993). This development, in turn, has its roots in the centralisation of state power and the increased control and surveillance of local agencies in the health, welfare, education and criminal justice fields (Wilding, 1992). The link between competence and managerialism emerges from Howe's (1991: 214) observation that:

> Managers seek to create regular and predictable task environments so that routine responses can be prescribed in set situations. They attempt to define both the work and the way the organisation's functionaries will react. Thus, in a pre-defined situation, the social worker is expected to act in a pre-programmed way. Work becomes both fragmented and standardised. By increasing rules, routines and procedures, the manager diminishes the area of professional discretion available to the social worker.

In organisations dominated by broad considerations of efficiency, effectiveness and economy, and permeated by notions of procedural correctness, training comes 'to be viewed not as a frill of an organisation, but rather an essential component that facilitates the effective operation of the agency' (Carter, 1991: 19). If certain objectives and targets are to be achieved, on a certain timescale, staff must act in pre-programmed, standardised ways. Competences identify these correct forms of practice and make it easier for managers to monitor if, and how, agency functions are being carried out. However, as the American literature on the subject makes abundantly clear, securing competence involves more than simply equipping staff with practical skills. As Carter (1991: 17) writes:

> . . . training should go beyond pre-service orientation to the employee's particular job assignment and provide an opportunity for the organisation to impart its mission, values, vision and culture. Too often in corrections, only worker skills are targeted for training, and the organisation misses a significant opportunity to communicate its vision and mission.

In organisations which do operate in this way, the distinction between management and training, as separate activities, begins to blur. Easterby-Smith et al.'s (1991) description of management as being 'essentially about controlling, influencing and structuring the awareness of others' could just as easily be said about the new forms of training, in which there is indeed a strong element of what Chomsky (1989) calls 'perception management'. Competences in the British public sector as a whole are embedded in a series of discourses (for example, consumerism and client rights, equal opportunities and quality assurance) which attempt to legitimate managerial authority in the eyes of the practitioners, and which may even be accepted as valid rationales by the practitioners themselves. With only these moderately important, but spuriously uplifting discourses to make sense of their world, practitioners can easily lose sight of the real political context in which they operate, the actual agendas of the organisations for which they work, and experience the reduction of their own role to that of functionary.

The greater the managerial influence, the greater the demand for uncritical employees and for competence-based practice. Although NCVQ was not involved in replacing CCETSW's failed three-year qualification with the new, two-year Diploma in Social Work (DipSW), the increasingly manager-influenced model of practice adopted by training councils led CCETSW (1989, 1991) voluntarily towards what might be called a *partial* rather than a *complete competence model* of generic practice. Agency influence over particular courses was again ensured by partnership with academic institutions, but specialisation was reduced to a 'particular area of practice', of which probation could be one, in the second year of the new DipSW course. The knowledge, values and skills identified as important in the DipSW were not, however, tied precisely to practice competences, and the competences themselves, rather than being derived from functional analysis, were derived from generic ideology and unrelated to the tasks of particular agencies. In reality, although the competences to which CCETSW and the courses attached special importance – those concerned with anti-oppressive, anti-discriminatory and anti-racist practice (the centrepiece of the DipSW value base) – were broadly welcomed and overdue, they came for a variety of reasons to be associated with quite simplistic concepts of power and language and deeply contestable notions of cultural purity and ethnic absolutism. The attempt to introduce into the core of social work and probation training hitherto ignored and neglected issues concerning general and specific forms of oppression was by no means representative of the most serious intellectual (and political) work going on in this field (Gilroy, 1992; Modood, 1992). The binding of anti-discriminatory competences to a well-intentioned but theoretically flawed perspective on race stands as a warning less of the rampant 'political correctness' feared by the Right (Pinker, 1993) and more of the inevitable simplification of complex issues, the eradication of ambiguity and legitimate differences of belief, that a managerially inspired, competence-based approach demands, especially when it is applied to values.

Towards punishment in the academy?

The launch of 'punishment in the community' coincided with the *Care for Tomorrow* (CCETSW, 1987) débâcle and the Home Office announced its new initiatives on probation training just as the DipSW was being established. CCETSW's lack of attentiveness to the issues raised by Fielding, Blythe and Hugman had left it ill prepared for the many legitimate criticisms of the Coleman review (Home Office, 1989) and the conclusions of the consumer research from the University of East Anglia (Davies, 1989a, 1989b). Coleman, an Oxford academic, was hired by the Home Office to ascertain the extent and quality of specialist training on the then 40 courses (in 32 institutions) which received sponsorships, and, in a more covert way, to appraise the degree of fit between them and the emerging policies on probation. Any recommendations he made were to be constrained by the need to preserve a reasonable spread of courses across the country, and to retain places for graduate, non-graduate and mature entrants.

His report was deeply critical, concluding that with the exception of a few universities and ex-polytechnics which offered probation training of a high standard, 'probation training is invariably taught as a minor specialism within generic social work' (Home Office, 1989: 11). He also added that even those courses with distinct probation streams (covering probation practice, court work, criminology, sentencing and related areas of law) devoted only 11 to 28 per cent of teaching time to it (Home Office, 1989: 12). Attention to the effectiveness of interventions with offenders was very variable and 'the impression was sometimes given that even to think in such terms was improper, and might have implications incompatible with social work values' (Home Office, 1989: 13). He criticised the Probation Inspectorate for its failure to exert more influence over training, proposed several possible ways of redistributing sponsorships, and identified the need for a training syllabus for probation students.

Martin Davies's 'receiving-end' research, based on a survey of the attitudes of main grade officers (some long-serving, some newly qualified) towards their training, complemented Coleman's essentially top-down approach and drew a number of similar conclusions about the relative insignificance of probation-specific material on social work training courses. Despite Davies's own known preferences for a correctional orientation in probation (Davies, 1982), he acknowledged that the survey respondents did not want to be trained as other than social workers: 'they just want to be *better* trained for the social work function of "holding the balance" in the penal system' (Davies, 1989b: 18; emphasis in original). This meant 'more teaching on criminology, penology, probation practice and the principles of sentencing' as well as more classroom teaching from practitioners (Davies, 1989b: 1).

The response from many social work educators to both Coleman and Davies was largely negative (Collett, 1989; Sanders, 1990; Williams, 1989). Both were seen as right-of-centre academics and therefore at odds with the progressive spirit of social work. The fact that some of the same issues had earlier been raised in left-of-centre critiques was conveniently ignored. Parsloe (1990, 1991) was particularly dismissive of Coleman for questioning genericism, and seemed to imply that if social work training was not about welfare, then it must be about punishment, with no conceptual middle ground between them. Although both Coleman and Davies were undeniably concerned with improving practice, the claim that they wanted training to produce 'robot-like workers, uniformly competent, moving within precisely calculated legal parameters with militaristic precision' (Hardiker and Willis, 1989: 328) seriously misrepresented their views. This diatribe was a caricature of what a complete competence model might entail, but it underplayed the extent to which both Coleman and Davies saw an autonomous role for a broadly conceived administrative criminology (that is to say, a criminology concerned with policy and practice) whose humanising values, though limited, are not to be underestimated (see, for example, Garland, 1992), within the academic curriculum.

In implying, furthermore, that the generic status quo had been a major source of intellectual and spiritual sustenance for the probation service, a tremendous conceit was in fact at work in many social work educator's criticisms. In the period during which CCETSW has had responsibility for probation training, major debates on probation theory and practice have been initiated at least as often from outside social work courses as from inside them (see, for instance, Bottoms and McWilliams, 1979; McGuire and Priestley, 1985).

DipSW, 'Annexes 2 and 3' and after

The Green Paper *Supervision and Punishment in the Community* (Home Office, 1990b) subtly distanced probation practice from 'social work' by emphasising the need for changes to working methods and new skills in addition to basic social work expertise (Home Office, 1990b: 3). As such, it went on, 'there will always be limits imposed by the requirements of training geared to general social work' (Home Office, 1990b: 9, 18), although it was prepared to consider that the new DipSW 'may facilitate better specialist training'. It mapped out four possible options, two of which involved remaining within the DipSW framework (temporarily or permanently), and two of which involved creating separate, specialist qualifications (either in tandem with an improved DipSW or as a complete replacement for it). These latter two options, which were acknowledged to be costly, were seen to require the devising of 'a training syllabus tailored to probation needs' which would then be 'put out to contract with universities and polytechnics' (Home Office, 1990b: 9, 18). Comment was also made on the need for improved induction training for the newly qualified, in-service training for established staff, management training for seniors and above, and a form of NVQ-based accreditation for ancillary staff, 'demand for whom is unlikely to slacken' (Home Office, 1990b: 9, 22).

Although no formal public commitment was made to any of these, in effect the Home Office opted to remain within the DipSW, albeit with larger numbers of sponsorships concentrated in fewer courses, and on the understanding that each course incorporated a training syllabus. In respect of sponsorship distribution, Coleman's ideal of a very small number of centres of excellence was deemed impractical at this point, not least because geographically restricted sites would limit access to students. The number of courses with probation streams was, however, reduced from 40 to 29 (19 universities, 10 polytechnics) in 1990, rising subsequently to 30. The total number of sponsorships was raised to 465 (approximately), although these were still insufficient to cover the service's annual recruitment needs.

A 'training syllabus' emerged in the form of two letters from CCETSW ('requirements' and 'advice') following a workshop initiated by the Home Office in March 1990. The 'requirements' (CCETSW, 1990a) set out basic principles, and outlined the knowledge, values and practice competences necessary for probation practice. Under knowledge, it listed offending behaviour and criminology theory, the organisation of the criminal justice system and the probation service, penal policy, law, civil work and anti-discrimination. Under values it cited understanding of the potential conflict between organisational, ethical and personal values; the promotion of policies and demonstration of practice which were non-discriminatory and anti-oppressive; and the management of tension between the demands of the court, the offender, the probation service, the family and the community. Under practice competence, it listed courtwork, assessment, supervision of offenders in the community, monitoring and anti-discrimination. The 'advice' specified that 'a minimum of 35%–40% of the content of the taught programme' be devoted to 'matters relevant to practice in the justice system' in both years (CCETSW, 1990b).

The requirements were a very positive development. They distinguished between basic principles, knowledge and values, on the one hand, and practice competence, on the other, and, even more so than the DipSW itself, did not specify a tight relationship between the two. Knowledge was considered important in its own right and not simply as the means by which specific competences could be informed. The requirements permitted debate, critique and argument about essentially relevant criminological and penal topics in a way that strict emphasis on competences alone would not, and allowed for the intellectually desirable possibility that different students would develop different, but equally valid orientations to crime and its control. Crucially, there was nothing overtly or covertly punitive about the requirements. Yet it cannot be said that they were particularly welcomed by CCETSW, or even by some courses, and even when they were incorporated as Annexes 2 and 3 in a new edition of Paper 30 (CCETSW, 1991), the Director's introduction made light of them.

While the annexes began to inform (in quite diverse ways) the construction of the DipSW around the country, other developments were taking place in the probation service which suggested that they might only be provisional. It was reckoned by most concerned parties that debates on the new Criminal Justice Bill and on 'national standards', which were only just beginning in 1991, would have implications for how competence was defined, and, in addition, the various calls for qualifying probation training to devote more time to crime prevention (Geraghty, 1991: 22), drug abuse (Advisory Council on the Misuse of Drugs, 1990: para. 35) and courtwork (Stone, 1989: 74) suggested, between them, that the 35 to 40 per cent maximum teaching time agreed by CCETSW and the Home Office would soon need to be increased upwards, or separate training arrangements be considered.

Further impetus for change came from a 'scrutiny' of in-service training in the probation service (Hadjipavlou et al., 1991), which suggested that the 60,000 person days per annum then being devoted to this were unrelated to the developing needs of the service (especially in regard to retraining staff to implement the forthcoming legislation) and criticised the lack of a national framework for such training. In order to remedy this situation, Hadjipavlou et al. (1991) recommended the establishment of a National Training Unit, which would replace (without requiring their immediate closure) the remaining Regional Staff Development Units. Each local probation service would in future be required to submit a detailed 'annual training plan' to the Unit, in which their training proposals would be tied more clearly than hitherto to official objectives, priorities and standards. In an effort to facilitate the development of a 'training continuum' stronger links were urged with qualifying training, and following the example of NCVQ and CCETSW the service was encouraged to adopt a competence-based approach in all its training strategies.

The Probation Training Unit (PTU) was established in June 1992. It was made part of the existing Home Office Probation Service Division and received its strategic guidance from a Probation Training Advisory Group chaired by a senior civil servant. Its mission was 'to promote good practice and the efficient use of resources in all aspects of the training and development of probation staff and trainees' (Home Office, 1992b: 1). As expected, it made an early commitment to a competence-based approach, candidly acknowledging that whatever benefits such an approach may have for individuals, its primary justification was managerial (Home Office, 1992b: 1):

> Competences geared to organisational aims and objectives ensure that staff training and appraisal are integral to service delivery rather than tacked on as an optional extra. . . . Effective services depend upon effective staff, and with a competence-based approach those who hold the purse strings can see a clear relationship between spending on staff development and results which are directly linked to organisational goals.

The content of qualifying training was just one among many aspects of the Unit's initial work. Its main foci were the revision of the sponsorship scheme (which resulted in probation students receiving essentially the same type of grant as other CCETSW-funded students) and (collaboratively with CCETSW) the monitoring and assessment of probation streams, the development and accreditation of practice teaching, the accreditation of agencies as 'competent workplaces' and the development of post-qualifying studies; plus the implementation of Hadjipavlou et al.'s (1991) 'scrutiny', middle management training and training for the performance appraisal of serving staff. Consideration was given, jointly with CCETSW, to revising Annexe 2 both to take account of the Criminal Justice Act 1991 and national standards, and to recast it in terms of competences and performance indicators, although this was delayed by the absence of a clear official view of what the core competences expected of basic grade probation officers actually were. A private consultancy was commissioned by the PTU to undertake this work (Joss, 1994).

In the course of 1993, however, there was a change in the climate in which the probation service and the PTU worked, as various items of public and political concern coalesced into a new law and order crisis. This, coupled with autumn expenditure cuts, meant that the Criminal Justice Act 1991 and 'punishment in the community' were never effectively implemented in the form intended. Crucial sentencing restrictions were quickly repealed and harder-line ministers at the Home Office sought to promote a crude 'prison works' philosophy. The range of responsibilities envisaged for the probation service were not ostensibly curtailed, but pre-sentence reports ceased to be mandatory, the overall ideological significance of community penalties was diminished and the proposed expansion of bail hostels was threatened. Probation training was directly affected by these developments. The 485 sponsorships that had once been envisaged for the 1994–5 period (Home Office, 1992a: 26) were lost, and the existing 465 cut back to 300, leaving approximately 10 students to each of the 32 courses. This reduction was a precursor to the Home Office announcement (guided by Treasury demands to save resources) of a 90-day review (Home Office, 1994a) which aimed to enlarge the range of entry routes into probation and to align training with the newly developed competences for basic grade officers (Home Office, 1994b), whose publication had itself been long delayed apparently because of ministerial resistance to residual traces of 'social work' in the early drafts. By the time the review began in May 1994, CCETSW's own first major review of the DipSW (forced on it by the government) was already well established: significantly, it was being undertaken in collaboration with the ever more influential Care Sector Consortium, 'in order', said CCETSW (1993), 'to establish more clearly the relationship of the DipSW to the framework of Vocational Qualifications'.

Thus 1994 was a time of great uncertainty for the probation service and for probation trainers. The Home Office reviewers consulted widely, if somewhat hurriedly, but never managed to convince probation or social work interests that their final report would be properly independent of ministerial desires to steer the probation service in a correctional direction. Their *Emerging Findings* (Dews and Watts, 1994) acknowledged widespread support in probation services and among sentencers for the improvements that had already occurred in the DipSW framework, but pleased no one because they then went on to propose quite fundamental changes. These included: first, devolving funding to consortia of local probation services, so as to better match training to the recruitment needs of the service; and, secondly, the proposal of a new qualification, tentatively called the Diploma in Probation Work, achievable for the majority through a direct entrant route using customised training packages designed according to trainee's previous experience, and for a minority ('of the calibre to lead change in probation practice') on a post-graduate course in '5 or 6 centres of excellence' in higher education.

Despite – or perhaps because of – the hostility which these views provoked among probation interest groups and their supporters no change was made to the Final Report (Dews and Watts, 1994), which simply reiterated them, with more detail and more supportive arguments. It was, however, published in conjunction with a government policy statement which in effect ruled a number of Dews and Watts' proposals out of court (Home Office, 1995a). This statement not only severed links between probation training and social work (which many had feared was inevitable), but it also made clear that it wanted to sever all formal links with higher education. Employment-based training was to be the only option from 1996 onwards, with services being funded to buy in whatever training they needed, from whatever source.

A strong coalition of probation, social work, educational and sentencers' interests formed to combat these proposals, taking account of the consultation period allowed by the Home Office (from March to May 1995), but no one was really confident that the policy statement was other than a fait accompli. The coalition campaigned for probation training to remain linked to social work training and to stay within higher education, and despite its manifest deficiencies chose to stay with the 'revised DipSW' that had emerged from the CCETSW review (CCETSW, 1995). Although this had been conducted with much greater openness than the Home Office review, the place of probation within the next DipSW did not emerge clearly until the end of the review period. Then, it became clear that despite having reduced generic work to six basic competences (into which, it was claimed, the Home Office probation competences could easily be fitted), CCETSW was committed to a strong and distinct 'probation pathway'. It acknowledged a distinct 'knowledge base', but not a distinct 'value' or 'skills base' for probation practice, a stance which neither met the challenge of the Home Office's arguments, nor did justice to what probation officers actually do.

Resources for a journey of hope

The Home Office decision to press ahead with its original plan regardless of the resistance (Home Office, 1995b), allows little cause for optimism. Rather than attempt to 'second guess', we will seek instead to outline the ingredients of a critical approach to probation training and leave readers to judge for themselves how well the new arrangements live up to them.

Certain things are clear. As we move towards 2000 probation training should reflect the fact that the service is much larger, more internally complex and has been moved into 'a much wider area of operation' (Home Office, 1990b: 8) than it was when CCETSW was first established. If 'more than ever before the probation officer will have to function as part of a criminal justice agency delivering a service to the criminal justice system as a whole as well as to individual offenders' (Home Office, 1990b), probation officers and those working with offenders will need knowledge and understanding of how 'the penal–welfare complex' the panoply of institutions (statutory, voluntary, private and informal) involved in the regulation of criminal and deviant behaviour (Garland, 1985), actually works, over and above mere understanding of 'competences' in working with offenders and knowledge of agency policy. It is beyond argument that much of this latter work, though informed by knowledge, is best learned in practice, on placement, and there is much to commend in recent CCETSW, Home Office and agency attempts to develop partnerships and improve opportunities for practice learning. There is also room, so long as its imperfections are recognised (Issit and Woodward, 1992; Kemshall, 1993; Smithers, 1993), for further experiment with competence-based assessments of placements, but in respect of the training courses as a whole a partial-competence model should be followed which does not bind the intellectual contribution solely to issues of immediate practice relevance. The intellectual contribution should foster uncompromising honesty, a critical consciousness and 'a spirit of scepticism, doubt and uncertainty' (Cohen, 1990: 18), political virtues which CCETSW, the Home Office and many courses seem mistakenly to have regarded as incompatible with committed professional action against oppression and discrimination.

It is in fact a moot point whether a more criminologically specialised probation training would best develop under CCETSW's auspices, or whether new partnerships (overseen by the Home Office Probation Training Unit or the Probation Inspectorate) should be made with university departments whose intellectual and practical input would have little taint of genericism (Nellis, 1993). Modern criminological theory has been distilled and combined from a range of social sciences in a way which has *prima facie* relevance to the practical, professional and political challenges faced by the probation service. Criminology and penology knowledge long ago broadened out from a positivistic concern with the causes of crime, and, from a variety of theoretical perspectives, they now take, without losing sight of aetiological questions, the products, practices and ideologies of legal, penal and welfare institutions as their object of inquiry. In their administrative, sociological and psychological forms they seek to serve, consolidate and reform these institutions, and to develop and evaluate new forms of effective intervention. There is a place for this in the training of probation officers, tied to traditional 'social work' emphases on methods such as counselling, groupwork and community work, but it does not exhaust all that criminology and penology could contribute to the culture and, indeed, the identity of the service as a whole.

Since its radicalisation in the 1960s and its continual engagement with the theoretical concerns of social science in its broadest sense, the study of criminology has become 'a subject of intellectual richness' (Cohen, 1990: 13). It has grown more aware of its own history and its complex relationship to crime control agencies, and has been drawn on by social movements (some of which involved 'social work') which 'were directed at weakening, by-passing or even abolishing conventional structures of legality, punishment, control and treatment' (Cohen, 1990: 14). Bottoms (1987: 263) sees criminology as being 'at the centre of debates about the basis of legal and social order at the end of the twentieth century', part of which involves developing feasible visions of what might be, locally and nationally, as well as analyses of what is (Carlen, 1990; Young, 1992).

Without such visions and analyses it is difficult to question official (government and management) versions of what the service is for and where it is going, to think and speak outside their parameters and to conceptualise genuine alternatives. Probation officers, and generally speaking those who work with offenders, who cannot relate the intricacies of criminal justice policy and probation practice to shifting patterns of political and economic domination, who know nothing of the politics of penal change, who cannot unravel the discourses which put an upbeat and seductive spin on repressive developments (managerialism, for example), and who are still distracted by generic 'material which is of only secondary use or importance' (Blythe and Hugman, 1982: 74) are in no position to critically evaluate their own or their agency's practice. Evaluating personal practice against the yardstick of agency policy and official orthodoxies, as against abstract ethical standards, broader political commitments and visions of what might be penologically possible, and even against the demands of conscience, is not in any meaningful sense a 'critical' evaluation. As managers such as Saiger (1992) imply, such closed forms of appraisal are a necessary means of fostering conformity and obedience to the agency, or ensuring that functionaries do neither more nor less than is required of them. Against this, however, one chief probation officer (Shaw, 1992: 136) has bravely emphasised not the notion of the dutiful, competent worker, but the notion of staff as an 'intellectual resource' who could help to shape the way that the service develops, as well as being skilful in practice. 'It seems not unreasonable', he states, 'to ask how managers can effectively mobilise the intellectual resources of staff in working with criminals if', among other things, 'there is a void in knowledge of criminology.'

It is not only knowledge, but also values, which a greater criminological and penal awareness could improve upon. There is an urgent need for distinctive probation values which actually sensitise practitioners to the repressive elements and dystopian leanings of contemporary penal policy (Christie, 1993; Mathiesen, 1990; Rutherford, 1993; Vass, 1990, 1996) and which facilitate reasoned resistance to them in a way that generic social work values, however well intentioned, have never done. Over the years generic values have in fact had a limiting rather than a liberating effect on the moral and political commitments of the probation service. It is one thing to suggest that compassionate and humanitarian values should be given expression in work with offenders (even confrontative work), and that criminal justice agencies should act in fair and non-discriminatory ways, but quite another to assume that this is all that can be said about probation values, or that all morally defensible interventions with offenders, or against crime, must conform to preconceived notions of generic social work.

Even when, as recently, 'social work' values have been framed in terms of anti-oppressiveness, they have failed to generate a compelling vision of society in which both crime and punishment might be reduced. Nor, except when they have been linked to racism and sexism, have such values been sensitive to the ways in which types of criminal activity and forms of punishment, especially the prison, can compound oppression and disadvantage (Campbell, 1992; Christie, 1993; Lea and Young, 1992; Mathiesen, 1990). As such debates are central to contemporary criminology (de Haan, 1990), so too are they central to the knowledge that should guide the practice of those who work with offenders. As has been argued elsewhere (Nellis, 1995), anti-custodialism, restorative justice and community safety, to which generic theorists have never paid attention, could form the core of a new probation value base, and these are all forms of anti-oppressive practice in which the probation service is uniquely placed to engage.

In a socially polarised and ever more authoritarian society (Galbraith, 1992; Hall, 1993) and in the intellectually restrictive, competence-oriented, managerial culture which increasingly suffuses it, it might indeed be possible to create the obedient, unreflective functionary that generic opponents of change in social work training project on to specialism (forgetting that 'generic technicians' are just as fearful as 'specialist technicians'). Although there is the distinct possibility that the worst may happen, i.e. the Home Office success-fully dismantling the process by which critical knowledge is fed into practice, it is not a forgone conclusion that it will. The demise of links with higher education, or with a genuinely intellectual and critical culture, would undoubtedly be a tragedy, but the demise of genericism itself and the development of more specialised forms of probation training (inside or outside CCETSW) need not be, if such training develops along the lines outlined here. The administrative, sociological and psychological components of criminology could usefully inform the new probation officer competences. However, if the service is to forge a new identity for itself as a community justice (rather than just a 'social work') agency – instead of having a wholly punitive and regulatory identity imposed upon it – a more complex array of ideas must be drawn upon. It is possible that regressive penal policies will continue to emerge from a rather unstable consensus of conservative and authoritarian interests (Radzinowicz, 1991); but it is from the critical analyses of these developments now being generated within criminology that 'resources for a journey of hope' (Williams, 1983) in the probation service will most readily come, if only trainees, practitioners and managers are encouraged to engage with them.

Note

1. The need for NCVQ's Care Sector Consortium to develop a criminal justice sub-group was identified by individuals from the Central Council of Probation Committees, the Northern Regional Staff Development Office and CCETSW. Without their input the Care Sector Consortium may not have had a specialist emphasis on criminal justice, and, indeed, not all probation areas were happy with

this (personal communication from Lionel Smith, CCETSW Probation Programme Head, 25 March 1994). In historical terms it is beyond argument that CCETSW as an organisation has had a poor record on probation training, although there have been individuals within it, of varying degrees of influence, who held more considered opinions as to what probation officers most needed to know.

References

Advisory Council on the Misuse of Drugs (1990) *Problem Drug Use: A Review of Training*. London: Home Office.

Advisory Council on the Penal System (1974) *Young Adult Offenders* (The Younger Report). London: HMSO.

Allan, R. (1990) 'Punishment in the community', in P. Carter, T. Jeffs and M. Smith (eds), *Social Work and Social Welfare Yearbook 2*. Milton Keynes: Open University Press. pp. 29–41.

Blumson, M. and Kerr-Rettie, J. (1993) *Investigation into Establishing an Employment-Based Route to Probation Option Training for the Diploma in Social Work*. Gloucester: Gloucestershire Probation Service.

Blythe, M. and Hugman, B. (1982) 'Social work education and probation', in R. Bailey and P. Lee (eds), *Theory and Practice in Social Work*. Oxford: Blackwell.

Bochel, D. (1974) *Probation and After-Care: Its Development in England and Wales*. Edinburgh: Scottish Academic Press.

Bottoms, A.E. (1987) 'Reflections on the criminological enterprise', *The Cambridge Law Journal*, 46 (2): 240–63.

Bottoms, A.E. and McWilliams, W. (1979) 'A non-treatment paradigm for probation practice', *British Journal of Social Work*, 9 (2): 159–202.

Campbell, B. (1992) *Goliath: Britain's Dangerous Places*. London: Methuen.

Carlen, P. (1990) *Alternatives to Women's Imprisonment*. Milton Keynes: Open University Press.

Carter, D. (1991) 'The status of education and training in corrections', *Federal Probation*, June: 22–9.

CCETSW (1978) *Paper 18: Learning to Be a Probation Officer. Report of a Study Group on Practice Placements in the Probation and After-Care Service*. London: Central Council for Education and Training in Social Work.

CCETSW (1987) *Care for Tomorrow: The Case for Reform of Education and Training for Social Workers and Other Care Staff*. London: Central Council for Education and Training in Social Work.

CCETSW (1989) *Paper 30: Requirements and Regulations for the Diploma in Social Work*. London: Central Council for Education and Training in Social Work (2nd edn, 1991).

CCETSW (1990a) *Requirements for Probation Training in the Diploma in Social Work*. Letter to probation tutors issued by CCETSW on 4 July 1990.

CCETSW (1990b) *Advice and Guidance Concerning Eligibility for Sponsorship in England and Wales*. Letter to probation tutors issued by CCETSW on 4 July 1990.

CCETSW (1991) *DipSW: Rules and Requirements for the Diploma in Social Work*. Paper 30 (2nd edn). London: Central Council for Education and Training in Social Work.

CCETSW (1993) *Review of the Diploma in Social Work*. Accompanying press release: 16 December.

CCETSW (1995) *DipSW: Rules and Requirements for the Diploma in Social Work.* Paper 30 (rev. edn). London: Central Council for Education and Training in Social Work.

Chomsky, N. (1989) *Necessary Illusions: Thought Control in Democratic Societies.* Montreal: CBC Enterprises.

Christie, N. (1993) *Crime Control as Industry.* London: Routledge.

Cohen, S. (1975) 'It's all right for you to talk: political and sociological manifestos for social work action', in R. Bailey and M. Brake (eds), *Radical Social Work.* London: Edward Arnold.

Cohen, S. (1990) 'Intellectual scepticism and political commitment: the case of radical criminology'. Inaugural Willem Bonger Memorial Lecture, University of Amsterdam, 14 May.

Collett, S. (ed.) (1989) *Skills, Knowledge and Qualities in Probation Practice: The Basis for Partnership?* Liverpool: Merseyside Probation Service/University of Liverpool.

Davies, M. (1982) 'Community-based alternatives to custody: the right place for the probation service'. Address to a conference of chief probation officers, 23 June.

Davies, M. (1989a) *The Nature of Probation Practice Today: An Empirical Analysis of the Skills, Knowledge and Qualities used by Probation Officers.* London: Home Office.

Davies, M. (1989b) *A Consumer Evaluation of Probation Training: The Courses Compared.* Submitted to the Home Office in February 1989 and supplied in confidence to the courses named in the report. Norwich: University of East Anglia.

Davis, J. (1992) 'Competences: flavour of the year or powerful investment? *Newsletter,* 2, December. London: Home Office Probation Training Unit. pp. 7–20.

de Haan, W. (1990) *The Politics of Redress: Crime, Punishment and Penal Abolition.* London: Unwin Hyman.

De Ville Report (1986) *Review of Vocational Qualifications in England and Wales: Report by the Working Group.* London: HMSO.

Dews, V. and Watts, J. (1994) *Emerging Findings of the Review of Probation Officer Recruitment and Qualifying Training.* London: Home Office.

Dews, V. and Watts, J. (1995) *Review of Probation Officer Recruitment and Qualifying Training* (The Dews Report). London: Home Office.

Easterby-Smith, M., Thorpe, R. and Lowe, A. (1991) *Management Research.* London: Sage.

Fellows, B. (1992) 'Management and empowerment: the paradox of professional practice', in R. Statham and P. Whitehead (eds), *Managing the Probation Service: Issues for the 1990s.* Harlow: Longman. pp. 87–96.

Fielding, N. (1982) *The Training of Probation Officers.* Occasional Paper No. 2, Sociology Department, University of Surrey, Guildford.

Fulwood, C. (1975) 'Control in probation, after-care and parole', in J.S. King (ed.), *Control without Custody.* Cambridge: University of Cambridge Institute of Criminology. pp. 23–47.

Galbraith, J.K. (1992) *The Culture of Contentment.* Harmondsworth: Penguin.

Garland, D. (1985) *Punishment and Welfare: A History of Penal Strategies.* Aldershot: Gower.

Garland, D. (1992) 'Criminological knowledge and its relation to power: Foucault's criminology and criminology today', *British Journal of Criminology,* 32 (4): 403–22.

Geraghty, J. (1991) *Probation Practice in Crime Prevention* Crime Prevention Unit Paper 24. London: Home Office Crime Prevention Unit.

Gilroy, P. (1992) 'The end of anti-racism', in J. Donald and A. Rattansi (eds), *'Race', Culture and Difference*. London: Sage. pp. 49–61.

Hadjipavlou, S., Murphy, S.C. and Green, G.A. (1991) *Report of a Scrutiny of Probation In-Service Training*. London: HMSO.

Hall, S. (1993) 'Thatcherism today', *New Statesman and Society*, 26 November.

Hardiker, P. and Willis, A. (1989) 'Cloning probation officers: consumer research and implications for training', *Howard Journal of Criminal Justice*, 28: 323–9.

Home Office (1962) *Report of the Departmental Committee of the Probation Service* (The Morison Report). Cmnd 1650. London: HMSO.

Home Office (1988) *Punishment, Custody and the Community*. Cmnd 966. London: HMSO.

Home Office (1989) *Review of Probation Training: Final Report* (The Coleman Report). London: Home Office.

Home Office (1990a) *Crime, Justice and Protecting the Public: The Government's Proposals for Legislation*. Cmnd 965. London: HMSO.

Home Office (1990b) *Supervision and Punishment in the Community: A Framework for Action*. Cmnd 966. London: Home Office.

Home Office (1991) *Organising Supervision and Punishment in the Community: A Decision Document*. London: HMSO.

Home Office (1992a) *The Probation Service: Three Year Plan for the Probation Service, 1993–1996*. London: Home Office.

Home Office (1992b) *Newsletter No. 1*. October. London: Home Office Probation Training Unit.

Home Office (1994a) *Home Office Review of Recruitment and Qualifying Training of Probation Officers*. Probation Circular 31/94. 28 April 1994.

Home Office (1994b) *Introducing Competences: Building on Strengths: a Guide for the Probation Service*. London: Home Office Probation Training Unit.

Home Office (1995a) *Review of Probation Officer Recruitment and Qualifying Training: Discussion Paper by the Home Office*. London: Home Office.

Home Office (1995b) *Review of Probation Officer Recruitment and Qualifying Training: Decision Paper by the Home Office*. London: Home Office.

Hood, C. (1991) 'A public management for all seasons', *Public Administration*, 69: 3–19.

Howe, D. (1991) 'Knowledge, power and the shape of social work practice', in M. Davies (ed.), *The Sociology of Social Work*. London: Routledge. pp. 202–22.

Issit, M. and Woodward, M. (1992) 'Competence and contradiction', in P. Carter, T. Jeffs and M. Smith (eds), *Changing Social Work and Welfare*. Milton Keynes: Open University Press. pp. 45–59.

Jones, C. (1989) 'The end of the road? Issues in social work education', in P. Carter, T.T. Jeffs and M. Smith (eds), *Social Work and Social Welfare Yearbook 1*. Milton Keynes: Open University Press. pp. 101–24.

Jones, D. (1989) 'The successful revolution', *Community Care (Inside Supplement)*, 30 March: i–ii.

Joss, R. (1994) 'CCETSW Paper 30 and competences for main grade probation officers'. Unpublished paper.

Kemshall, H. (1993) 'Assessing competence: scientific process or subjective inference? Do we really see it?', *Social Work Education*, 12 (1).

Lea, J. and Young, J. (1992) *What is to be Done about Law and Order?* (2nd edn). London: Pluto.

Matheson, D. (1992) 'The probation service', in E. Stockdale and S. Casale (eds), *Criminal Justice under Stress*. London: Blackstone Press. pp. 142–59.

Mathiesen, T. (1990) *Prison on Trial*. London: Sage.

McGuire, J. and Priestley, P. (1985) *Offending Behaviour: Skills and Stratagems for Going Straight*. London: Batsford.

Modood, T. (1992) *Not Easy Being British: Colour, Culture and Citizenship*. London: Runnymede Trust and Trentham Books.

NAPO (1987) *Course Content*. Training Committee Discussion Paper: 29 May. London: National Association of Probation Officers.

Nellis, M. (1993) 'Criminology, crime prevention and the future of probation training', in K. Bottomley, T. Fowles and R. Reiner (eds), *Criminal Justice: Theory and Practice* (British Criminology Conference 1991: Selected Papers, Vol. 2). London: British Society of Criminology/ISTD. pp. 135–64.

Nellis, M. (1995) 'Probation values for the 1990s', *Howard Journal of Criminal Justice*, 34 (1): 19–44.

Parsloe, P. (1990) 'Future of social work education: recovering from care for tomorrow', in P. Carter, T. Jeffs and M. Smith (eds), *Social Work and Social Welfare Yearbook 2*. Milton Keynes: Open University Press. pp. 150–71.

Parsloe, P. (1991) 'What is probation?', *Social Work Education*, 10 (2): 50–9.

Pinker, R. (1993) 'A lethal dose of looniness', *The Times Higher Education Supplement*, 10 September.

Radzinowicz, L. (1991) 'Penal regressions', *Cambridge Law Journal*, 50 (3): 422–44.

Raine, J. and Willson, M. (1993) *Managing Criminal Justice*. Hemel Hempstead: Harvester Wheatsheaf.

Ralphs, E. (1985) *The Probation Service: Topic Papers on Community Service 1:9*. Birmingham: Department of Social Administration, University of Birmingham.

Rutherford, A. (1989) 'The mood and temper of penal policy: curious happenings in England in the 1980s', *Youth and Policy*, 27: 27–31.

Rutherford, A. (1993) *Criminal Justice and the Pursuit of Decency*. Oxford: Oxford University Press.

Saiger, L. (1992) 'Probation management structures and partnerships in America: lessons for England', in R. Statham and P. Whitehead (eds), *Managing the Probation Service: Issues for the 1990s*. Harlow: Longman. pp. 173–80.

Sanders, A. (1990) 'Training: on dealing with those who have let us down', in D. Woodhill and P. Senior (eds), *Criminal Justice in the 1990s: What Future(s) for the Probation Service?* Sheffield: Pavic. pp. 41–50.

Scott, D.M. and Dawes, J. (1986) 'Beyond the twilight of a sacred privacy', *International Journal of Offender Therapy and Comparative Criminology*, 30 (2): 141–9.

Shaw, R. (1992) 'Corporate management in probation', in R. Statham and P. Whitehead (eds), *Managing the Probation Service: Issues for the 1990s*. Harlow: Longman.

Smithers, A. (1993) *All our Futures: Britain's Educational Revolution. A Dispatches Report on Education*. London: Channel 4 Television Programme.

Stone, C. (1989) 'New work for the probation service in the courts', in R. Shaw and K. Haines (eds), *The Criminal Justice System: A Central Role for the Probation Service?* Cambridge: Institute of Criminology, University of Cambridge. pp. 66–75.

Timms, N. (1991) 'A new diploma for social work or Dunkirk as total victory', in P. Carter, T. Jeffs and M. Smith (eds), *Social Work and Social Welfare Yearbook 3*. Milton Keynes: Open University Press. pp. 158–72.

Vass, A.A. (1990) *Alternatives to Prison: Punishment, Custody and the Community*. London: Sage.

Vass, A.A. (1996) 'Crime, probation and social work with offenders', in A.A. Vass (ed.), *Social Work Competences: Core Knowledge, Values and Skills*. London: Sage. pp. 132–89

Wilding, P. (1992) 'The British welfare state: Thatcherism's enduring legacy', *Politics and Policy*, 20 (3): 201–9.

Williams, B. (1989) 'Skills, knowledge and qualities', *Probation Journal*, 36 (3): 119–20.

Williams, R. (1983) *Towards 2000*. Harmondsworth: Penguin.

Young, P. (1992) 'The importance of utopias in criminological thinking', *British Journal of Criminology*, 32 (4): 423–37.

Younghusband, E. (1978) *Social Work in Britain: 1950–1975 – A Follow-Up Study*. London: George Allen and Unwin.

2

The Essential Skills of Probation Work

Gwyneth Boswell

The contextual backcloth to this chapter is a radical reappraisal of penal policy by a government preoccupied with 'punishment' and the improvement of efficiency and cost-effectiveness in the criminal justice system. Increasingly over almost 90 years, probation officers have come to play a crucial part in the sentencing, supervision and rehabilitation of offenders. They have done so, by and large, via social work training and social work methods. However, their identity as social workers in the penal system has, in the 1990s, been more critically examined than at any other time over the last nine decades. Qualifying training, already radically reviewed by Davies et al. (1989) and the Central Council for Education and Training in Social Work (CCETSW, 1991, 1995) is (as the previous chapter referred to) under further threat by the Home Office (see Dews and Watts, 1995; Home Office, 1995a, 1995b). The concern is that at worst a service consisting of ex-armed services personnel given a short burst of training to punish offenders in the community is threatened. At best, on present evidence, the knowledge and skills of probation seem likely to be reduced to interminable lists of output-linked 'competences' operating at a variety of levels before, during and after qualifying training.

In this chapter we present a research-based account of ways in which experienced probation staff themselves have described the fundamental skills, knowledge and qualities required to perform their job. We re-examine the notion of competence, describing the essential nature of day-to-day skills involving *communication, assessment, intervention* and *professional relationships*, and highlight the need for *knowledge* and dynamic *critical analysis*. The implications for pre- and post-qualifying training and for probation service management will be discussed. Finally the unambiguous social work identity which emerges from the research will be placed within the current criminal justice framework in an attempt to look realistically at the nature of probation work and its accompanying skills in the penal system.

Competence in probation

In its *Rules and Requirements for the Diploma in Social Work* (CCETSW, 1991), CCETSW became the first body officially to introduce the notion of competence in the social work profession. It was a word which caught on fast, coming to be used in the plural more often than in the singular, and with a variety of spellings: competence, competences, competency, competencies. It became the cornerstone of National Vocational Qualifications (NVQs) which produced lists of 'units and elements of competence' for criminal justice services standards (Criminal Justice Services Standards Group, 1992). In 1994 the notion of competences for probation staff was introduced to be used as the basis for staff appraisal and probably, in due course, performance-related pay (Home Office, 1994).

The notion of competence, especially in the plural, is difficult to conceptualise let alone operationalise (though see Vass, 1996a, 1996b, 1996c for such an attempt). The Diploma in Social Work (DipSW), best known as Paper 30 (CCETSW, 1991, 1995), renders a trainee competent, in an overall sense, to practise, by virtue of the fact that s/he has demonstrated a given set of skills, knowledge and values. That set of skills, knowledge and values is intended to be broadly transferable across the wide range of tasks in social work settings. When one looks at the format of competences set down in Paper 30 (and in the amendments of requirements: CCETSW, 1995), in the NVQ document (Criminal Justice Services Standards Group, 1992) and the introduction document on competence for probation staff (Home Office, 1994), it can be seen that most of them amount to skills, roles or tasks. An example in Paper 30 is to 'assess needs, strengths, situations, risks'; in the NVQ document 'to support clients who are substance users'; in the probation document for probation officers to 'record, store and maintain information'. Assessment is a skill; support is a role; recording information is a task. The word 'competence' defies true meaning at these micro-levels and long lists of them are confusing and stultifying as many practice teachers struggling to produce some sort of evidential narrative, based on Paper 30, have testified in the post-CQSW era. The *Oxford English Dictionary* describes 'competence' as 'the ability to do', and 'competent' as 'adequately qualified to do.' Thus the Diploma in Social Work renders trainees adequately qualified to practise as a probation officer. Skills, knowledge and values applied to a range of tasks form the constituent elements of this overall competence. Attempts to couch these in sets of mini-competences seem superfluous. It is simply one layer too many for the already hard-pressed probation organisation. What is important at post-qualifying level is to continue building on knowledge, reappraising values (including checking them against personal qualities in terms of delivery) and in particular to concentrate on skill development and transferability. A skill, the *Oxford English Dictionary* says, is '*practised* ability or expertness': to be skilled means to be 'highly trained or experienced'. It would seem desirable for this to be the direction which main grade officers follow as they move through confirmation, into specialism and perhaps towards promotion.

It has been argued that competences as they are employed in this 'long list' format quickly become dated, are prescriptive, making little allowance for professional discretion, and are increasingly likely to become political (Hayman, 1993). The interim paper on core competences for probation officers derives its authority from the Home Office's 'statement of purpose' for the probation service (Home Office et al., 1992) and makes the point that 'the competence approach is based on the idea that relevant inputs and processes are only desirable and important in as much as they contribute to delivering the required outputs.' The expression 'required outputs' is unavoidably political as well as resting on a mistaken assumption that probation personnel have total control over these outputs in an agency whose major activity is containing difficult, damaged, disorganised and unpredictable members of society. This scenario is further bedevilled by a scanning of the 'statement of purpose', which reveals that the 'required outputs' are generated from a document which, oddly, as has been pointed out elsewhere (Boswell et al., 1993), sets out its objective first, its tasks second, its values third and its goals last. There is a list of 11 goals, only the first part of the first listed goal, 'Reducing and preventing crime', constituting anything other than an objective or an abstract ideal. Other 'goals', for example, include 'Achieving excellence in management' and 'Promoting community involvement, voluntary effort and partnership in work with offenders', but none of these explains to what end or goal this activity is to be directed. Where there is lack of clarity about goals there is bound to be uncertainty surrounding the objectives which stem from them, the tasks which need to be undertaken to meet the objectives, and the methods by which the tasks will be effectively performed. It is no wonder that, with this tenuous underframe, the notion of competence as it has come to be used in probation provides confusion and complexity rather than clarity, and irrelevance in place of facility. It is simply another of those attritional assaults on a long tradition of professional autonomy couched in an alien language which serves only to sideline the holistic skill of ongoing critical analysis and the seizing of the '*kairos*', the moment of creative opportunity (Elliott, 1988), in work with offenders. As Hayman (1993: 182) suggests, 'It is this sense of reflective and innovative ingenuity in response to diversity that is so woefully absent from almost all current formulations of competences'.

As with any activity focused around changing behaviour, it is a question of how probation officers and offenders relate to each other and to the organisations and communities of which they are a part. It is a question of whether people can have minds of their own and a capacity for imputing meaning (which includes criticism and challenge) to their actions and events. It is, most of all, a dynamic, risk-taking process, constantly open to review and redefinition, which depends for its success on the continued refinement of the skills of communication, assessment and intervention. In illustration of this quintessential process, the substantive section of this chapter will draw upon a qualitative study of main grade probation officers conducted by the author in the late 1980s (Boswell, 1989) based upon the ingredients of skills, knowledge and qualities for probation practice.

Background to the study

This in-depth survey of 62 probation officers from four contrasting probation areas formed a less publicised section of a four-part national study focusing on the relevance of qualifying training to probation practice (Davies et al., 1989). The survey in question (Boswell, 1989) centred on the views of a sample of experienced probation officers with a minimum of five years' service about the skills, knowledge and qualities they employed in day-to-day practice. Thirty-two officers were female, 30 male, 25 with generic caseloads, 37 in full-time specialisms. The Criminal Justice Act 1991 was in prospect but not implemented. However, the fundamental business of purposeful interaction with offenders, colleagues and organisations formed the basis of the hour-long interview schedule, and despite the penal and other changes since the administration of that schedule, there is no reason to believe that the guiding principles for effective interaction between workers and offenders have changed since 1991. Indeed, as argued in the introduction of this book, many things may change but certain issues, contexts and outcomes remain the core areas of knowledge and practice for probation. Furthermore, as will be observed, the six core competences identified following the major review of the DipSW (CCETSW, 1995; Doherty and Pierce, 1994) show a close, if not remarkable, resemblance to the essential skills identified and discussed here.

Communication with clients

Almost without exception, when recalling how they had established human contact with particular clients, the officers in this study spoke of the importance of putting them at their ease, in order to create an atmosphere of trust and confidentiality in which the purpose of the contact and relationship between officer and offender could then be explored. Some officers found it necessary to be 'up front' by stating their purpose immediately, but most preferred to approach it more gradually, making formal introductions brief and trying to relax clients first, offering them coffee and informal conversation, establishing common human links rather than storing up problems of alienation by emphasising role differences early in the relationship.

As was the case throughout the interview schedule, some officers found difficulty in analysing processes which they regarded as skills, but felt they performed, for the most part, instinctively, sometimes automatically. Several officers, indeed, admitted that on what they called an 'off' day, because of their long experience in the job, they could switch onto 'automatic pilot' in their communication with clients, though none of them was particularly proud of this practice. However, when pressed about the ways in which they put people at their ease, it became clear that many officers put considerable thought into this endeavour by asking their clerical staff not to interrupt them on the telephone, arranging chairs in a fashion calculated to aid communication, and then greeting the clients by shaking hands and giving them their proper titles. This was seen as the beginning of a process which affords people status and respect, one of the traditional social work values, which these probation officers clearly still regarded as paramount in their work. Several officers mentioned the importance of signifying that they themselves were relaxed, particularly by the use of their own body language, smiling, making direct but unthreatening eye contact, and speaking in warm, reassuring tones. One described this process in the context of her work with a young female heroin addict, whose drug abuse was out of control and who was reluctant to engage in discussion about her life-style when they first met, in the following terms:

> I needed to enable her to know I'd be there however often she failed. I wanted to overcome the restrictions of my office and my role – I didn't want my role to be another pressure on her. I wanted her to see me as friendly and unshockable. I used my own personality and warmth to give her the message, 'I've got time for you'.

Some officers who worked in probation centres or had other informal settings available to them spoke of the usefulness of establishing common human contact by sharing an activity, such as a game of pool, in which conversation which one described as being of a 'non-directive, non-intrusive nature' took place, where again an atmosphere of relaxation and space-giving (also regarded as important by a number of people) could be created. The need for such a climate in the officer/offender contact was probably best justified by a prison probation officer who said:

> In a formal setting, a client may give you information such as the fact that he split up with his wife in 1972. What you have to do is to create a sufficiently relaxed atmosphere for him to tell you how he *felt* about that, and to become more transparent.

Given that nearly all the probation officers spoke at some point in their interviews of engaging with offenders' feelings in order to help bring about real change in their lives, it becomes clear that the ability to relax people sufficiently to own their feelings is the first, and perhaps most crucial, skill upon which all subsequent probation skills hinge.

The fact that this process has to take place in the context of a clear sense of purpose seemed to be agreed by most respondents in the survey. They were aware that whilst they might be giving the appearance of engaging in aimless social chit-chat, they were in fact laying the foundations for the work which they hoped to be able to do with offenders. They were also employing what one civil work specialist called:

> A series of awarenesses – holding onto purpose, observing the effect you're having on a person, identifying the effect they're having on you – in fact using your learned skill of continuous· social assessment. You assess all the time their statements, their actions, their living conditions if it's a home visit.

The skill of timing was one which seemed next to be brought into play. Officers spoke of the need for adaptability and flexibility in their approach, and whilst most had, over the years, developed a personal model for communicating with offenders, it was one which allowed for the unpredictability of what might be presented to them. 'Starting where the client is at' was a phrase used frequently, so that if offenders presented themselves in a business-like fashion, and were clearly more at ease with formality, and immediate discussion about purpose, role and function, then that would come first on the agenda. If, on the other hand, offenders were visibly distressed, then both formal and informal discussion would be put in abeyance whilst the emotion of the situation was directly addressed. In other words, the officers were concerned to keep down barriers and blocks to communication, so that they could begin to work effectively with the offender.

Learning to listen, *really* listen, was how several officers emphasised another important communication skill. This referred to the
uniqueness of the individual, and the danger of slotting them into
pigeon-holes and stereotypes without really taking in the meaning
for them of what they are saying. Observing their facial expressions,
body language, their silences and interactions with other family
members was also an intrinsic part of listening. One officer
suggested thus:

> If you *really* listen, you provide yourself with the necessary clues about
> when to ask questions too, and when to gently prompt. You need to gain
> a lot of information about the client to be able to work usefully with
> them – it's like slowly painting a portrait and getting the shadings and
> angles right. You don't get a picture of quality by stabbing at it with a
> brush – you paint a bit here and there when it feels right. It's the same
> with finding out about a client. If you overwhelm them with questions
> and talk, you might get some information, but it won't tell you much
> about colours or feelings.

The need to show genuine interest in offenders was stressed by
many officers, and the process of listening was again very important
here. 'Honesty' and 'genuineness' were words used over and over
again in the context of relationships with offenders. It was clear
that officers felt that they have to be accredited as human beings
first before they are accepted and responded to as probation
officers. This also involved appropriate self-disclosure, humour,
sometimes anger, sometimes body-contact if an offender appeared
distressed (though remaining alert to the risks and taking particular
care to recognise social boundaries and avoid distortion in the
message conveyed and received). A minority but not insignificant
skill mentioned was being able to recognise cultural diversity and if
possible communicate with deaf offenders, and to speak offenders'
native languages.

Setting limits in the relationship was seen as important by almost
everyone. Additionally drawing the line between the personal and
the professional was viewed as crucial, although 'breaching' (that is
to say, prosecuting offenders) was not enshrined in a national
standards system at that time (as it subsequently has been: Home
Office et al., 1992, 1995). Most people had established thresholds of
permissiveness and probation centre workers in particular were very
firm about the need to breach when contracts of behaviour were
broken. One established her limits via honesty about the nature and
purpose of the relationship, the contract and the authority invested
in the probation officer. 'People breach themselves!', one explained.
Another officer put the case in these terms:

> I breach people a lot more here than I did in a district team because you have to be absolutely consistent working with groups. There is a skill in mixing the friendly approach and establishing limits with a rigid framework. You need to work through it, wrestle with it a bit, get it wrong a few times. Getting the balance right, becoming comfortable with it yourself, that takes time.

Although the process of enforcement of requirements and the violation of those requirements by offenders leads officers to consider initiating formal proceedings against the defaulters, this is a much more complex relationship than these responses reveal (see, for instance, Vass, 1984). The discomfort of not being empowered enough to set and apply limits was evident in the responses. Several officers expressed their frustration with courts and the Home Office for not supporting their recommendations for 'breach action' or for recall of prisoners on parole licence, and for the overall lack of 'teeth' in young offender licences. This view may not be entirely accurate in the 1990s. The Home Office has produced guidelines and national standards (Home Office et al., 1992, 1995) whose purpose is to create structure and consistency. However, the officers felt that it was difficult to go on demonstrating consistency in their relationships with offenders, or to receive credibility from them, if the various parts of the criminal justice system cannot work together towards a consistent approach to the disposition of offenders. Knowing where to draw the line on the care and control continuum and having the authority to do so was very necessary for these officers.

Perhaps not surprisingly, discussion with 62 probation officers produced an almost inexhaustible list of the qualities they felt were needed in order to be able to communicate with offenders. The two most frequently cited, however, were honesty and warmth. They saw these qualities as 'given' and not amenable to be automatically learned by resort to training, though training could help 'polish up' the act. As one officer put it:

> Honesty and warmth are qualities which cannot be learned. You are either honest and warm or you are not and the client will always sense it and respond accordingly!

Another officer suggested that warmth, respect and sincerity are interpersonal cues which are given, felt and experienced in the context of social interaction, and that they are 'sensed by people, and you need to have them inside you before you can learn any social work skills'.

In addition to these personal and interpersonal qualities, a knowledge of human behaviour was seen as a vital tool with which to measure the effectiveness of communication with offenders. One officer described it thus:

> It's whether I'm heard; whether it's retained and seen as relevant. But it's not always what's said – it's the mood of the contact. For example, one client with great problems hid behind his hair and wouldn't look at me for weeks. Now he does look at me so I know I've had an effect. Another client went from not caring about himself to being quite positive, and is now saying he actually doesn't want to go to prison, he wants to be on probation. That is the result of years of probation officers sticking with that man.

The probation officer with good communication skills, then, is someone with a sense of timing and modes of awareness, who relaxes people whilst holding on to purpose, who really listens, tries to draw a balance between personal and professional, care and control, who possesses qualities of honesty and warmth in particular, can work with diverse people and in different contexts, and has a good knowledge of human behaviour, crime, crime prevention, sentencing and outcomes. Having established this level of communication, skills and knowledge are needed for the process of making assessments of offenders and taking appropriate action.

Assessment

The process of assessment, whether for report-writing or record-keeping purposes, measuring progress or needs, or considering action and outcomes, constitutes one of the major tasks of the probation service.

The majority of responses to the subject centred on interviewing and information-gathering skills, 'practice wisdom' and life experience, knowledge of psychology, sociology, criminology, knowledge of local resources and inter-agency activity, court procedure, sentencing and the tariff, offending behaviour and relevant law. It was often emphasised that the communication skills described in the previous section, having operated both to relax and engage offenders, had to be continued and interwoven in the process of assessment, so that the two sets of skills and knowledge were simultaneously at work. In other words, knowledge and practice were seen as inseparable. This is in fact the substance of what we have covered in Chapter 1 and in the issues, contexts and outcomes covered in the rest of this book. The need for knowledge and understanding of relevant issues, their contexts and outcomes were viewed by these respondents as being fundamental for competent practice.

The skill of interviewing itself appeared, in the main, to be a matter of structure. This structure refers to a beginning, a middle and an end, during which the purpose was stated and hopefully fulfilled. In conjunction with a structure, though, care must be given as to the clarity of the questions put, the ability to ask the right question at the right time, to listen to the replies (as with communication, but this time with correct assessment as a more specific end-product), and to gather, prioritise, analyse and summarise information, ideally involving the offender in the entire proceedings.

Although most officers did not, in the main, work to definite formulae, many of them referred to the need to blend interviewing and diagnostic skills with particular bodies of knowledge, and to 'fit them all', as one officer said, 'into the bag of tricks'.

An experienced officer gave a useful account of such a process by stating:

> Learning how to ask questions which don't pre-empt the answer. Getting the client to talk but not letting it turn into a chat. Keeping the flow going by asking prompting questions in a way which doesn't seem controlling. Listening on two levels – first to the words that are fed back and second to other indications like tone of voice, fastness or slowness of response, the ease or difficulty of it. Always weighing up if what the client tells you fits in with how you've perceived them. Applying a well-digested knowledge of human growth and development – not the kind you've just taken in and spat out again. For example, knowing that there are three levels (psychological, sociological and physical) of impact on a person of a condition like, say epilepsy – and that you have to respond to them. You may not always know what they are, but you know they exist and you know where you can go and look them up!

Many officers spoke of the importance of verifying information and collecting as well as contesting the evidence, and of telling offenders that this process would take place. This was, according to the respondents, a major way of avoiding being 'conned'. One officer described this skill as 'detective work' and doing relevant research such as collecting information and checking facts. Another talked of his cautiousness in the interviewing process. He said thus:

> It's about being streetwise. If you get a lot of vagueness, you go over things with a find tooth comb. The same if their account is too neat or there are logical gaps with no explanation. Whether I feel pressurised – sold a line. You need to check even more with those people. The thing is they're often 'conning' themselves too.

Being able to communicate their assessments to good effect on paper was universally seen as vital. 'Simple English; short sentences; clear, familiar concepts; brevity; simplifying complexity,' was how one officer put it. Another spoke of the importance of keeping written assessments lively and interesting:

Give a good pen picture – bring the client to life on paper. Show the reader the real person rather than just their behaviour or the fact that they're a drug user. That is part of our professional skill. The layperson would just take the media view of a DSS defrauder as a scrounger whereas we see the personal difficulties and sometimes hopelessness which have led to that offence. It doesn't mean we excuse them, but unless we can bring them and their realities to life for the court, the questions of 'why' and 'how can we stop them doing it again' will never be answered. I suppose it's a way of putting across your commitment to helping the client as well.

In sum, the skills which were identified as being necessary in making assessments are: interviewing and information-gathering (incorporating previously identified communication skills such as listening and timing); interpretation; analysis; practice wisdom; ability to challenge; ability to identify readiness to change; good English usage; the provision of structure; clarity, conciseness, summarisation, flow; using appropriate methods and styles for the achievement of purpose (notably by 'bringing the client to life' on paper); the effective communication of messages; abstraction and deduction; the ability to differentiate between opinion and fact; balancing the interests of court and client. The broad bodies of knowledge identified, some of which were earlier described as also being necessary for communication were: psychology; sociology; criminology; relevant legislation; sentencing disposals and tariff; court; prison and parole procedures; means of fact verification; and self-knowledge (particularly in terms of a practitioner's own value system).

Implicit in the assessment process generally, have also been the presence of a number of qualities to which officers have referred to or reiterated, such as honesty, warmth, intuition (based on life and work experience), risk-taking and acceptance. This serves to remind those working with offenders that such factors are as inextricably linked with assessment as they are with communication. As they described the place of particular skills, knowledge and qualities in assessment, many officers also explained that the process sometimes required, for its success, the injection of social work methods of intervention. It is to this area of probation officers' work which the next section will turn.

Modes of intervention with offenders

Of the 62 probation officers interviewed, 50 said that they felt clear about the overall purpose of their intervention with clients, and that they, therefore, had specific goals in mind as they worked with them. Three officers did not feel clear, and a further three felt clear at times and hazy at others. Of the former group one probation centre specialist said that sometimes he found himself doing group exercises and had lost track of their purpose. Two of the vacillating group pointed to some confusion and depression in their practice because of the difficulty of achieving anything with clients on young offender licences, drug addicts, those with chronic debts or bad housing conditions. Both, however, acknowledged that they still aimed to reduce offending behaviour and to provide alternatives to custody.

As respondents outlined the respective purposes of their intervention it became apparent that the most frequent of these revolved around crime prevention and attempts to stop offenders from reoffending. Some officers spoke in more modest terms of objectives which they would aim for in the course of this process, such as serving the court; advising, assisting and befriending clients; and helping clients to make alternative choices, and to identify their own potential. One officer described the usual pattern of her practice thus:

> I go to each visit thinking 'Why am I going?' and 'How am I going to ask the questions which will give me the information I want?' Often I do this instinctively, but I can usually work out why afterwards.

Another officer preferred to be more precise:

> The main skill is in bringing theory and practice together. Every PO *does* have a clear theoretical perspective, even though they don't acknowledge it. You have a view of offending, of sociological and other influences, and how your clients fit into this. A general consensus about this often emerges in teams but it differs across areas. Part of the perspective is how you use authority. People do go through a period of painful adjustment when they find the world isn't as they thought. The danger after ten years is that you can stop thinking – I know I go onto automatic pilot some days. Values need to be in the perspective too. Someone from outside, not trained for this job, would not operate from such a broad theoretical base.

Certainly an implication of these two views is that if theory and practice do, as they should, inform each other, then a crucial part of the skill of intervention must be to think and articulate what theories, disciplines and methods are being drawn upon in any given situation.

Although there was a modicum of resistance to labels, it was clear that most officers made use of a wide range of social work methods, notably casework (often in conjunction with other methods such as social skills training and alcohol education) and groupwork. Specialists found their existing skills considerably enhanced by their concentration and often learned previously untried skills and new bodies of knowledge which they found they could then usefully transfer back to the field. Right at the heart of the skills needed for intervention was still the skill of effective communication. Most officers felt they spent much of their time talking, listening, confidence-building and giving practical help, and that these activities were both prerequisites for and integral to the process of successful intervention. In order to sustain this often stressful long-term process, officers needed personal qualities of resilience, patience, honesty, humour, tolerance, curiosity and finally the ability to define professional and personal boundaries and 'switch off' from it all when appropriate.

Functioning as a probation professional

The skills of making and sustaining good internal and trans-agency professional relationships – largely those of communication – involved honesty, tolerance and sensitivity, in parallel with the process of supervising or controlling offenders. The art of public speaking emerged as being particularly important in court, as did that of steering a middle course between court and client. In short, functioning as a probation officer and working with offenders calls for skills that allow a process of negotiation to come into play so that the diverse expectations and demands of different parts of the criminal justice process (for example, personal and professional culture, organisational goals, offenders' needs, courts' expectations, among others) are accommodated and resolved. As a specialist court officer put it:

> Your central role is to be a bridge between all the different factions in the court. It takes the gravel out of life's vaseline. If you can, for example, explain a client's problems to the police and the difficulty of the police's job to clients, you get people to shift their positions. It's the same in court because this is the central skill throughout the job. An offender is out of step with society. If you can build the bridge that helps him/her step *with* society, you've fulfilled your role!

An enormous body of knowledge in relation to court work was seen as vital, as was a knowledge of self, personal values and traditional probation service ethos – viewed in terms of standing with and retrieving the offender for society.

'No-one is irretrievable. I believe you should never turn your back on another human being, no matter what they've done,' said one of the respondents, whilst another expressed the view that '[b]elieving in the self-realisation and maximising of potential of offenders – and believing it is worth challenging them till they get there' is the driving force in working with offenders. Similarly, there was an emphasis on '[l]oving the unlovable, but without forgetting the victim', leading to the reconciliation role played by officers.

The skill of workload organisation and balancing this with offender contact was important, as were differential methods of relating to line management and negotiating autonomy. Dissatisfaction and disaffection in respect of lack of consultation with the main grade officers in matters such as job mobility left unanswered questions about the skills, knowledge and qualities needed by managers for the effective supervision and servicing of probation staff.

Differential styles and skills were revealed between individual officers, between specialists and the mainstream, and between probation and other professions. Those in specialisms demonstrated the need for particular combinations of skills, knowledge and qualities for success in their fields, and indeed the way in which the three factors interacted had emerged as an important issue throughout. The philosophy of retrieving the law-breaker for society meant that the probation officer had to engage with the law-maker to attain understanding and compromise. This was the centrality of the skill of mediation, holding the balance between court and offender, for which the skill of autonomy management was also needed, as it was in most areas of probation activity. Whilst the existence of structure and boundary awareness were important, the wide-ranging nature of autonomy and balance, the two essential ingredients of being a probation officer, pointed to the potential strength which lay in the diversity of the approaches to working with offenders, courts and the communities they represent.

Research implications and challenges

It is important to emphasise that the ideas expressed in the above extracts are not the product of external observers but have been wholly generated by experienced serving probation officers working at the interface between the criminal justice system and the offender. Their comments and reflections have been reproduced at some length precisely to show that they are not employing their social work skills within some kind of simplistic and ad hoc 'helping' vacuum, but that they are doing so within a criminological and penological framework and with a concern to prevent and reduce crime (see, however, a broader view in Chapters 11 and 12). They speak from an accumulated self-critical practice wisdom. They are, as Davies (1969) suggests, operating at the point where criminology meets casework. They cannot, of course speak authentically for probation students, managers or other grades, but what they suggest in these pages is that whatever the current legislation, the latest fashion in sentencing practices, the political culture in regard to types of penalties and disposal of offenders, the required quota of offenders per annum in a probation hostel, and so on, they will still require relevant knowledge and will still need to deploy skills which fit the task. Irrespective of social and penal change, they portray a determination to be there working it out, staying with the offender, posing the 'Why?' and 'How?' questions, researching and re-evaluating practice, wrestling with uncertainty, holding the balance between court and client and applying critical and diverse knowledge acquired in the course of training. That is a living, breathing, critically analytical process which static lists of competences (even those encompassing buzz words such as 'positive and proactive', on which Davis [1993] pins her hopes) cannot adequately capture. Such lists serve merely to reduce the complexity of that process to bluntness and colourlessness and make the interaction between worker and offender a mechanical experience. One is reminded of Jeremy Cameron's amusing but none the less telling vignette of an appraisal/performance-related pay interview (Cameron, 1993: 177) in which a staff member's workplans are characterised thus:

> I plan to put out many outputs in my prospective performance. I also aspire to pin under a modest number of underpins whilst never losing sight, of course, of implementing the core requirements of my competences.

Whilst this is a send-up, the reality is getting closer. There is, we suggest, something about this use of vacuous language which protects those with responsibility for critically assessing issues such as crime, crime prevention and sentencing practices from a set of powerful fears about encroaching issues such as race, nationality, poverty, environmental change and cultural well-being, with which the criminal justice system barely engages and to which it certainly offers few answers. The language of competences and outputs helpfully masks the fact that high proportions of offenders suffer from .desperate economic and social problems, the alleviation of which is not within the gift of the probation service but lies within broader social structures. Thus the service faces its own distinct version of a challenge which, in common with other organisations and bodies, it is still struggling to understand. There are no instant solutions now, any more than there ever were, as experienced probation officers have highlighted above in their own terms. It is not a matter for dispute that probation staff should work to lucidly stated goals and be accountable for matters over which they have control. However, if the right knowledge, skills and qualities (which some prefer to reframe as values) have been employed but the overall competence which centres on the 'required output' has not, for reasons which are, as they often will be, beyond the staff member's control, then the staff member should not be held accountable (and potentially financially penalised) for this omission. The distinct challenge, then, is to find a succinct, manageable and fair way of expressing effective probation practice for all professional grades which potentially offers the freshness of daily produce (resisting the allure of a packet of frozen food), which gives credence to professionalism with a critical edge and to professional discretion in general.

Servicing your own machine

In their discussion of the management of criminal justice, Raine and Willson (1993) argue that the very nature of the work requires personnel 'who can exercise discretion and deal with the unexpected' (see also Vass, 1982, 1990). They suggest that standardisation techniques such as competence requirements can only be temporary, for 'like a Band-aid, if left on too long it stops promoting healing and makes the site go soggy' (Raine and Willson, 1993: 96). They note (in similar terms to May, 1991) the dangers of an organisation moving from a problem-solving to a performance focus, evaluating and controlling instead of valuing and enabling its staff. Addressing this tension directly, Raine and Willson (1993: 97) outline the basis of a contract for the professional with the agency which proposes these terms:

> If you will ensure my exercise of discretion then I will undertake to work within the parameters of agency policy and to keep the agency informed of what demands are being made of me and how I am addressing my work.

In reverse, the contract for the agency with the professional may read thus:

> If you will agree to work within the basic parameters of our policies and will provide systematic information about the work in which you are involved, then we will support the exercise of your discretion.

The difficulty here is how such an arrangement can be translated meaningfully into practice. We suggest that the art of self-monitoring and self-evaluation be taught to students during qualifying training and that they are helped to apply this integrally to a small set of core skills (limited to a manageable number) within the framework of the criminal justice system. One choice (based on our experience as educators and long discussions and associations with colleagues who have run student training units) for these skills would be as follows: *communication*; *assessment*; *intervention*; *oral and written skills*; *relating theory to practice*; *professional relationships*; *workload management*; *use of self* (which is frequently omitted from competence lists). In all these skills, there is one distinct phase which runs through and unites them. This is the acquisition of intellectual qualities which are rooted in the very substance of working with offenders: a knowledge base which serves to enlighten and critically evaluate the issues, contexts and outcomes of intervention (see Vass, 1996d).

Without that core knowledge and understanding of one's social world, self-evaluation and critical self-appraisal is meaningless. Without proper self-evaluation, which can check practices, intervention and outcomes become a risky business. For self-evaluation almost unavoidably brings in the otherwise excluded narrative, chronicles the material interaction and, most importantly, addresses the dimension of quality and informs social change. Pirsig, in his acclaimed book *Zen and the Art of Motorcycle Maintenance* (1974), explains that you can either choose to service your own machine and set standards for its performance or you can let someone else do it for you. An organisation can and should tell its staff what it expects of them in terms of performance, and staff are accountable for that. However, they are also trained professionals with a licence to practise and with much to offer to the servicing of their own machine. Unless the content and process of their work has internal meaning for *them* it is unlikely that their own abilities and motivations as professionals will be brought into play. They are the people who provide continuity of performance and standards in their own careers within a climate of organisational change. The most important skill they have to learn, therefore, is that of being in charge of their own performance, especially in unpredictable and volatile situations. It is that unpredictability and the dynamic nature of their tasks which calls into question the practical value of the mechanistic nature of a wholly competence-based culture of working with offenders.

A simple framework for self-monitoring and self-evaluation as a basis for action could operate along the following lines:

1   Decide on the goals of the process (which will include reference to desired standards).

2   Decide on the means of carrying through those goals and the means of evaluating progress.

3   Ask 'what knowledge do I have and how can it help me understand the issues, contexts and outcomes?' 'What are my perspectives?'

4   Collect and collate the data (which should answer the question, 'How am I doing?').

5   Interpret the findings (which should answer the question, 'What does all this information mean?').

6   Use the findings to make recommendations (for example, 'What do I need to read, learn, change, in order to improve my performance?').

7   Review the performance at a later stage in the light of developments and changes undertaken.

This kind of framework, once carefully taught and integrated into practice, can form a firm basis for meaningful interaction about professional competence with a line manager who is quite legitimately charged with the job of eliciting evidence for accountability and quality assurance. It does not answer all the questions but neither, we suggest, do the interminable lists of competences. In the end, training practitioners to work with offenders must mean that courses instil into them an intellectual, personal and professional culture which is both self-critical and critical of broader practices at both the situational, micro-level and within the wider structure. Similarly, organisations have to depend on their own selection processes to ensure that they recruit people equipped with a critical (and self-critical) faculty, who see information and evaluation systems, as Raynor et al. (1994) suggest, as the essential prerequisite for satisfied curiosity.

Conclusion

It is clear from all that experienced probation professionals have outlined in these research excerpts that fundamental social work skills which have been referred to (for example, communication, assessment, intervention, among others) and which are taught in depth at university are vital to the task of working with offenders towards purposeful change. Such skills have to be placed firmly in the context of criminological and penological perspectives and students taught to analyse and evaluate their own performance in this sphere. This foundation is vital for an organisation which rightly requires high-quality work geared towards the reduction of crime; and which can also depend on its professionally trained staff to set and achieve its own sound standards for practice by interacting energetically with change and holding paramount its unique bridge-building role between society and the offender.

References

Boswell, G.R. (1989) 'Holding the balance between court and client', Research Report 4, in M. Davies, G. Boswell and A. Wright, *Skills, Knowledge and Qualities in Probation Practice*. Norwich: Social Work Monographs, University of East Anglia.

Boswell, G., Davies, M. and Wright, A. (1993) *Contemporary Probation Practice*. Aldershot: Avebury.

Cameron, J. (1993) 'Appraisal and PRP', *Probation Journal*, 40 (3): 176–7.

CCETSW (1991) *DipSW: Rules and Requirements for the Diploma in Social Work*. Paper 30 (2nd edn). London: Central Council for Education and Training in Social Work.

CCETSW (1995) *DipSW: Rules and Requirements for the Diploma in Social Work*. Paper 30 (rev. edn). London: Central Council for Education and Training in Social Work.

Criminal Justice Services Standards Group (1992) *Listing of Units and Elements of Competence*. Care Sector Consortium, London: National Council for Vocational Qualifications.

Davies, M. (1969) *Probationers in Their Social Environment*. London: HMSO.

Davies, M., Boswell, G. and Wright, A. (1989) *Skills, Knowledge and Qualities in Probation Practice*. Research Reports 1–4. Norwich: Social Work Monographs, University of East Anglia.

Davis, J. (1993) 'Competences – flavour of the year or powerful investment?', *Home Office Probation Training Unit Newsletter*, 2 (December).

Dews, V. and Watts, J. (1995) *Review of Probation Officer Recruitment and Qualifying Training* (The Dews Report). London: Home Office.

Doherty, G. and Pierce, R. (1994) *Review of the Diploma in Social Work: Final Consultation Papers* (November), Paper 1: Overview Paper. London: Central Council for Education and Training in Social Work.

Elliott, C. (1988) *Signs of Our Times*. London: Marshall Pickering.

Hayman, V. (1993) 'Re-writing the job: a sceptical look at competences', *Probation Journal*, 40 (4): 180–3.

Home Office (1992) *The Probation Service: Statement of Purpose*. London: Home Office.

Home Office (1994) *Introducing Competences: Building on Strengths: A Guide for Probation Service Staff*. London: Home Office Probation Training Unit.

Home Office (1995a) *Review of Probation Officer Recruitment and Qualifying Training: Discussion Paper by the Home Office*. London: Home Office.

Home Office (1995b) *Review of Probation Officer Recruitment and Qualifying Training: Decision Paper by the Home Office*. London: Home Office.

Home Office, Department of Health and Welsh Office (1992) *National Standards for the Supervision of Offenders in the Community*. London: Home Office Probation Service Division.

Home Office, Department of Health and Welsh Office (1995) *National Standards for the Supervision of Offenders in the Community*. London: Home Office Probation Training Division.

May, T. (1991) *Probation: Politics, Policy and Practice*. Milton Keynes: Open University Press.

Pirsig, R. (1974) *Zen and the Art of Motorcycle Maintenance*. London: Corgi Books.

Raine, J. and Willson, M. (1993) *Managing Criminal Justice*. Hemel Hempstead: Harvester Wheatsheaf.

Raynor, P., Smith, D. and Vanstone, M. (1994) *Effective Probation Practice*. BASW Social Work Series. Basingstoke: Macmillan.

Vass, A.A. (1982) 'The probation service in a state of turmoil', *Justice of the Peace*, 146: 788–93.

Vass, A.A. (1984) *Sentenced to Labour: Close Encounters with a Prison Substitute*. St Ives: Venus Academica.

Vass, A.A. (1990) *Alternatives to Prison: Punishment, Custody, and the Community*. London: Sage.

Vass, A.A. (1996a) 'The quest for quality', in A.A. Vass (ed.), *Social Work Competences: Core Knowledge, Values and Skills*. London: Sage. pp. 1–7.

Vass, A.A. (1996b) 'Crime, probation and social work with offenders', in A.A. Vass (ed.), *Social Work Competences: Core Knowledge, Values and Skills*. London: Sage. pp. 132–89.

Vass, A.A. (1996c) 'Competence in social work and probation practice;, in A.A. Vass (ed.), *Social Work Competences: Core Knowledge, Values and Skills*. London: Sage. pp. 190–219.

Vass, A.A. (1996d) *Social Work Competences: Core Knowledge, Values and Skills*. London: Sage.

3

Discrimination and Anti-discrimination in Probation

David Denney

One of the most contentious and complex areas of debate within probation education and practice focuses on discrimination. The contention has been created by a growing awareness of the existence of widespread forms of overt and covert forms of discrimination within social work generally and the probation service specifically. The complexity is created by the many contradictions and fundamental questions which are inevitably raised in this area. A chapter of this length cannot capture the dynamism and anger which has fuelled current debates, since it seeks to encompass such a diversity of issues including class, gender, 'race' and discrimination directed against disabled, gay and lesbian people. The chapter can only raise some questions and consider broad theoretical positions in relation to penal policy which have a direct bearing on the development of anti-discriminatory practices.

First, a discussion of the meanings attributed to the vocabulary of anti-discrimination as it applies to probation work will be explored. Secondly, the forms of discrimination experienced by probation service users and employees will be discussed. Some of the managerial responses to discrimination in probation will then be considered. Finally, some future possibilities for the development of anti-discriminatory practices will be broadly discussed.

The context

Anti-discriminatory policies were developed promoted and formulated within probation training under the aegis of the Central Council for Training in Social Work (CCETSW). Paper 30 (CCETSW, 1991a), which set out the rules and requirements for the Diploma in Social Work (DipSW), appeared to herald a new and bold approach which was at odds with the dominant anti-collectivist thrust of social policies which since 1979 had dominated political discourse. The starting point for CCETSW's analysis were the contradictions within contemporary social structures which give rise to institutional forms of discrimination. This can be seen most clearly when in November 1988 CCETSW's 'Black Perspectives Committee' approved the following policy statement (CCETSW, 1991b: 46):

> CCETSW believes that racism is endemic in the values, attitudes and structures of British society, including those of social services and social work education. CCETSW recognises that the effects of racism on black people are incompatible with the values of social work and therefore combats racism in all areas of its responsibilities.

All qualifying social workers were therefore required to show the ability to 'understand and counteract the impact of stigma and discrimination on grounds of poverty, age, disability, and sectarianism' (CCETSW, 1991a: 16).

Qualifying social workers were also expected to demonstrate an awareness of both individual and institutional racism and sexism whilst expecting students to address such issues directly in their training. CCETSW appeared unequivocally committed to ensuring that anti-discriminatory policies formulated in Paper 30 were not relegated to tokenistic statements of intent.

With specific respect to probation officers, Paper 30 (CCETSW, 1991a: 40) clearly states that at the point of qualification a probation student must be able to:

> Demonstrate and operate antiracist, antisexist and other forms of discriminatory policy and practice in order to enable them to work effectively within a multiracial and multicultural society.

Although CCETSW required qualifying students to demonstrate 'an awareness of the interrelationship of the processes of structural oppression, race, class and gender' (CCETSW 1991a: 16), primacy appears to have been placed upon the importance of tackling racism.

Challenges to anti-discriminatory practice

A concerted media campaign directed at attempts being made by CCETSW to implement anti-discriminatory policies followed in the wake of the refusal of Norfolk County Council adoption panel to allow Jim and Roma Lawrence permission to adopt a 'mixed-race' child in July 1993. Melanie Phillips in two articles published in 'quality' newspapers argued that 'what was going on' in social work departments was not benefiting black people. The drive to eradicate all 'politically incorrect' attitudes was an abuse of power and a corruption of traditional liberal values of open-minded education and honest inquiry (Phillips, 1993a). Other articles followed in the same vein (Amiel, 1992; Appleyard, 1993; Phillips, 1993b).

It became clear that social work was being utilised in the production of a social category, political correctness, exclusively situated on the left of British politics, in order to create a form of moral panic. Dominant ideas fundamentally affecting probation practice emanating from the right (for example, market testing of services, curfews) were not described in terms of political correctness. Despite the allegations made in the media, numerous more seriously considered critiques of anti-discriminatory practice have been formulated by academics from a number of differing perspectives.

Ballard (1992) has argued that anti-discrimination within social work can now be regarded as a form of conventional wisdom, which he refers to as 'deprivationism', having its conceptual foundations rooted within Fabian socialism. The conflation of racial divisions with class divisions has led commentators to concentrate on the need to expose the extent of racism which exists in society. Such a limiting account suggests that the 'victims' of exclusion lack the capacity to change their own destiny. People are not pawns, unable to negotiate the terms of their own existence. The deprivationists, in their preoccupation with urban proletarianisation, often fail to understand the part that differing cultures have played in the effectiveness of the resistance to hegemony demonstrated by the 'migrant minorities'. Creative human energy can be effectively utilised to circumvent or resist oppression. Thus hegemonic ideologies which oppress can be challenged through the establishing of alternative conceptualisations of reality based on what Ballard (1992) refers to as mental, spiritual and cultural resistance.

Webb (1991) to some extent mirrors the concerns expressed by Ballard, when he notes a regrettable change in emphasis from statements reflecting self-doubt and hesitancy (CCETSW, 1976) to a position of certainty based in a commitment to social justice. Certainty for Webb has become a feature of the way in which ideas are presented by neo-conservatives (Webb, 1991). Dominelli, who has challenged the critics of anti-discriminatory practices, contends that anti-discrimination was not simply a response to perceived discrimination driven by CCETSW, but resulted from the efforts of black people and feminists who have compelled CCETSW to take their position. She also denies that certainty is a feature of anti-discriminatory ideas since many controversies exist between those who advocate anti-discriminatory practice (Dominelli, 1991a).

Culturalists, reflecting the position taken by Ballard, appear to place the responsibility for anti-racist action on black people and some form of cultural strength, and not the social work institutions which, like other institutions, may create and reproduce racism. Such a posture fails to demand an understanding of the institutionalised position of subordination which is occupied by black people and supported by the activities of those involved with the delivery of the probation services (Bourne and Sivanandan, 1980).

The significance of these attacks, particularly those launched through various forms of media attention, should not be underestimated. CCETSW has reviewed the manner in which anti-discrimination is presented in a reformulation of Paper 30, whilst the future of the 'Black Perspectives Committee', as presently constituted, is still under review. The revised DipSW (CCETSW, 1995) has in many respects turned the 'clock back', with an emphasis on six core competences which hardly refer to any issues of discrimination and anti-discrimination. The issue of discrimination and challenges to it surfaces rather hesitantly under CCETSW's *Equal Opportunities Statement* (CCETSW, 1995), where less than four short paragraphs are devoted to it. This is in sharp contrast to the original requirements for the DipSW (CCETSW, 1991a), which made anti-discriminatory and anti-oppressive practice the fundamental focus of social work and probation training and practice.

In a sense, the change in direction may have a lot to do with charges levied against CCETSW, and social work in general, of 'political correctness'. Such an attack was taken to the extreme by the media and critics. We are right to suggest that part of the reason for this 'U-turn' in policy and the new requirements for the DipSW, which, on first sight, appear to downgrade the importance of anti-discriminatory practice, lies with exaggerated interpretations and meanings imputed to anti-discrimination statements within the original DipSW requirements. Rightly or wrongly, as argued earlier in this volume, though broadly welcomed, such anti-discriminatory prescriptions came to be associated with simplistic notions of very complex social issues and relationships. They were subsequently turned, in the hands of a few overzealous interpreters, into a 'straitjacket' within which every personal, interpersonal and social activity should fit, irrespective of context and circumstances.

As an issue, anti-discriminatory practice must remain an important, indeed a core, value of probation work and those working with offenders in general. Practitioners working with offenders are placed in a social context which allows them unique opportunities to observe and experience discrimination if and as it takes place. Their own personal observations and experiences – within their own organisations, the courts, the police, prisons and inter-agency work – coupled with knowledge offered by research findings, can often guide them in recognising discrimination when and where it takes place, and encourage them to do something about it through anti-discriminatory and anti-oppressive practice. We believe that as long as practitioners are genuinely able to consider the issues, are assisted and guided to maintain a desire to consciously work towards an anti-discriminatory practice, and are given information about both good and bad practices, the revised DipSW requirements may not, in themselves, be significant as long as the study of discrimination and oppression and ways of alleviating it (in a practical sense) remain important requirements in both the curriculum and in practice.

Meanings and perspectives

The controversies which exist with regard to discrimination and anti-discrimination are related to complex meanings which can be ascribed to the forms that anti-discriminatory practice can take. Taylor and Baldwin (1989) have conceptualised discrimination in terms of the systematic use of power by some powerful groups which devalue other less powerful groups on the basis of perceived difference. Such differences can be conceptualised in terms of 'race', ethnic or national origin, religion, age, gender, class, sexuality or disability. Oppression is then conceptualised in terms of being the consequence of discrimination. Thus ideas which connect negative beliefs about particular user groups, and differential practices, constitute the essence of discrimination in probation. Attention should be focused on the relationship between ideas and practices if we are to understand the origin, transmission and impact of discrimination.

In regard to gender, Ramazanoglu (1989: 21) has argued that oppression can be seen in terms of 'the various ways in which men have been seen to dominate women, and in which structural arrangements have been seen to favour men over women'. However, some feminists would object to the use of a single term like 'oppression' to describe the experiences of women, black, disabled and gay people, instead preferring the word 'subordination'. However, use of the term 'oppression' does not preclude qualifying terms like 'subordination', 'discrimination' and 'exploitation'. The struggle of women, like that of black, disabled and gay people, constitutes what Ramazanoglu (1989) refers to as 'historically and culturally specific sets of practices in social situations' in which individuals have conflicting interests.

Although anti-discriminatory practice is established within probation training and practice vocabulary, the term is fraught with conceptual differences and raises fundamental and, as yet, un-answered questions. This is not surprising given that intra-group divisions ensure that terms used to describe the relations between men and women, white people and black people, heterosexuals and homosexuals, disabled and able-bodied people will depend on the perspectives from which the form of oppression is conceptualised (Ramazanoglu, 1989). Thus the importance of the relationship between ideas and practice is of fundamental importance when considering any aspect of anti-discriminatory practice.

The different theoretical approaches which embody the competing perspectives have been most thoroughly rehearsed in the literature relating to social class, black people and women. Of these, social class appears as the overarching form of oppression. Cavadino and Dignan (1992), in an extensive study of bias in the criminal justice system, reached the conclusion, albeit not a new one in criminology, that although official statistics do not provide data relating to social class, the penal system's subjects are overwhelmingly working class.

It is difficult to relate to statistics as an absolute truth for 'they are socially constructed' (Vass, 1996). In addition to other in-built biases, they also camouflage invisible crime such as corporate and 'white-collar' crime, thus overemphasising particular, and more visible, types. Notwithstanding this qualification, whilst some criminologists would describe such overrepresentation in terms of the contradictions inevitably inherent within capitalism (Quinney, 1977), conservative criminologists, according to Brake and Hale (1992), disregard social conditions as being relevant to crime. Criminals, according to this view, exercise free will and choice in the commission of their acts and are therefore responsible for such acts. Such a view can be reflected in probation service policy (May, 1991). Between these two extreme positions, there are numerous shades of positioning. Young (1986) has argued that criminologists on the left have failed to analyse sufficiently the negative impact of working-class crime on working-class people. Such 'new realism' concentrates more on engaging with all forms of crime, with the specific intention of its reduction.

Probation officers veering towards the former position would recommend that middle-class probation officers should always consider the relevance of class on the way in which they work (Devlin, 1993). Walker and Beaumont (1985), for example, describe constructive 'help to clients' as constituting the 'central purpose' of a socialist approach to probation work. More punitive measures incorporating tougher community sentences reflect the individualist class perspective in probation. In a revealing study, Boswell (1989, but see also Chapter 2 in this volume), found that in a sample of 62 experienced probation officers, 8 were willing to accept the idea of electronic tagging without qualification, whilst 23 were willing to provide qualified acceptance. At first sight, whilst this may imply the acceptance of more punitive community penalties, the actual intention may be different. They may still regard that choice as a way in which offenders can be 'helped' and diverted from harsher punishment. If the practitioners' goal is to keep people out of custodial institutions, supporting or employing tougher community regimes as an alternative to imprisonment may appear far more attractive and acceptable to practitioners than seeing offenders incarcerated (see Vass, 1990).

Early social writing on social work and black people is expressed in individualised terms of a deficit model, with intensive casework constituting the prescription for successful assimilation of the 'immigrant' community (Fitzherbert, 1967). By the early 1970s liberal pluralists described social work with black people in more integrationist terms, as occurring in a society composed of a system of élites each deriving their power from a variety of military, economic and political sources (Cheetham, 1972). Critical social work perspectives which developed during the mid-1970s, whilst emphasising the importance of class exploitation, tended to be Eurocentric (Corrigan and Leonard, 1978). Anti-racist perspectives appearing in the 1980s then located racism as being a product of the contradictory state ideologies found within capitalism (Dominelli, 1979). Black perspectives, virtually absent from the social work and probation literature until the mid-1980s, emphasised the knowledge, experience and aspirations of black communities, drawing attention to institutionalised racism existing within social work practice (Divine and Patel, 1992).

However, the analysis offered by black writers of the powerlessness experienced by black people over public policy and service delivery marked the single most significant development in the social work literature (CCETSW, 1991b; Gilroy, 1987; Northern Curriculum Development Project, 1994). Mullard (1991), for example, suggests that assimilationists discount other cultures altogether, their norms, languages and religions, whilst the liberal pluralists' insistence on integration does not fully question the dominant power relations which enable social workers to create discrimination. In the first place, cultural pluralist ideas appear on the surface to tolerate racism since the political structures which give rise to racism are not fully analysed, whilst the advocates of structuralism ignore the role that racism might play in the formation of both capitalist and communist oppression. Mullard therefore calls for the development of black perspectives which locate 'the problem' in terms predicated upon black definitions of reality and experience.

With regard to women, Williams (1989) has described 'libertarian' feminists as identifying the state as the cause of women's oppression. Whilst the libertarians emphasise the importance of individualism and minimalist state intervention in all aspects of welfare, liberal feminists advocate the case for greater eligibility to state-admin- istered welfare services. Socialist feminism, on the other hand, emphasises the importance of conceptualising discrimination in structural terms of patriarchy and capitalism. Black feminism encompasses various critiques of the welfare state, whilst arguing for the creation of black provision which will challenge current social and racial division of labour.

In terms of sexuality, Weeks (1986) has identified an absolutist position which conceptualises sex outside the nuclear family as dangerous, disruptive and anti-social. Probation work within this approach would encompass tight and authoritarian regulation of sexuality. In rejecting both classical Marxism and functionalism, Weeks argues that sexuality is moulded through complex and overlapping mechanisms which create domination, opposition, subordination and resistance. Weeks (1986: 41) states thus:

> Instead of seeing sexuality as a unified whole, we have to recognise that there are various forms of sexuality: there are in fact many sexualities. There are class sexualities and gender specific sexualities, there are racial sexualities and there are sexualities of struggle and choice.

Oliver (1990) argues that social workers operationalise an 'indi- vidualist personal tragedy theory', which results in a form of state intervention which compensates victims for the tragedies which have befallen them. Disability arises from the functional or psychological limitations of impaired individuals. Consequently social work intervention is geared towards helping individuals to adjust to their limitations.

Like the assimilationist position described in relation to black people, personal tragedy theory is essentially a deficit theory. Liberal pluralism, on the other hand, emphasises the disabled person's diminished ability to adapt to the demands of a hostile environment and the disadvantages experienced by disabled people in a less than perfect society (Wood and Badley, 1978).

The social construction of disablement and associated discrimi- natory practices affecting sick and disabled people are strongly influenced by cultural variation, ranging from rejection to the according of honour and privilege (Safilios-Rothschild, 1970). According to Oliver (1990), such differences cannot be explained by cultural relativism alone, since such cultural differences are produced by the relationship between the mode of production and the central values of the society concerned.

Oliver espouses a social oppression theory of disability based on a structural critique which empowers disabled people and argues thus (Oliver, 1990: 47):

> The idea of disability as individual pathology only becomes possible when we have an idea of individual able bodiedness, which is in itself related to the rise of capitalism and the development of wage labour. Prior to this, the individual's contribution had been to the family, the community, the band in terms of labour, and while, of course, differences in individual contributions were noted, and often sanctions applied, individuals did not in the main suffer exclusion. Under capitalism that is precisely what happened and disability became individual pathology.

Linking discrimination, ideas and practice

The form in which oppression is conceptualised by the probation officer will have a crucial bearing on the way in which offending behaviour is explained and considered by the courts through pre-sentence reports and other forms of official discourse, which will, in turn, link to the methods and theories which are utilised in practice. Although many probation officers are aware of discrimination within the criminal justice system, the combination of legal and professional convention leads them to speculate in an individualised, subjective and quasi-scientific manner on the casual factors which lead to offending behaviour. This highly individualised approach which dominates probation practice can lead to what Morris and Giller (1987) have referred to as a 'free-floating catalogue of pathology', resulting in some offenders being sentenced on the basis of the offence, their pathological problem and their potential for future deviance.

Probation service users can also carry the added burden of the negative connotations used by probation officers in relation to particular user groups. Thus when service users cite discrimination as a 'causal factor' associated with their offending, they are more likely to be subjected to a correctional code which emphasises the threat that they then pose to the social structure. This can lead to the greater likelihood of a non-custodial outcome in court decisions (Denney, 1992).

Evidence ranging over a 20-year period suggests that probation officers consistently overestimate the degree of risk faced by individuals upon whom they make a report, and apparently feel the need, on occasions, to sound tough (Rumgay, 1989). Drakeford has argued that the Criminal Justice Act 1991 has led to probation officers overestimating the seriousness of offences in reports partly as a result of an atmosphere in which they are in fear of being singled out by sentencers as proposing unrealistic penalties. Within the culture of the oversimplified individualised severity which currently appears to dominate the courts in England and Wales, any possibility of bringing about an anti-discriminatory and anti-oppressive perspective is bound to be both threatened and threatening (Drakeford, 1993).

User groups: probation, discrimination and black people

In considering specific forms of discrimination within probation service practice it is important to appreciate that oppression may have a different meaning to different user groups. As Williams (1989: xv) suggests:

> Each oppression has to be considered as specific: they are not parallel forms. Gender, for example, is a biological construct, whereas 'race' is a social construct; disability denotes physical impairment but also reflects as much the disabling norms of able-bodied society.

One may disagree with Williams's understanding of 'gender' and 'disability' for in both cases it is not the biological aspect which defines the social consequences but the social definitions of those terms. That is to say, gender and disability, as in the case of race, are similar in the sense that they *are socially constructed*. However, the point that there may be different meanings and experiences attached to each specific area may be important in ensuring that practitioners avoid a 'blanket' approach to every example of discrimination and oppression.

In looking generally at the criminal justice system it is worth emphasising that black people are overrepresented within it, although the reasons for this overrepresentation are complex when all the evidence is examined (Reiner, 1989). In London 42 per cent of men on remand are black. Black people are also sentenced to longer periods of imprisonment (James, 1992). However, as Vass (1990) has pointed out, although there appears to be an over-representation of black people in custodial establishments, the one single ethnic minority group which remains almost totally forgotten and about which little is known is what criminal statistics conveniently label 'Other, unknown'. This social group, as Vass has observed, though small in numbers, is remanded for far longer periods in comparison to any other group and serves some of the longest prison sentences. Notwithstanding this observation, and until further knowledge is provided about this social group, black people appear to run a higher risk of imprisonment even though they may be convicted for similar offences to white offenders. Thus, for example, in an extensive empirical study, Hood (1992) found that black offenders had a greater probability of being sent to prison by the Crown Courts. Furthermore, as Vass has also argued, there are serious questions to be asked about the way in which community penalties (for example, community service order, probation with requirements and day centres) are used or misused in relation to minority ethnic groups and in relation to women (see, for instance, Vass, 1984, 1990; Vass and Menzies, 1989; Vass and Weston, 1990; and Chapter 8 in this volume).

In addition to the way in which black offenders are treated in the criminal justice system, it must also be acknowledged that the probation service is dominated by white people. In 1989 black probation officers represented only 1.9 per cent (127) of the 6,651 probation officers employed at all grades within the services (NAPO, 1989).

Two general findings have been generated from the numerous studies which have examined the relationship between racial discrimination and the probation service. First, evidence would seem to support the view that probation officers perceive black offenders in a manner incorporating complex forms of overt and covert racism. Secondly, probation officers, although they may hold anti-racist perspectives and possibly aim at anti-racist practice, are constrained by structures and conventions imposed by the courts, the criminal justice system and the probation service, and are then led to include irrelevant and exclude relevant material from pre-sentence reports on black offenders; or not enough is done, in an institutional sense, to account for variations in the recommendations made for community penalties as alternatives to immediate imprisonment. Such practices increase the possibility of custodial sentences being imposed (Carrington and Denney, 1981; De la Motta, 1984; Pinder, 1984; West Midlands Probation Service, 1987).

The question as to whether white probation officers are more or less likely to recommend probation for black offenders in reports is a contentious and relatively well-researched issue. Some work suggests that there is little difference in the rate of recommendation, and that 'race' is a marginal issue in court proceedings (Guest, 1984; Waters, 1990). Other studies discovered no difference in recommendations whilst finding that black people were less likely to receive probation (Mair, 1989; Shallice and Gordon, 1990). Such findings point to the possibility that positive recommendations must also be consistent with the body of the report in order to be successful.

In attempting to understand the manner in which black people are treated by probation officers, a number of possible areas have been researched. The potentially discriminatory affects of constructing reality through official discourse has been a relatively new development within social work literature (Rojek et al., 1988; Stanley, 1991; Stenson, 1993). The deconstruction of official discourse can reveal complex linguistic processes through which discrimination operates. Although all offenders are presented to the courts in individualistic terms, white offenders are frequently presented as victims of cruel circumstances, which serves to minimise the amount of blame that can be attributed to the individual. Such explanations, which adhere to conventional forms of probation discourse, tend to constitute pleas for the mercy of the court. However, when explaining black offending to the courts via court reports, probation officers often combine familiar conventional accounts based on such factors as traumatic family background and alcohol dependency with less familiar and unconventional explanations like 'anti-authoritarianism' and 'irresponsibility' (Denney, 1992).

Sexual orientation

When it comes to sexual orientation, no specific legislation exists to make discriminatory behaviour against gay and lesbian people an offence. However, ineffective legislation does exist in the case of gender and race (the Race Relations Act 1976 and the Equal Opportunities Act 1975). In that sense, as NAPO (1993a: 11) argues:

> The 1980s licensed oppression of lesbians and gay men. Clause 28 of local government legislation prohibited local authority employees from promoting homosexuality in their services. Clause 25 of the 1991 Criminal Justice Act unhelpfully and deliberately confused consensual homosexual offences with offences of sexual abuse, and placed more gay men at risk of being treated more punitively than ever by the courts.

Britain thus encourages a level of institutionalised judicial discrimination against gay and bisexual citizens which is greater than in any other European member state. In 1989, according to official Home Office figures, the cost of criminalising men for consenting gay behaviour cost the taxpayer some £12 million and resulted in 3,500 prosecutions (Tatchell, 1991).

The literature on probation practice and sexual orientation is remarkable for its paucity. A lack of research also applies to work with gay and lesbians in residential work (Lloyd, 1993). The absence of research in this area may suggest that heterosexism is inextricably linked to power in society. This power is heterosexist in origin, a term defined by Buckley (1992: 35) thus:

> An activity based on and enforced by judgements and statements about lesbians and gay men arising from prejudice and homophobia and the assumption that heterosexuality is the only appropriate and morally acceptable way of exercising choice. Homophobia is an irrational fear of the same sexuality.

Half of probation services currently do not have sexual orientation in their equal opportunities statements (Senior, 1992). The rationale for this has never been clearly articulated. Schofield (1994) reports that in reformulating national standards for probation practice, the Home Office proposes to remove sexual orientation from the issues on which discrimination can occur in the writing of pre-sentence reports.

One of the key issues which must be addressed is the extent to which sexuality is seen as a relevant issue in practice. Robertson (1993) suggests that many officers do not consider discussing sexuality unless it is raised by the service user. Such an approach, it is argued, allows probation officers to assume heterosexuality, compelling gay people to indicate their difference from the norm.

Issues of disability and impairment

The Disabled Persons Act of 1986, although conferring certain rights of procedural fairness on disabled people, has not been properly implemented (Doyle and Harding, 1992). The development of services for disabled people and the role of the probation officer in empowering disabled people to claim their rights to services has yet to be systematically examined. Disabled people are in every sense a neglected probation user group. Despite the presence of numerous local probation services 'equal opportunity posters', disabled people see institutional discrimination as the major obstacle they face, and challenge the right of able-bodied officials like probation officers to distribute services which affect their lives.

The number of disabled people who come into contact with the probation service in any context as employees or service users is shrouded in mystery. There appears to be no information. In April 1991 a NAPO sub-group on disabled people wrote to all probation areas seeking information about policies on disability. Only one met the conditions laid down under the Employment of Disabled Persons Act 1944, which requires 3 per cent of disabled staff to be employed. The 1944 Act also requires exemption certificates from the above requirement. Only 15 areas were applying for exemption certificates. Very few probation areas indicated that they were taking into account issues relating to service delivery. Further, little if any attention appears to be given by probation services to the need for ramp access. Although a number of areas expressed good intentions in affirming that they are committed to non-discriminatory services, policies appeared to hinge on terms like 'whenever possible'. Some areas admitted that they were doing nothing in connection with issues raised by disability, whilst others made reference to general statements about equal opportunities. Specific measures which were thought to be necessary to the majority of probation areas who responded to the questionnaire included circulating job advertisements to a disablement resettlement officer and ensuring that all new buildings are adapted to the need of those who have mobility problems. Probation areas in this study appeared to equate disability with motor disability, making few references to hearing loss or visual impairment (Bodlovic, 1992).

Attention must be focused upon the wide range of delivery service issues raised by this research. For example, particular attention should be paid to service users who are not able to hear clearly in court due to lack of a public address system. Other vitally important priorities include the access to buildings for disabled service users and employees and the needs of those with learning difficulties. The National Association of Probation Officers is committed to dismantling the 'barriers which are constructed by lack of thoughtfulness and lack of resources, and which transform disability into a handicap' (NAPO, 1993b: 2). However, the declaration against discrimination has a long way to go before it is transformed into a practical and effective action.

Women and the probation service

Dominelli has argued that attending to issues connected with gender and race requires 'differential handling' since they occupy different 'positions within the profession'. Whilst black people are conspicuous by their absence, the presence of women makes gender inconspicuous (Dominelli, 1991b).

In effect, gender issues are marginalised within social work and probation practice due to the fact that women form the majority of the workforce, which helps to obscure the location of gender divisions within practice.

According to Crook (1993), half the basic-grade probation officers are women, whilst women occupy only 32 per cent of senior probation officer posts. Some 23 per cent of assistant chiefs and deputy chief probation officers and 15 per cent of chief probation officers are women. The probation service as an organisation is currently dominated by white men and is driven by a form of management which, in an era of managerialism, as Chapter 1 in this volume has argued, is strategic decision-oriented, and gives the impression of being tough and aggressive. This has, according to Crook, led to notions of skill being 'gender constructed'. As Senior (1992: 50) suggests:

> Promotion for women brings with it assertions from men that such a move was motivated not by ability, but simply because 'she was a woman', a charge rarely levelled at the many incompetent male managers.

Other writers have argued that criminology and deviancy studies are similarly male-dominated (Gelsthorpe and Morris, 1988); and much focus is placed on the virtues of 'masculinity' – being 'tough' and 'acting tough' – which translates in practice (in working with offenders and penal policy in general) as a 'tough-minded' approach by 'tough-minded' professionals and policy-makers (see Chapter 5 in this volume; Hudson, 1989, 1993).

In the early 1980s recorded offending by women represented 17 per cent of all offending, a figure which Worrall (1993) argues has remained relatively unchanged. During the 1980s women were overrepresented on probation, constituting 33 per cent of all orders made. By 1991, this figure had reduced to 18 per cent. This occurred whilst the number of men on probation increased from 24,000 in 1981 to 36,000 in 1991. Worrall (1993) argues that women who are not being placed on probation are more likely to be cautioned. It may also possibly be the case that women are more likely than men to be fined or given conditional discharges and thus less likely to be placed on probation for a first offence. At the other end of the sentencing tariff the indicators are not as encouraging. Whilst the number of women placed on community service orders has increased from 1,600 in 1981 to 2,300 in 1991, the number of women placed on community service orders with no previous convictions has increased from 18 per cent in 1981 to 30 per cent in 1991.

A number of explanations have been given for these differential rates. The report of the HM Inspectorate suggests that probation centres and associated programmes are rarely geared up to the needs of women, which could affect the way in which reports are being written (Vass and Weston, 1990; Worrall, 1993). Similarly, in community service the low representation of women may be explained by the presentation of this community penalty as 'masculine' punishment not suited to the female and more 'subtle' gender. As Vass (1984: 34) observed in his participant observation study of community service:

Probation officers and courts do not seem particularly keen on recom-
mending or imposing community service orders on women, probably
because the idea of a woman having to perform manual tasks . . . may
appear . . . morally unacceptable and practically undesirable. Instead,
female criminality seems to receive the 'therapeutic' treatment by the law.
. . . Whatever the reasons for the disproportionate use of community
service orders in respect of male and female offenders, where females are
involved in community service tasks they are by and large given tasks
akin to the dictum that a 'woman's place is in the home': preparing tea
for the male offenders and supervisors, given cleaning jobs, cooking,
shopping and caring for the old, the young and the disabled.

It is also relevant to add that the above penalty as well as most
other community penalties which are presented as having 'harsh'
regimes and are seen as tough punishment in the community are
'working-class' penalties. Vass (1984: 34) sums up this, thus:
'Another important feature of community service is that it is a
working-class penalty. It is essentially for the young, male, unskilled
or skilled manual worker and the unemployed labourer'. Similar
explanations have been offered by Mair and Brockington (1988),
who concluded that women's offending behaviour is more likely to
be seen by the courts and probation officers as evidence of underlying problems remediable by a more 'caring' type of intervention
which has an emphasis far more on supervision, guidance and help
rather than punishment. However, where the crime committed could
be seen as 'unwomanly', the risk is for women to receive higher
tariff community penalties or immediate imprisonment at a
relatively early stage when compared with men.

Other research has focused on the way in which analysis of
official forms of discourse can assist in understanding the position of
women within the criminal justice system. Worrall (1990) and Eaton
(1986) have described magistrates' decisions as being constituted by
the ideology of common sense and the material conditions of a
privileged existence, whilst solicitors' discourse reflects the ideology
of legal representation. This requires solicitors to repackage female
law-breakers according to typifications of 'normal' women which
can be discursively recognised by 'magisterial common sense'.

Psychiatric discourse is dominated by the ideology of forensic
medicine, which authorises psychiatrists to make medical, moral and
judicial judgements of women law-breakers and which also renders
them understandable within the discourse of magisterial common
sense. These ideologies create a narrow range of gender-stereotyped
classifications. The form of discourse used by probation officers is
constituted within social work ideology, requiring both care for and
control of women as key figures in the maintenance of the nuclear

family. It may be that probation officers reproduce explanations of offending which are acceptable to the courts, anticipating that any alternative to legal discourse will negatively affect the outcome for the service user.

Whereas white women are frequently presented to the courts as being 'neurotic' and 'irrational', black women can be presented in less conventional and mythically constructed terminology which encompasses pathological unpredictability and, in some instances, maniacal religiosity (Denney, 1992). Black women therefore bear the burden of the sexist assumptions relating to 'normal' female irrationality, whilst also being subjected to conceptualisations based on racist assumptions. Although the overrepresentation of black people in the criminal justice system is the subject of debate (Reiner, 1989), the 'double jeopardy' faced by black women could arguably be reflected within the black prison population. If the prison population is viewed in total, it can be seen that 15.5 per cent are black men whilst an alarming 24.2 per cent are black women. This figure has to be compared with the proportion of black men and women in the general population, which is currently approximately 4.5 per cent (NACRO, 1991). Of course, this issue, though of serious concern, has to be qualified. Such comparisons must be put in context and other variables than race or gender may be at play. For example, a particular ideology which may be fashionable with politicians and courts at a particular time with regard to a particular type of offence (for example, drug trafficking and 'mules', that is to say, carriers of drugs) may explain the statistics. A high proportion of black women, particularly from certain parts of Africa, are imprisoned because of their involvement in this type of offence and for fitting the stereotype of a 'mule'. In other words, they come under closer surveillance. Subsequently, black women may attract more severe custodial penalties than other people because they fit the current profile of a culpable person, of a particular social and ethnic origin, of a particular residence, of a particular gender, and of someone who is capable of committing a very serious crime for profit.

Looking at gender issues from another perspective, Dominelli (1991b), in a study of sex offenders, identified a masculist ideology as providing the main legitimating force in a sex offender's behaviour which enables him to transcend acceptable behaviour. Men who are unable to exercise power in a public domain will exercise power in private over less powerful women, children or other men. Again, this issue is far more complex than it is commonly assumed and may go beyond just implicating men against women. For example, sex offences by children against children, by women against women, by men against men and even by women against men are gradually receiving attention by researchers and indeed legislators. As an illustration, the Criminal Justice and Public Order Act 1994 introduces for the first time sex offences, including rape, against men. Gender relations, therefore, should be a fundamentally important element in probation work and particularly with sex offenders. Interestingly, Dominelli (1991b) concludes that gender does not appear to rank as a high-priority issue for probation officers working with this type of offender.

Equally, increased priority must be given to both the victims and perpetrators of domestic violence in probation practice. Although some probation work is being developed in domestic violence units, more focused attention should urgently be given to assisting women who need safe alternative accommodation and protection (Merchant, 1993).

The organisational response

Discrimination within the probation service has met with a differentiated managerial response in respect to particular user groups. Black people have received most attention, whilst other groups, most notably disabled people, have been virtually ignored. Partly this can be explained by a reactive and defensive style of management which has come to dominate public services in management in the last decade. In its 1993–6 plan, published by the Home Office, the stated goal of the probation service nationally is to 'achieve equality of opportunity throughout the service' (Home Office, 1992a: 3). Section 95 of the Criminal Justice Act 1991 (Home Office, 1992b) requires the secretary of state in each year to publish such information as 'he' considers 'expedient' for the purposes of:

> Facilitating the performance by persons engaged in the criminal justice system in a way which avoids discrimination against any persons on the grounds of race or sex or on any other improper grounds.

It seems puzzling to see how such goals can be achieved when in other official policy documents dealing with the probation service fundamental concepts which are ostensibly related to rights and quality are conflated with other polemical aspects of policy more closely related to the financing and administration of public services. Such a process can be seen in a Treasury policy document, *Competing for Quality* (Treasury, 1992). This simply asserts that: 'Competition is the best guarantee of quality and value for money' (Treasury, 1992: 1).

In official circles such an equation now appears to be so self-evident that no further official elaboration is thought justified. However, the inconsistencies in Home Office policies are clearly apparent when one considers both the introduction of section 95 of the Criminal Justice Act 1991 and the simultaneous disregarding of this requirement in terms of Home Office-prescribed probation performance indicators. As Walsh (1993) has argued, key perform-ance indicators ignore the views of service users and any indication of how probation officers are operating in a non-discriminatory manner. In practice, the proposed indicators lack any requirement relating to anti-discrimination. Thus, the right to be treated equally by the probation service is not officially regarded as a factor worthy of performance indication despite stated policy to the contrary. In an attempt to remove the concept of quality from finance-led agendas, Kemshall (1994) has argued effectively that the only quality measure which has real significance is the impact that the work being done has on the lives of service users, and their subsequent offending.

Despite an emphasis on improvements in national standards and quality of service, the service users' views can easily be ignored in a court report or in the actual context of supervision following sentence. It is possible, for example, for supervision to be arranged at inconvenient times which clash with the person's child-care needs. It also seems possible for a probation user to be subjected to a discriminatory form of practice without any form of regularised institutional redress.

Towards rights

So far it has been argued that the extent to which the needs of particular groups are ignored emphasises the absence of clearly expressed rights for employees and service users. Any discussion of rights and the quality of public services should, as Wilding (1994) rightly argues, be approached with caution, since the dangers associated with such an approach are legion. Such issues include the requirement of complex and expensive organisational back-up for rights enforcement, the difficulty of defining precisely the quality of service to which the user is entitled, and the ultimate use of charters of rights to protect the service provider. Wilding also warns against the overemphasis on the adversarial struggle for rights, which could detrimentally affect the user and provider relationship. Probation officers attempting to practise in an anti-discriminatory manner by, for instance, mentioning structural oppression in official reports are right to fear the possible negative outcome for the service user.

Although Senior (1992) detects a slow improvement in equal

opportunities with respect to employee conditions, the level of resistance to change is still entrenched. At present it is unclear as to what a service user who suffers any form of discrimination can do to gain redress and assistance. Rights clearly understood and accepted by both employers, employees and service users are basic to the development of non-discriminatory services. If probation service users are to be valued more, and their views about improving and changing services are to be heard, then a number of basic rights must be considered. Notwithstanding the practical obstacles and indeed problems in implementing such a policy, service users should have more influence in deciding how the probation order should progress in terms of aims, duration, location, frequency and content of contact and outcome. Points of disagreement should be discussed, written down and reviewed. An overemphasis on quantitative 'outcomes' as measured by performance indicators ignores the qualitative process of supervising or being the subject of a probation order. Most importantly, there needs to be an independent complaints system. A probation ombudsperson, independent of the funders of probation, is also necessary to receive and investigate specific complaints relating to discriminatory practices. With specific regard to anti-discriminatory practices, all probation areas must formulate and implement an equal opportunities policy, with specified objectives and results which are then made public and published in every probation office. All service users should have the right to receive service only from staff who have been properly trained and who within that training have covered knowledge about anti-discriminatory theory and practice in a critical fashion. Although there are dangers of increasing paperwork, this should not be an excuse for not finding out from service users the quality of service received. This could be done through written and or verbal opinion on the outcome and quality of service they have received through, for example, an exit survey or evaluation form given to users (Broad and Denney, 1992). A broader and unresolved issue concerns the applicability of a charter to service users who have 'chosen' and continue to commit crime.

It is also important to take cognisance of the need to create practical strategies for responding to users who engage in oppressive behaviour. An instruction to attend appointments might make a stipulation which prohibits '[l]anguage or conduct that might reasonably give rise to serious offence in probation staff, other persons under supervision or members of the public' (Cooper and Cooper, 1994: 16).

Monitoring processes must go beyond a counting and categorising exercise and provide a method whereby probation officers can 'think before they write'. Monitoring should also include value judgements, identifying disparaging comments and projecting dominant cultural assumptions which might detrimentally affect all groups of service users.

The roots of institutional discrimination are laid in training where probation officers learn the professional conventions which can differentially affect women, minority ethnic groups, disabled, gay and lesbian people. Training should enable probation students to critically examine and evaluate the ramifications of institutionalised discrimination in relation to penal policy, rights and procedures under the anti-discriminatory legislation such as it is, as well as aspects of criminology. This cannot be achieved by watering down the role of higher education in the training of practitioners. They need a knowledge base which critically examines the issues and their context. Inevitably, anti-discriminatory practice cannot be achieved without a critical understanding of the society in which social relations take place. Furthermore, the practice of 'buying in' anti-discriminatory teachers can make equal opportunity issues appear separate to the mainstream of social work and probation education, thus shifting the responsibility for anti-discriminatory practices to outside 'experts'.

Conclusion

Developing anti-discriminatory training in an atmosphere of change and uncertainty combined with a media apparently geared to label such developments as 'politically correct' provides a daunting challenge for probation trainers and managers. Although the oppressive position occupied by some probation user groups has been partially recognised through equal opportunities statements, stated intentions have not been coherently reflected in practice. A reactive rather than proactive managerial approach has led to particular groups being temporarily targeted for attention at particular points, whilst the needs of others are consistently ignored. From another side, there is also a risk that such reactive approval without much happening in practice translates into an obsessive preoccupation with slogans rather than positive action, which create, in themselves, a false belief that much is done when actually nothing happens in real terms. Thus, discrimination faced by gay, lesbian and disabled people appears to remain unaddressed and virtually unresearched within the probation service. What emerges in relation to black people and women is a weak and apparently contradictory set of policies which may lead employees and service users to regard equal opportunities statements as little more than a public relations exercise. The emergence in the 1990s of generally framed good intentions creates the impression that 'something is being done'. The ineffectiveness of policies to be translated into action is dependent on a number of factors including specificity as to what constitutes discriminatory practice, the meaning of 'quality service' and more developed user rights. Without an engagement with these issues and a firmly directed desire for change, there is a danger that equal opportunities statements will simply become a smoke-screen for inaction; thus enabling institutionalised discriminatory practices to continue. Probation staff at all levels must incorporate the experience of oppression as experienced by service users and themselves into their daily practices.

References

Amiel, B. (1992) '"Lady Bountiful's" lethal little society list', *The Sunday Times*, 11 October.

Appleyard, B. (1993) 'Why paint so black a picture?' *Independent*, 4 August.

Ballard, R. (1992) 'New clothes for the emperor: the conceptual nakedness of the race relations industry in Britain', *New Community*, 18 (3): 481–92.

Bodlovic, M. (1992) 'Disability-responses of probation areas to a survey by sub-group on disability', *NAPO News*, 36: 4–5.

Boswell, G. (1989) 'Holding the balance between court and client', Research Report 4, in M. Davies, G. Boswell and A. Wright, *Skills, Knowledge and Qualities in Probation Practice*. Norwich: Social Work Monographs, University of East Anglia.

Bourne, J. and Sivanandan, A. (1980) 'Cheerleaders and ombudsmen', *Race and Class*, 21: 331–52.

Brake, M. and Hale, C. (1992) *Public Order and Private Lives*. London: Routledge.

Broad, B. and Denney, D. (1992) 'Citizenship, rights and the probation service: a question of empowering or oppressing probation service users', *Probation Journal*, 39 (4): 170–5.

Buckley, K. (1992) 'Heterosexism, power and social policy', in P. Senior and D. Woodhill (eds), *Gender, Crime and Probation Practice*. Sheffield: Pavic. pp. 35–47.

Carrington, B. and Denney, D. (1981) 'Young Rastafarians and the probation service', *Probation Journal*, 28 (4): 111–17.

Cavadino, M. and Dignan, J. (1992) *The Penal System: An Introduction*. London: Sage.

CCETSW (1976) *Values in Social Work*. Paper 13. London: Central Council for Education and Training in Social Work.

CCETSW (1991a) *DipSW: Rules and Requirements for the Diploma in Social Work*. Paper 30 (2nd edn). London: Central Council for Education and Training in Social Work.

CCETSW (1991b) *One Small Step towards Racial Justice*. London: Central Council for Education and Training in Social Work.

CCETSW (1995) *DipSW: Rules and Requirements for the Diploma in Social Work*. Paper 30 (rev. edn). London: Central Council for Education and Training in Social Work.

Cheetham, J. (1972) *Social Work and Immigrants*. London: Routledge and Kegan Paul.

Cooper, P. and Cooper, J. (1994) 'Enforcing instructions against oppression', *Probation Journal*, 41 (1): 14–18.

Corrigan, P. and Leonard, P. (1978) *Social Work under Capitalism*. London: Macmillan.

Crook, F. (1993) 'Discrimination in the criminal justice system', in P. Senior and B. Williams (eds), *Values, Gender and Offending*. Sheffield: Pavic. pp. 23–35.

De la Motta, K. (1984) 'Blacks in the criminal justice system'. Unpublished MSc thesis, University of Aston.

Denney, D. (1992) *Racism and Antiracism in Probation*. London: Routledge.

Devlin, J. (1993) 'Class oppression as if it mattered', *Probation Journal*, 40 (2): 72–8.

Divine, D. and Patel, N. (1992) 'Shaping responses', *Community Care*, 24 September: 10–12.

Dominelli, L. (1979) 'The challenge to social work education', *Social Work Today*, 10 (25): 27–9.

Dominelli, L. (1991a) '"What's in a name?": A comment on "Puritans and paradigms"', *Social Work and Social Sciences Review*, 2 (3): 231–5.

Dominelli, L. (1991b) *Gender, Sex Offenders and Probation Practice*. Norwich: Novata.

Doyle, N. and Harding, T. (1992) 'Community care: applying procedural fairness', in A. Coote (ed.), *The Welfare of Citizens*. London: Institute for Public Policy Research/Rivers Oram. pp. 69–83.

Drakeford, M. (1993) 'The probation service, breach and the Criminal Justice Act 1991', *Howard Journal of Criminal Justice*, 32 (4): 291–303.

Eaton, M. (1986) *Justice for Women: Family, Court and Social Control*. Milton Keynes: Open University Press.

Fitzherbert, K. (1967) *West Indian Children in London*. London: Bell.

Gelsthorpe, L. and Morris, A. (1988) 'Feminism and criminology in Britain', in P. Rock (ed.), *A History of Criminology*. Oxford: Clarendon Press. pp. 93–111.

Gilroy, P. (1987) *There Ain't No Black in the Union Jack: the Cultural Politics of Race and Nation*. London: Hutchinson.

Guest, C. (1984) 'A comparative analysis of the career patterns of black and white offenders'. Unpublished MSc thesis, Cranfield Institute of Technology.

Home Office (1991a) *Discussion Document: Towards National Standards for Pre-sentence Reports* (November). Unpublished.

Home Office (1991b) *Organising Supervision and Punishment in the Community: A Decision Document*. London: Home Office.

Home Office (1992a) *The Probation Service: Three Year Plan for the Probation Service, 1993–1996*. London: Home Office.

Home Office (1992b) *Race and the Criminal Justice System*. London: HMSO.

Hood, R. (1992) *Race and Sentencing: A Study in the Crown Court*. Oxford: Clarendon Press.

Hudson, B.A. (1989) 'Discrimination and disparity: the influence of race on sentencing', *New Community*, 16: 23–34.

Hudson, B.A. (1993) *Penal Policy and Social Justice*. London: Macmillan.

James, M. (1992) 'A duty not to discriminate – what this might mean for probation practice', in B. Williams and P. Senior (eds), *Probation Practice after the 1991 Criminal Justice Act*. Sheffield: Pavic. pp. 31–9.

Kemshall, H. (1994) 'Quality: friend or foe?', *Probation Journal*, 40 (3): 122–7.

Lloyd, M. (1993) 'Lesbian and gay clients and residential work', in C. McCaughey and K. Buckley (eds), *Sexuality, Youth Work and Probation Practice*. Sheffield: Pavic.

Mair, G. (1986) 'Ethnic minorities probation and magistrates' courts: a pilot study', *British Journal of Criminology*, 26 (2): 147–55.

Mair, G. and Brockington, N. (1988) 'Female offenders and the probation service', *Howard Journal of Criminal Justice*, 27: 117–26.

May, T. (1991) *Probation: Politics, Policy and Practice*. Milton Keynes: Open University Press.

Merchant, D. (1993) 'Gender: a management perspective', in P. Senior and B. Williams (eds), *Values, Gender and Offending*. Sheffield: Pavic. pp. 41–69.

Morris, A. and Giller, H. (1987) *Understanding Juvenile Justice*. London: Croom Helm.

Mullard, C. (1991) 'Towards a model of anti-racist social work', in CCETSW, *One Small Step towards Racial Justice*. London: Central Council for Education and Training in Social Work. pp. 10–20.

NACRO (1991) *Race and Criminal Justice*. Briefing Paper. London: National Association for the Care and Resettlement of Offenders.

NAPO (1989) 'Black probation staff', *NAPO News*, 23: 5.

NAPO (1993a) 'Speech made by Chair of NAPO to the TUC on lesbian and gay rights', *NAPO News*, 46: 11.

NAPO (1993b) *Disability Pack*. London: National Association of Probation Officers.

Northern Curriculum Development Project (1994) *Improving Practice in the Criminal Justice System*. Leeds: Central Council for Training and Education in Social Work.

Oliver, M. (1990) *The Politics of Disablement*. London: Macmillan.

Phillips, M. (1993a) 'Oppressive urge to stop oppression', *The Independent*, 1 August.

Phillips, M. (1993b) 'Antiracist zealots drive away recruits', *The Observer*, 1 August.

Pinder, R. (1984) *Probation and Ethnic Diversity*. Monograph. Leeds: University of Leeds.

Quinney, R. (1977) *Class, State and Crime*. London: Longman.

Ramazanoglu, C. (1989) *Feminism and the Contradictions of Oppression*. London: Routledge.

Reiner, R. (1989) 'Race and criminal justice', *New Community*, 16 (1): 5–21.

Robertson, T. (1993) 'Probation and sexuality: a study of attitudes to sexuality in Hereford and Worcester probation service'. Unpublished MSc dissertation, University of Oxford.

Rojek, C., Peacock, S. and Collins, S. (1988) *Social Work and Received Ideas*. London: Routledge.

Rumgay, J. (1989) 'Talking tough: empty threats in probation', *Howard Journal*, 28: 177–86.

Safilios-Rothschild, C. (1970) *The Sociology and Social Psychology of Disability and Rehabilitation*. New York: Random House.

Schofield, H. (1994) 'Revision of national standards', *NAPO News*, 59: 5.

Senior, P. (1992) 'Gender-conscious service delivery: implications for staff development', in P. Senior and D. Woodhill (eds), *Gender, Crime and Probation Practice*. Sheffield: Pavic. pp. 47–59.

Shallice, A. and Gordon, P. (1990) *Black People, White Justice: Race and the Criminal Justice System*. London: Runnymede Trust.

Stanley, S. (1991) 'Studying talk in probation interviews', in M. Davies (ed.), *The Sociology of Social Work*. London: Routledge. pp. 123–47.

Stenson, K. (1993) 'Social work discourse and the social work interview', *Economy and Society*, 22 (1): 42–76.

Tatchell, P. (1991) 'Speech to fringe meeting at the National Association of Probation Officers', *NAPO News*, 27: 7.

Taylor, P. and Baldwin, M. (1989) 'Travelling hopefully: anti-racist practice and practice learning opportunities', *Social Work Education*, 10 (3): 5–32.

Treasury (1992) *Competing for Quality* (June). London: HMSO.

Vass, A.A. (1984) *Sentenced to Labour: Close Encounters with a Prison Substitute*. St Ives: Venus Academica.

Vass, A.A. (1990) *Alternatives to Prison: Punishment, Custody and the Community*. London: Sage.

Vass, A.A. (1996) 'Crime, probation and social work with offenders', in A.A. Vass (ed.), *Social Work Competences: Core Knowledge, Values and Skills*. London: Sage. pp. 132–89.

Vass, A.A. and Menzies, K. (1989) 'The community service order as a public and private enterprise: a comparative account of practices in England and Ontario, Canada', *British Journal of Criminology*, 29: 255–72.

Vass, A.A. and Weston, A. (1990) 'Probation day centres as an alternative to custody: a "Trojan Horse" examined', *British Journal of Criminology*, 30: 189–206.

Walker, H. and Beaumont, B. (1985) *Working with Offenders*. London: Macmillan.

Walsh, G. (1993) 'Performance indicators', *NAPO News*, 52: 5.

Warwick, L. (1991) *Probation Work with Sex Offenders: A Survey of Current Practice*. Monograph. Norwich: University of East Anglia.

Waters, R. (1990) *Ethnic Minorities and the Criminal Justice System*. Aldershot: Avebury.

Webb, D. (1991) 'Puritans and paradigms: a speculation on the form of new moralities in social work', *Social Work and Social Sciences Review*, 2 (2): 146–59.

Weeks, J. (1986) *Sexuality*. London: Routledge.

West Midlands Probation Service (1987) *Report on the Birmingham Crown Court Social Enquiry Monitoring Exercise*. Birmingham: West Midlands Probation Service.

Wilding, P. (1994) 'Maintaining quality in human services', *Social Policy and Administration*, 28 (1): 57–72.

Williams, F. (1989) *Social Policy: A Critical Introduction*. Cambridge: Polity.

Wood, P. and Badley, N. (1978) 'An epidemiological appraisal of disablement', in A. Bennet (ed.), *Recent Advances in Community Medicine*. London: Heinemann. pp. 23–46.

Worrall, A. (1990) *Offending Women*. London: Routledge.

Worrall, A. (1993) 'The contribution to practice of gender perspectives in criminology', in P. Senior and B. Williams (eds), *Values, Gender and Offending*. Sheffield: Pavic. pp. 35–41.

Young, J. (1986) 'The failure of criminology: the need for a radical realism', in R. Matthews and J. Young (eds), *Confronting Crime*. London: Sage. pp. 4–31.

4

Values in Context: Quality Assurance, Autonomy and Accountability

Ellis Finkelstein

This chapter is concerned with accountability in the probation service, but before this can be explored in the agency context it seems appropriate to address some of the wider issues which will help to create a backdrop against which more focused concerns can be raised. Because of its status as a public service the probation service should be accountable for the work which it undertakes and for the management of its finances. In this sense it should be no different from other public services, such as the police and prison services, which have generated so much attention about their operation and on the relationship between them and the citizen.

For the past three decades concerns about accountability have been growing across the range of public service agencies. Beginning in the 1960s, when concerns were expressed about the police, the literature on accountability has mushroomed. Led by Marshall (1965), who was concerned with the accountability of the constable, Oliver (1987) and Jefferson and Grimshaw (1984) have studied the accountability of the organisation and administration of the police. Similar inquiries have been conducted into education (see Elliott, 1981; McCormick et al., 1982) and the prison service (see MacGuire et al., 1985; Ryan, 1983; Wagner, 1989). However, probation has escaped the critical scrutiny which has made several public sector agencies more accountable to the public. Although this chapter is concerned with internal accountability in the probation service, the arguments and concerns which pertain to public accountability set the stage for understanding the issues within the agency setting.

Background

Since the Conservatives came to power in 1979, accountability has occupied a prominent position on the political agenda. This would appear, in part, to be a result of the government wishing to make public bodies more responsive to parliament, but on another level of analysis it may also relate to a genuine belief in the right of citizens to know about and to question the work of government and its administrative and social control agencies. Shortly after 1979 the government began to implement its philosophy, almost in a theological sense, to reduce its costs and to pursue value for money, which converged on notions of accountability. Measures such as the Financial Management Initiative (FMI)[1] were undertaken in order to curb the various agencies of state by exercising greater control over their costs, which made them more accountable for their funding. Later legislation was enacted to prevent local councils from meeting in secret and the post of ombudsman for local government was created to ensure that citizens were treated fairly; finance and insurance scandals led to the creation of ombudspersons in the corporate sector in order to allow self-regulation and to forestall possible government intervention. These measures effectively raised the level of expectations of people to complain about services and, along with public inquiries about child abuse cases and hospital maladministration, increased the pressure in all spheres to provide more information to members of the public.

These initiatives not only helped to keep accountability on the political agenda, but raised levels of awareness of surrounding issues. For example, do Members of Parliament have a greater right to question agencies of state than aggrieved citizens? If one represents the interests of the other, why should accountability be indirect? To what lengths do Members of Parliament go to pursue the interests of others? What are the rights of ordinary citizens? How are these determined? These questions raise, to some extent, the complexities inherent in the subject matter.

Those issues which are concerned with the nature of accountability between the citizen and the state, and between the organs of state and parliament, fail to capture an essential ingredient in relation to the methods of internal accountability used by organisations to ensure that staff are providing optimum services. For this purpose, accountability as a concept extends beyond the basic notion of 'taking account of' and includes asking a series of other questions about the control of employees. What processes and methods are used to ensure that staff achieve a satisfactory level of service? How do agency values and culture respond to changes in duties, function and organisation or services? What effect do these have on members of staff and their perceptions of the way in which the organisation operates? These appear key issues for the study of accountability in organisations.

Following the change of leadership in the Conservative Party and the formation of a new government under John Major, 'Majorism', in contrast to 'Thatcherism', attempted to resolve some of these issues by the notion of a so-called 'Citizens' Charter' which encouraged all agencies of state and its public services, such as British Rail, the health service and education, to provide consumers with details of the standards of service which they could expect and possible redress if these were not achieved. In view of the fact that information about standards of service is held in the public arena, relations between the citizen and the organisation can be more direct, making interference from third parties, such as ombudspersons and Members of Parliament, redundant. Standards also facilitate control over staff who provide services; the failure to provide a satisfactory level of service makes members of staff accountable to others in the organisation.

This second kind of accountability, that of the employee to the employer (organisation), has featured in the literature of economics which examines the issue in terms of principals and agents. Although this distinction and language may sit uneasily with the reader, it is none the less important in understanding some of the critical issues. Principal and agent relationships occur when, as Strong and Waterson (1987: 18) put it,

> . . . one party to a contract (the principal) engages another party (the agent) to take actions on his behalf in situations of asymmetric information. More specifically, it is assumed that the principal has less information concerning the agent's actions than the agent does himself so the agent has some scope to pursue his own interests undetected by the principal.

The probation context

The immediate problem raised by the notion of principal in the probation context is that of identity. The Criminal Justice Act 1925 gave magistrates powers to employ, pay and oversee the work of probation officers, beginning a long-established practice of appearing before magistrates to report on the progress of probationers, thus creating a level of accountability between the magistracy and probation officers. These case committee meetings were largely formal occasions until the early 1970s, when their formality was reduced along with a focus on probationers' progress. The requirement for case committees was dropped in the Criminal Justice Act 1991, though, as Chapter 6 in this volume argues, probation committees still have a role to play in the provision of probation service work. Indeed their relevance may increase further if the government's proposals to remove probation training from higher education (Home Office, 1995a, 1995b) are enacted. In many respects they will not only be the 'employers' but also the 'trainers', managing resources of future employees.

As the probation service became more bureaucratic and its officers professionally trained and supervised, the need for oversight from the magistracy was reduced. Alongside this trend the Home Office became more involved in probation service activities, exerting more and more influence on its work and the part which it would play in criminal policy planning. This influence was advanced by increasing financial control over area budgets. Thus, on a macro-level, the principal has changed from magistrate to Home Office. This picture, admittedly simplistic, involves probation officers in a principal–agent chain whose links consist of overlapping dyads so that the principal (Home Office)–agent (chief probation officer) on one level becomes the chief probation officer (principal)–assistant chief probation officer (agent) on another. A different representation would be chief probation officer (principal)–all probation staff (agents). Numerous variations on the principal–agent theme are contingent on organisational variety as well as the reader's frame of reference. Two points are important about this relationship.

First, the principal must find a means to police the agent's work. In the contract between principal and agent, enforcement poses no problems when the agent abides by the contract. Policing becomes an issue when the principal is uncertain about the agent's perform-ance; it extends beyond detection and acts as a force for condition-ing. Crozier and Friedberg (1980) point out there is no conditioning without constraints. According to North (1990: 33), this requires that institutional constraints operate in such a way that 'self-interested behaviour will foreclose complex exchange, because of the uncertainty that the other party will find it in his or her interest to live up to the agreement'.

Secondly, the nature of the asymmetrical relationship between principal and agent is qualitatively different in probation than in commercial firms studied by economists. Probation officers hold professional qualifications in social work and membership in rele-vant professional associations which link them to a code of practice-based ethics and values. This provides probation officers with opportunities to oppose the promulgation of agency policies and to thwart its policing activities based on adherence to core values and probation practice.

Educationalists have also made a unique contribution to the accountability debate that is now critical in understanding events which are now taking place in the probation context. Sockett takes accountability to mean improvement and argues that it is necessary 'to *prove* that this is being done'. He goes on to draw a distinction between 'accountability for *results and outcome* and accountability to *codes of practice*' (Sockett, 1982: 7–8; emphasis in original).

This chapter is concerned with accountability and autonomy *in* the probation service, which requires that attention must be directed to relationships *among* members of staff. Since the inception of the probation service its officers have considered themselves professionally autonomous workers who exhibit a high degree of personal responsibility in their work. Reports[2] which have examined the work of the probation service have commented favourably on the personal responsibility which probation officers take and consequently have recommended that they should be paid higher salaries than local authority social workers in order to take these factors into consideration. This is partly due to the way in which probation areas have been organised.

Historically, probation officers assumed responsibility for a geographical area (patch) in which they possessed a high degree of autonomy and personal power. This was enhanced by an organisation which was hierarchically shallow, lacking in formal structure (bureaucracy) and high in staff homogeneity. The limited structure which was available to oversee the work of probation officers was based on a casework supervision model (King, 1969; Monger, 1972) and not on notions of the management of staff. This changed with the reorganisation of local government in 1974, which reduced the number of probation areas from 103 to 56. The enlargement of probation areas, and an increase in tasks such as community service, meant that chief officers were required to seek ways to control the provision of services and staff. At the same time the role of the senior probation officer underwent a change from supervisor to manager, reflecting the change in the nature of work undertaken by seniors *and* the various probation areas. A function of management is the control of staff, who, as agents, become accountable for their work.

The nature of management in probation has been the subject of some degree of controversy, initiated by McWilliams (1990) and responded to by Shepherd (1990) and Lacey (1990). McWilliams approaches the 'problem' of management by suggesting that for most of its history probation was not managed. Beginning with the 1970s, management 'vocabulary' began to enter probation relations and practice and probation areas began to issue guides for good practice; they started becoming more bureaucratic, but not necessarily more effective. McWilliams notes that his arguments are an 'ideal' in that they stake out the extremes, which is helpful in encouraging discussion and debate as well as measuring real events against these heuristic devices.

It is not the purpose here to consider the rebuttals to McWilliams by Shepherd (1990) and Lacey (1990), nor to enter a debate about the value of management. What seems important, however, is to understand that organisations change and evolve and that management is necessary in order for people to coordinate and cooperate in pursuing their work. McWilliams's approach to management in the probation service seems to be driven by nostalgia in which probation officers practise according to certain professional codes of ethics and values for which no evidence is given. It would be remarkable if all probation officers shared and applied the same ethics and values in all their work and were able to evaluate each other's work accordingly. Without a form of management to which probation officers are accountable, their work inevitably would become idiosyncratic.

Deeply embedded in probation culture is the legacy of the lone probation officer who works a 'patch', assumes responsibility for a court, supervision of offenders, exercises discretion, and thus upholds professional standards. However, as we know, the reality is far different, and beginning with the 1960s, as probation areas expanded, officers began to work in teams. They were no longer working alone but were part of larger organisations which assumed responsibilities for the work undertaken by its staff. During the 1970s the growth in specialisms, such as court welfare, after-care and prison secondment, meant that some posts were unpopular, requiring chief officers to direct staff accordingly. McWilliams's view does not consider the principal–agent relationship which occurs in an organisational setting. The probation officer as professional worker may be compared with the general practitioner who operates as an independent contractor subject to National Health Service guidelines, but when the GP works in a NHS facility, say, for example, an AIDS clinic, the nature of the working relationship changes and the practitioner becomes the agent carrying out work for the principal. The GP in the NHS and the probation officer are not protagonists in their respective organisational settings: the relationship between them and the wider organisation is asymmetrical *and* cooperative. The GP who practises outside NHS facilities and/or those who are completely private are still regulated by the General Medical Council, which can strike a doctor off the register for malpractice or misconduct. The same is not true for probation officers, or social workers, who may lose their employment due to misconduct or malpractice but retain their professional status and be available to practise elsewhere.

Working in an organisational context, then, involves the principal and agent in an asymmetrical power relationship. The agent's failure to comply with the instructions of the principal may lead to breach of contract and loss of employment. This is extreme. But tensions do take place over the quality of work undertaken by the agent. Davies (1972) examines these issues in terms of efficiency and effectiveness: the former is the organisational objective, the latter is the functional (worker) objective. He suggests that the two are not mutually exclusive and that one objective may interfere with the other.

Accountability in probation began to emerge as an issue when areas increased in size and complexity. Managers began to develop priorities for their areas and, with the onset of management by objectives in the 1980s, developed strategic plans which targeted services available to offenders. This created a backdrop against which probation areas and members of staff could be held accountable. Initially, this was to probation committees (see Chapter 6 in this volume) reflecting local priorities, but it was not until the early 1980s that probation areas found themselves increasingly accountable to central government.

Perhaps because of its comparatively small size and relatively modest budget, probation did not loom large on the government accountability agenda. However, as the 1980s wore on, and as government attention became increasingly preoccupied with reducing the nation's burgeoning prison population, probation moved up the political agenda. In the early to mid-1980s the Home Office asked probation areas to respond to a document entitled *Statement of National Plans and Objectives for Probation* (SNOPS). Local areas submitted their local plans and objectives (SLOPS), which prepared the way for an increase in community-based programmes. However, SLOPS demonstrated a weakness in area management which the Home Office could not ignore and recommended that measures be taken to sharpen up area plans and delivery of service. The Home Office recommended the use of management consultants to provide the help necessary to assist local probation areas (see Humphries, 1991) in that respect. By the late 1980s management by objectives (MBO) became, as one chief officer put it, 'the flavour of the month'. In response, virtually all areas produced strategic plans for corporate strategies according to the MBO formula worked out by one particular firm of consultants. The decade also witnessed an expansion in community service, bail hostels, day centres, groupwork and the introduction of intensive probation schemes which helped to enhance the position of the probation service as a key player in criminal policy planning. At the same time its growth encouraged greater governmental oversight leading to an inquiry by the Audit Commission (1989). This confirmed the key role which probation plays in the criminal justice system as the only agency involved with defendants at all stages of the criminal process.

Although probation plays a key 'administrative' part in the criminal justice system, the government, when convenient and politically expedient to do so, has been preoccupied with punishment and 'efficiency', which led to the passage of the Criminal Justice Act 1991 and the Criminal Justice and Public Order Act 1994. The 1991 Act related punishment to deprivation of liberty so that the more serious the offence, the greater the loss of liberty. Insofar as probation is concerned, the Act transformed probation into a sentence in its own right incorporating loss of liberty. Crudely speaking, this one piece of legislation changed probation from a welfare-oriented social work service to one based on punishment in the community. Now probation officers were required to alter their working methods and practices in order to achieve the punishment aims of the legislation. Although the 1994 Act shifted the emphasis on punishment to prison, changes in philosophy appeared to have led to conflicts and low morale among members of staff (May, 1991), a situation well predicted by Vass (1982) in his critical analysis of changes in legislation, ethics and direction in criminal justice policy in regard to probation.

On another level of analysis, May (1991) describes the conflicts which take place between different levels of probation staff and the organisational tensions which occur when agency policies appear to contradict expectations for work and job satisfaction. This portrayal to some extent illustrates the ways in which probation officers felt as though some of the values which underpinned their practice were being eroded by the agency. Some seniors, for example, believed that they were restricted from offering a service to clients, which was one of the reasons that stimulated their application to become probation officers. In other words the agency was inhibiting seniors from undertaking the work for which they had undergone training and for which they entered probation.

These tensions, which were localised when May conducted his research, may have become more general in scope with national standards (Home Office et al., 1992, 1995) which were implemented with the Criminal Justice Act 1991. These standards were the first attempt to create a nation-wide set of guidelines for service delivery in which the expectations for contact between probation officer and offender were set out as well as the responsibilities of probation officers when offenders do not meet their obligations to report as instructed, notify change of address, and so forth. National standards are silent, however, on the redress of offenders when probation officers do not deliver an acceptable level of service (this is an area addressed in Chapter 3 in this volume). Nevertheless, local probation areas may make use of disciplinary procedures in order to achieve compliance with national standards. While probation officers are accountable to agency managers, Home Office administrators and courts, there is no direct accountability to those subject to supervision. In this respect probation differs from other public services where attempts are made to be accountable to the citizen, though the probation service is currently developing a 'charter of rights' for offenders.

Accountability and autonomy

In order to examine some of the issues relevant to accountability and autonomy, research was undertaken in a medium-size probation area called Hills[3] where staff were invited to respond to a postal questionnaire on professional autonomy. This was followed by semi-structured interviews with a number of staff who indicated that they wished to be further involved.

The initial postal survey was undertaken in May 1993, some seven months after the implementation of the Criminal Justice Act 1991 and the associated national standards. Respondents were contacted for interviews about eight months later. This was deliberate in order to see if experience working with standards had shaped and altered the opinions of the probation officers, who were initially sceptical. The imposition of national standards generated a considerable degree of insecurity among probation officers, who thought that their professional autonomy was under threat, and it therefore seemed to make some sense to defer interviews until people had the opportunity to work with the new system for a while. This part of the research is still in progress and any findings contained in this chapter are preliminary.

Forty-four members of staff, including nine senior probation officers and four ancillaries/projects officers, completed questionnaires. This amounted to around half the members of staff, but the number is too small to make for significant statistical sampling. However, there is a range of opinion on the issues which allows us 'to paint with a broad brush' and also to point out some of the problem areas which require further investigation. Given their location in the organisation and their obligation to monitor national standards data, senior probation officers are also used and compared with information supplied by main grade officers. It is important, though, to qualify comparisons by recognising that people occupying different organisational niches may possess different perspectives and are involved in different sets of experiences, which leads to problems when attempts are made to generalise. Additionally, the responsibility of senior probation officers is to monitor national standards, whereas the responsibility of main grade officers is to implement.

Before examining some of the issues which may appear important to the nature of accountability and/or professional autonomy, it might be useful to establish a conceptual framework. Here we use the notion of concept rather than definition because, for empirical purposes, the latter may well be too restrictive and incapable of encompassing a variety of viewpoints and opinions. Secondly, and of equal importance, a definition imposes the researcher's point of view onto the subjects of the study which may be both discriminatory and oppressive (see Agar, 1980, for a discussion of anti-oppressive research with specific reference to questionnaires).

While accountability may mean different things to different people, the concern here is with the ways in which it affects probation officers operationally. This means that in order to understand it we must first ask 'accountable to whom and for what?' The phenomenon does not exist in a vacuum, but takes place against a backdrop of expectations about what people think they are expected to do and the ways in which they perform their tasks according to the instructions of others. The tasks which probation officers are required to undertake are set out in *The Probation Rules* (Home Office, 1984), but the arrangement of probation officers into specialist teams means that not all probation officers perform all the tasks required. Probation officers serve at the discretion of the chief probation officer, who assigns staff to their duties and delegates certain responsibilities to others, such as senior probation officers, who manage teams of probation officers. Aside from other duties the organisational hierarchy monitors the work of probation officers to ensure 'quality control' and that agency objectives are being achieved. This provides a basic framework for a discussion of accountability particular to probation and also detaches it from the 'feelings' approach taken by Boswell (1982), which personalised informants' points of view so that the issue could not be taken further.

Respondents were asked several indirect questions which related to accountability. This was done in order to construct an impression of what people thought, and in some cases *did*, about their level of accountability, rather than projecting the author's point of view onto them. One question asked, 'What factors outside staff affect probation policy?' The choices, in order form, were Home Office, probation committee, Association of Chief Officers of Probation (ACOP), Association of Probation Committees (APC), National

Association of Probation Officers (NAPO), parliament, the media
and the local authority. Respondents were asked to rank order the
choices available. This revealed a fairly even split between those
who thought that parliament or the Home Office exercised the
greatest influence. A few respondents placed the two equal first; five
responded by indicating that only two choices, the Home Office and
parliament, were important; the others did not count. The responses
suggested that opinion may have shifted in probation circles away
from the previously important influence exerted by probation
committees as the employing and paying agency to a recognition of
the position of the Home Office (and thus central government),
whose influence has been growing since 1979. The response to this
question suggests that officers are aware of the political part played
by Home Office officials and ministers in constructing an agenda for
the probation service.

Probation officers cannot avoid experiencing the impact of the
Home Office and the concomitant reduction in importance of the
probation committees. Officers have been aware of the growing
influence of the Home Office through new policy and legislation and
measures such as the FMI (Humphries, 1991), SNOP, management
by objectives, in which staff underwent training, and the introduction of national standards, which will be discussed in more detail
below. These initiatives have taken place despite the reservations of
chief officers and probation committees, whose role and rationale is
undergoing change directed by the Home Office.

As choices moved away from those with direct relevance to
probation, there appeared to be a lack of agreement about the
influence exerted by, for example, local authorities and the media.
The former provides around 20 per cent of the probation budget
and has a financial stake in the work of probation, although this
may be more obvious to those occupying more senior managerial
posts in probation. Insofar as the latter are concerned, many
probation officers know that issues raised in the media shape
political opinion, which may bear on the work of the probation
service.

Another question asked, 'What level of staff should be responsible
for policy-making?' Four choices were available: chief officers'
management team, assistant chief probation officers with specialist
responsibility, team/specialist senior probation officers and individual probation officers. This question was asked in order to
understand how officers perceived the internal structure of the
organisation and where they fit within it. The notion of 'fit' is
important from an organisational point of view because it locates
members of staff in relation to others. This does not mean that

positions are rigid or that staff are unable to exercise influence over policy.

The answers to this question generated some interesting information. First, 20 respondents (total 44) placed the chief officers' management team (COMT) first by recognising the hierarchical nature of the contemporary Hills Service. This does not mean, however, that these respondents believed that the COMT policy-making position was unassailable. One senior probation officer suggested that she had the right, if not the duty, 'to challenge policies which impinge on her speciality'. She thought that part of her job was to use the specialist knowledge acquired in her post to inform COMT about policy-making. Although she placed COMT in the first position, she had particular views about the way in which it should construct its policies: through discussion and dialogue with those who are engaged in operational work. Another senior probation officer answered the question by suggesting that policy-making is continuous. He sketched an outline in which the Home Office set the broad policies, which are then filled in by Hills' management. For him, 'the further down the organisation the more detailed the policy gets'.

Detailed policies affect those at the 'sharp end' more than those occupying managerial posts. The former may feel that policies are being imposed on them and that they are mere instruments. One main grade officer suggested that all policies should be based on discussion and negotiation but that, 'at the end of the day, COMT has to be the final arbiter'. This recognises the hierarchical reality of the structure of the organisation but in a way which is not perceived as negative. It shows an awareness that conflicts occur among members of staff which need to be reconciled and that these cannot always be resolved by discussion and debate. However, some discussion and debate among staff is necessary in order to generate issues relevant to policy-making. The important point is the way in which these take place. Management style may encourage or stifle discussion and debate.

One way to test out the 'open' or 'closed' nature of agency management style is to understand if officers have opportunities to engage in policy formation or create their own policies. This was achieved by asking several questions. 'Are you a member of a team?' 'Do you think that team members should arrive at collective decisions within the framework of county policy?' Except for those occupying specialist posts, almost all respondents regarded themselves as members of a team. Three took the opportunity to comment on what appeared a simple yes/no question. One suggested that he was part of a team in name only. Another suggested that although he was part of a team he undertook specialist practice teaching duties. A third wrote that colleagues got on well together socially, but there was a lack of consensus about goals and a propensity to share.

These sentiments raise questions about the nature of team work in probation, which, although they extend beyond the parameters of this chapter, none the less raise issues about accountability to colleagues. In a hierarchical organisation vertical accountability is assumed, but horizontal accountability *appears* to receive little attention. Are probation officers accountable to members of the team in which they work, or only to the hierarchy?

To some extent this question is difficult to answer without reference to the feelings approach discussed by Boswell (1982): if officers *feel* as though they belong to a team they will *feel* accountable to colleagues. Horizontal accountability may be understood in the context of mechanisms which anticipate a collective approach. All offices in Hills use gatekeeping procedures in which colleagues review each others' pre-sentence reports (as well as other work) in order to ensure that proposals are in accord with county policies and objectives: if not, the report is returned for rewriting. Gatekeeping is not regarded as a simple monitoring task but as a serious attempt for all probation officers not only to adhere to county objectives, but also to ensure that pre-sentence reports achieve a high standard. Loyalty to colleagues does not interfere with this process, indicating a degree of responsibility and clarity of purpose. This takes place in addition to the monitoring work undertaken by senior probation officers as part of their supervisory duties and which places them in a hierarchical position vis-à-vis the main grade probation officer. This is an example of the policing function noted by North (1990), which has become more prevalent as probation areas have become more formal.

The question relating to collective decision-making within the team also raised some issues which will require further investigation, in part because some of the more elaborate replies impinge on the notions of teamwork. Although most responded affirmatively to the question, a number of written comments suggested that things are not all that clear. The following responses provide a flavour of some of the problems inherent in interpretation: 'ideally', 'usually if possible', 'cannot answer this question with a yes or no', and 'I've been saying this for a long time, but others don't seem to share this view'. These statements may suggest that probation officers lack clarity about the notion of team and their responsibilities *to* it. The word '*to*' is used in order to draw a distinction between the responsibilities to undertake certain tasks and not the scrutiny of those tasks which relate to issues of quality (concepts concerned with quality of work are discussed in Chapter 2 in this volume).

The problems inherent in attempting to understand the nature of teams in a probation setting become more confused when the question of policy-making at team level is considered. Various responses suggested that teams *should* be able to make policies within the framework established by COMT, but there is little evidence that this takes place. Insofar as the information contained in the questionnaire is concerned, policy-making at team level is an abstraction. Of course, this is not to deny the fact that in administrative and operational terms, as Vass (1984) has argued, probation officers (as other 'middle-management' workers in all organisations) act as 'policy-makers in miniature' (see also Chapter 8). That is to say, although they *may* appear not to have powers to create policy, in discrete settings those who are expected to administer and enforce policies are found to reinterpret, distort, evade and reformulate policies to satisfy their perspectives ('world views') and meet organisational demands about efficiency and effectiveness.

This has a direct bearing on notions of accountability and professional autonomy. There is general agreement among respondents that they are part of a team in which some aspects of their work are gatekept by colleagues and/or monitored by the senior probation officer. This may indicate the existence of horizontal and vertical accountability which does not manifest itself in terms of team policy-making.

One respondent suggested that teams do not formulate any 'serious' policies, suggesting that the senior's job is to convince probation officers that 'policy made by those above was actually created by the team'. In other words this appears to give the impression that policy is created in an open, democratic fashion which creates a 'false conscienceness' that power and responsibility are distributed in various parts of the service. In a sense, this appears to confuse one of the roles undertaken by senior probation officers, namely to act as a communication link between the team and head office, but there may be other reasons why probation officers do not appear to have achieved team policies. First, some of the policies may be about practice issues and therefore may not be understood as policies which are related to administration, goals and objectives. Secondly, the creation of policy at team level may lack formality or the status of policy directed from above. Thirdly, creating policy by team agreement means that all members must accept responsibility for their adherence, diminishing the ability to work in autonomous (idiosyncratic) ways.

National standards

The introduction to national standards sets out as its objective (Home Office et al., 1992: 1; emphasis in original)

> . . . to strengthen the supervision of offenders in the community, building on the skill and experience of practitioners and service managers: . . . by enabling *professional judgement* to be exercised within a framework of *accountability*.

National standards (see also Home Office et al., 1995) arrived at the end of a decade of Home Office interference in the work of the probation service. It was the first occasion on which an attempt was made to 'enforce' Home Office policy on the work of individual officers rather than the employing areas through the respective chief officers. Previously, many probation areas adopted their own standards or guidelines for good practice without much reference to each other.

By imposing national standards, the Home Office has thus exerted direct influence in the supervision of offenders. National standards are not exclusive to probation; they have been imposed on other agencies dealing with offenders, such as social services departments which supervise juveniles. Therefore, the desired effect of national standards is to create uniformity in the supervision of offenders irrespective of agency. What do Hills probation staff think of national standards?

Of those who responded to the questionnaire, 12 disagreed that national standards were necessary to the work of the probation service while 30 agreed. Respondents were asked to weigh their answers on a +10/-10 scale. Although some placed themselves at the extreme ends of the scale, most chose to place themselves closer to the middle. This question was not as important as the following question, which was designed to shift people from the abstract to the specific in order to describe the ways in which national standards affected the work of staff.

Those who disagreed were asked to 'describe how these standards have affected the preparation of court reports, supervision of cases, etc.' One suggested that the focus of report writing has changed: the 'offence is now more important than the offender'. Other officers made similar comments about the focused nature of reports, which they did not present unfavourably, although one suggested that reports were 'unduly constrained'. There were also comments on the increase in the amount of paperwork, while others expressed fear of prescription, with one indicating that it has 'cramped my style'.

The larger group of those who agreed that national standards are necessary to the work of probation provided broadly similar responses to those who disagreed about the ways in which standards have affected the preparation of reports and so on. They commented favourably on more focused work and structure; four expressly mentioned that national standards had little impact because local standards were more stringent. Although some officers may think that this is the case, they offered little to substantiate this point of view. Indeed, there is evidence to the contrary. One probation officer, who recently transferred from another area, suggested that Hills lacked a 'breach culture'. Shortly after arriving, he claims to have prosecuted, 'breached', three probationers and wondered whether national standards would lead to changes in 'breach' activity.

Some probation officers expressed concerns that national standards contained the potential for seniors to take a too prescriptive approach to their supervision, but there was no evidence that this had happened. A senior probation officer thought that some of his colleagues who occupied specialist posts might be too prescriptive and that they could take the easy way out and use the standards in order to achieve continuity across the board.

The real test of the effect of national standards on probation officers is to see if their implementation has affected accountability. Twenty-eight members of staff agreed that national standards had made them more accountable to their line managers. But based on the responses elsewhere in the questionnaire and in interview with some members of the Hills Probation Service, there is no indication that this level of accountability is more demanding or prescriptive. Indeed, 21 respondents answered the question 'Have national standards interfered with your ability to work as a professional?' negatively, meaning that officers believed that they could use their professional discretion and discuss cases with their line managers without fear of prescription. It may also add further support to our argument in Chapter 8 that 'policy is one thing, its application in practice another'.

If processes such as the FMI and SNOP were attempts to make probation areas more accountable to central government, then national standards may be seen as an attempt to change the nature of the relationship between probation officers, area managers and the Home Office by making individual probation officers, as well as others, more directly accountable to courts (and thus parliament) for their work with offenders. This may be only the first in a series of standards (see, for example, new amendments in Home Office et al., 1995) which could become more prescriptive, but it is also the first governmental attempt to police the staff, which may change the nature of the principal and agent relationship.

National standards present an attempt to construct a set of rules for, inter alia, the supervision of offenders. But rules do not command behaviour; they set out expectations (Emmet, 1964), which may be susceptible to various meanings and interpretations and hence practice. Rules which are drawn too tightly will restrict professional autonomy; those which are drawn too loosely will inhibit accountability. National standards provide a framework for service provision across the country by making probation officers accountable for its delivery. They also generate dilemmas in practice where their application extends beyond what probation officers consider good practice.

Those who framed national standards sought uniformity of service; this is difficult to gauge and impressions thus far are that such uniformity has not been achieved. The reasons are varied. One senior probation officer noted that one sub-area district lacked an office, requiring probation officers to make home visits because of lack of resources. Even if such a place existed, lack of public transport would inhibit probationers meeting their reporting obligations. The senior pointed out that this could lead to discriminatory practice as offenders were required to make a greater effort to report than those who merely waited at home. Thus, national standards expose the failure of criminal policy planning to address wider social and demographic issues. These need not be broader social concerns – they can be local concerns, for example population density and transport which affect the consumers' access to services and the allocation of resources to providers, and which can force particular probation teams to 'invent' their own methods of dealing with official obligations and duties (see Vass, 1984). This, in turn, can create a climate which fosters the kind of discretion (professional autonomy) which national standards have attempted to eradicate.

Conclusion

The growth of Home Office influence, in its attempts to control offenders in the community by increasing its control over professional workers, has added another dimension to accountability in the probation service (and other agencies involved with offenders). In the probation setting this has changed the principal and agent relationship and has threatened professional autonomy and has led to more prescriptive standards and may de-professionalise the agency, particularly if Home Office plans to train professionals 'on-the-job' (Home Office, 1995a, 1995b) are implemented.

Historically, professional autonomy has meant that probation officers were free to engage with 'clients' of the service in ways which would allow them to adhere to a deeply held probation value

– the primacy of the individual who is unique and should be treated as such. But, more importantly, professional autonomy has allowed probation officers the freedom to extend the range of opportunities available to offenders and to take 'risks' in their supervision.

Professional autonomy, however, does not exist in a vacuum but is integral to a code of ethics and values, which form the basis for the supervision of offenders in the probation setting. This growth inevitably has led to a more formalised organisation and specialists that require increased accountability and, consequently, a reduction in autonomy in order to establish uniformity of operation.

As the government seeks ways to increase its control over workers who supervise offenders it runs a high-risk strategy (see May, 1991; Vass, 1982, 1990). More accountability to central government through a number of means, including national standards, may be welcomed because of attempts to eradicate inconsistencies and diversity of operation. However, it may also distort the relationship between principal and agent, officer and offender from being one that is negotiable to one that is prescribed and externally regulated. This can make the relationship mechanistic and inflexible, thus reducing or eroding opportunities for creativity and co-existence in a highly demanding and fast-changing social and penal environment. It may become one of 'performance-related practice' guided by 'competence' (measured by 'administrative' tasks and achievements) rather than one of 'relating to and with' on social terms which are meaningful to all participants. However, at the same time, it is important to recognise that national standards, though they may serve political expediency, go a long way in addressing many of the inconsistent probation practices of the past and introduce or focus attention on areas which had hitherto been neglected. As Chapter 7 in this volume argues, national standards for pre-sentence reports brought to the fore the promotion of anti-discriminatory practice and introduced a more refined 'team scrutiny' and 'monitoring' of reports on defendants. In some sense, therefore, *accountability*, which runs contrary to *autonomy*, may in some instances create a feeling of loss of professional 'liberties' and choice; but equally, if used appropriately, it may create and promote the value of a better practice and thus quality assurance.

Notes

1. See Humphries (1991) for the effect of FMI on probation.
2. See, for example, the Butterworth inquiry.
3. This area is fictionalised for the purposes of this publication and certain of its features have been changed to preserve its anonymity.

References

Agar, M.H. (1980) *The Professional Stranger: An Informal Introduction to Ethnography*. New York: Academic Press.

Audit Commission (1989) *The Probation Service: Promoting Value for Money*. London: HMSO.

Boswell, G. (1982) 'Goals in the probation and after-care service'. Unpublished PhD thesis, University of Liverpool.

Crozier, M. and Friedberg, E. (1980) *Actions and Systems: The Politics of Collective Action*. London: University of Chicago Press.

Davies, M. (1972) 'The objectives of the probation service', *British Journal of Social Work*, 2 (3): 313–22.

Elliott, J. (1981) *School Accountability: The SSRC Cambridge Accountability Project*. London: McIntyre.

Emmet, D. (1970) *Rules, Roles and Relations*. London and Basingstoke: Macmillan.

Home Office (1984) *The Probation Rules*. London: HMSO.

Home Office (1995a) *Review of Probation Officer Recruitment and Qualifying Training: Discussion Paper by the Home Office*. London: Home Office.

Home Office (1995b) *Review of Probation Officer Recruitment and Qualifying Training: Decision Paper by the Home Office*. London: Home Office.

Home Office, Department of Health and Welsh Office (1992) *National Standards for the Supervision of Offenders in the Community*. London: Home Office Probation Division.

Home Office, Department of Health and Welsh Office (1995) *National Standards for the Supervision of Offenders in the Community*. London: Home Office Probation Training Division.

Humphries, C. (1991) 'Calling on the experts: the financial management initiative (FMI), private sector management consultants, and the probation service', *Howard Journal of Criminal Justice*, 30 (1): 1–18.

Jefferson, T. and Grimshaw, R. (1984) *Controlling the Constable: Police Accountability in England and Wales*. London: Frederick Muller in association with the Cobden Trust.

King, J. (1969) *The Probation and After-Care Service*. London: Butterworth.

Lacey, M. (1990) 'The management ideal: a CPO's view', *Probation Journal*, 38 (3): 110–16.

McCormick, R., Bynner, J., Clift, P., James, M. and Morrow-Brown, C. (eds) (1982) *Calling Education to Account*. London: Heinemann.

MacGuire, M., Vagg, J. and Morgan, R. (1985) *Accountability and Prisons: Opening Up a Closed World*. London: Tavistock.

McWilliams, W. (1990) 'Probation practice and the management ideal', *Probation Journal*, 37 (2): 60–7.

Marshall, G. (1965) *Police and Government: the Status and Accountability of the English Constable*. London: Methuen.

May, T. (1991) *Probation: Politics, Policy and Practice*. Milton Keynes: Open University Press.

Monger, M. (1972) *Casework in Probation*. London: Butterworth.

North, D. (1990) *Institutions, Institutional Change and Economic Performance*. Cambridge: Cambridge University Press.

Oliver, I.T. (1987) *Police, Government and Accountability*. Basingstoke: Macmillan.

Ryan, M. (1983) *The Politics of Penal Reform*. Longman.

Shepherd, G. (1990) 'Management: short of ideals', *Probation Journal*, 37 (4): 176–81.

Sockett, H. (1982) 'Accountability: purpose and meaning', in R. McCormick, J. Bynner, P. Clift, M. James and C. Morrow-Brown (eds), *Calling Education to Account*. London: Heinemann. pp. 7–9.

Strong, N. and Waterson, M. (1987) 'Principals, agents and information', in R. Clarke and T. McGuiness (eds), *The Economics of the Firm*. Oxford: Blackwell. pp. 18–41.

Vass, A.A. (1982) 'The probation service in a state of turmoil', *Justice of the Peace*, 146: 788–93.

Vass, A.A. (1984) *Sentenced to Labour: Close Encounters with a Prison Substitute*. St Ives: Venus Academica.

Vass, A.A. (1990) *Alternatives to Prison: Punishment, Custody and the Community*. London: Sage.

Wagner, R.B. (1989) *Accountability in Education: A Philosophical Inquiry*. London: Routledge.

5

Masculinity, the Probation Service and the Causes of Offending Behaviour

Karen Buckley

Exploring the impact of the Criminal Justice Act 1991 on the probation service, Canton (1993: 8) writes, 'The theoretical vacuum created by the Services' rejection of the treatment model was never adequately filled by "alternatives to custody". It is now clear that "just deserts" will not meet the case and the Service is once again at risk of losing direction.'

Canton (1993) goes on to argue for a reaffirmation of what we stand for, which is, in his terms, an 'ability to work demandingly, creatively and humanely with people'. The question which this chapter seeks to pose is how that can be achieved; and how a baseline can be developed for the understanding of masculinity and its relevance to offending behaviour. By exploring some of the ethical dilemmas which have beset the management and operation of the service, we shall aim at outlining how they may have arisen from a failure to acknowledge the impact of stereotypical masculinity on male behaviour. By concentrating on masculinity and related themes, the purpose is to identify which parts of probation management and practitioner-based discourse are relevant and, conversely, which can best be ignored.

At the time of writing, the author has been working in the probation service for 25 years. Over that time our understanding of what causes offending behaviour, and our methods of tackling it, have changed considerably. Those probation officers who trained for social work in the 1960s, on a diet of Freud and biology, have moved willingly or reluctantly through a range of philosophies and methods of combating offending. The job itself has moved from vocation to employment, as colleagues have espoused groupwork, community work, focused problem-solving, behaviour modification and radical non-intervention, to name but a few. These types of intervention, seen as radical at the time, have been pioneered by groups of officers, sometimes gripped whole services and have often been reflected in changing patterns of management activity and service policies. Managers are largely ex-practitioners, whose activity or direction may frequently be of a type which philosophically reflects abandoned practice. Training for service managers has of itself been variable in style and quality over the same period.

In more recent years the twin spectres of increased accountability and limited budgets have forced on the service considerable change. These changes are centrally led and symbolised for officers in increased recording, monitoring and surveillance both of offenders by officers and of officers by managers. National standards and increased inspection type activity, both local and national, represent just how far officers have come from the dogged independence of 25 years ago. However, whether this process will provide real answers, effective analysis or simply new challenges, successes or failures remains to be seen.

In many ways the last 25 years have seen theories of offending come round full circle. The notion of individual culpability was strongly influenced by psychoanalysis, and the famous one-to-one casework relationship homed in on teaching the offender better coping strategies. Two decades or more later, after working with poverty, alienation, community strategies, 'alternatives to custody', and so forth, practitioners are returning, or are firmly returned by changes in penal policy, to notions of personal responsibility and the 'just deserts' notion, no more firmly espoused than in some current work with sex offenders (Cowburn et al., 1992). Interestingly, the impact of feminism on social work theory has produced an outcome that feminists may not have anticipated: a ready identification with the notion of individual responsibility for behaviour whatever the circumstances. If sex offenders are totally responsible for their behaviour, then why not shoplifters or burglars? Thus, as a result, some services have already begun behaviour challenge programmes for everything and everybody referred to them under the banner of 'offender'.

Meanwhile offending continues to be on the increase, and indeed more victims are prepared to come forward, make complaints and demand their recompense through victim support groups. It seems a timely moment, therefore, to review the causes of offending and their implications for practice. The study of masculinity and its relationship to offending may provide a means of exploring that relationship and one which may offer a perspective on good management and practice.

Social work theory and literature is, one can suggest, permeable by outside influences, which can be regarded as positive. The impact of feminism on criminology provides one example of that. Notwithstanding that knowledge, permeability can sometimes be a disadvantage, as colleagues can seem to struggle with or even become hostile to each other's perspectives. In short, rather than create a synergy, it can lead to competing perspectives and confused practice. Thus, as Cordery and Whitehead (1992: 24) point out in relation to probation officers' use of theories, 'we tend to pick and choose between them rather like going to a wardrobe and putting on a suit of clothes for the occasion'.

Any new perspective adopted needs to offer unity and coherence and provide a way in which current social work methods and management activity can be re-evaluated. The study of masculinity offers just such a framework.

Men: the unresearched gender?

Over the past 25 years or so, many questions have been posed as to why people offend. Social work texts are littered with such questions and attempts to answer them but to no avail (see Vass, 1996). Interestingly there is one matter which, though obvious, has, until recently, been ignored. National statistics indicate that about 18 per cent of offences are committed by women. Heidensohn (1985: 19) observes thus:

> Recent studies confirm that what distinguishes the pattern of female from male criminality is its frequency, scope and seriousness. . . . Women commit fewer crimes than men, are less likely to be recidivists or professional criminals and contribute very little to the tariff of serious violent crime.

Curiously, therefore, there has been an extensive literature concentrating on why women offend, including studies which aim at finding out whether they are dealt with more leniently than men (see, for instance, Farrington and Morris, 1983).

On the other hand, no one seemed too anxious to ask the question 'Why do men break the law?' Men are not examined as a homogeneous group, rather they are seen as young men, black men, sex offenders, angry men or impoverished men. The rationale for this can only be that men are seen as the norm, the baseline by which all others are judged, and since being 'male' is regarded as normal, it follows that offending is also seen as 'normal' for men.

Traditionally, men have produced the bulk of published research and related studies, but they have taken manhood for granted as not requiring explanation. Segal (1990: 259) goes so far as to suggest that 'men have preferred to study neither God nor man but "women", defined as the particular sex – the different, the difficult, the problematic sex. It is women and not men who have traditionally been the object of scrutiny'. Perhaps it is more appropriate to say that a lot has been written about men, especially in the criminal justice field, but the conceptual tools to deconstruct masculinity are not available, especially in social work-related literature.

One of the strengths of such literature has been, however, its capacity to be susceptible to external influences. Thus, the late 1960s and 1970s saw a boom in feminist books, from *The Female Eunuch* (Greer, 1970) onward. The same decade saw an upsurge of feminist analysis by female criminologists like Smart (1976). The late 1980s have seen the beginning of an exploration of masculinity which can perhaps be used to reflect on aspects of male offending behaviour and is beginning to be reflected in some social work-related writings.

This current exploration is based on what might be termed a 'structural conflict' view of society. It moves away from notions of biological determinism that men are born like that and the world must cope with it, and also from the inheritance of psychiatry which explores individualised interpretations of behaviour focused on developmental issues and experience. It also moves on from Marxist analysis which sees the individual as a pawn in the game of social life shaped and fashioned by economic systems and the definitions of those in power.

All of these theories have informed probation practice and management. Managers are, after all, the practitioners of yesterday and it is sometimes possible to date someone's training by his/her approach to his/her work. It is also not uncommon to find oneself being discreetly, if amateurishly, psychoanalysed by a member of senior management whilst at the same time one's job is being reshaped by another senior manager in order to make it less dysfunctional for the current objectives of the organisation. In posing the question 'What does the study of masculinity have to offer probation practice?', we must thus ask what it has to offer management practice also. In order to do this we need first to address what may appear to be the components of stereotypical masculinity in our society.

Masculinity: what a man's gotta do!

Brannon and David (1976: 16) attempted to define the components of masculinity thus:

(a) no sissy stuff – avoid all behaviours that even remotely suggest the feminine;
(b) be a big wheel – get success and status and they confer masculinity;
(c) be a sturdy oak – reliability and dependability are defined as emotional and affective distance;

(d) give 'em hell – exude an aura of manly aggression: 'take no prisoners'.

Commenting on this view, Kimmel (1990) suggests that this specifies a white, middle-class, heterosexual masculinity against which all others are judged. However, it is the prevailing view and the view subscribed to by those males who control the economic and political power in our society. Thus it has corrupted or even sometimes obliterated alternative forms and constructs. Reviewing the male role, Bowl (1985) points to key themes of competence and competition and aggression which underlie the breadwinner role for which all men are intended. He goes on to describe how these themes are connected to form an idealised role which is difficult to maintain or achieve. It requires, therefore, strategies for its maintenance such as the rituals contained in sexual innuendo, or 'the male obsession with demonstrating their strength and unity through sport' (Bowl, 1985: 13). Bowl goes further in examining the implications of the male role when he comments that, 'taken to its limits, not expressing emotion must lead to not experiencing it. Thus comes less insight, less awareness of one's inner self and a self-descructive non-recognition that things are going wrong' (Bowl, 1985: 14). Other works have pointed out, as critical, the centrality of sexual competence and bravado to the male self-image. Willis (1977) and Kagan and Moss (1962) both point out that central to maintaining a traditional masculine identification is a preoccupation with and an ostentation about sexual knowledge. Individuals show they are men by announcing concern with and prowess in sexuality. Similarly, as Vass (1984) observed in his participant observation study of community service, the 'tough guy' masculine type, who boasts of plenty of sexual exploits and presents as a 'casanova' and a 'womaniser' to incite others to challenge requirements and obligations, is a regular feature of community service organisation with regard to men, whilst the few women offenders who are put in that male-dominated organisation become the subordinates to the 'macho' culture: they look after male offenders' needs by serving tea and being in the kitchen. Such strands are central to the oppression of women and to the many damaging and offending ways that men behave towards them (Buckley, 1991). What is also clear is that men are not by and large comfortable with challenging such stereotypes of themselves. Alison Thomas (1990: 152), in her research into male attitudes, found 'a strong denial of acting unconventionally for one's gender' coupled with 'a preoccupation with rather than resistance to conventional standards of masculinity'.

The present author's own involvement with running workshops on masculinity indicates a surprising correlation of images around what a man is supposed to be and considerable adherence to them (Buckley and Williams, 1992).

The common themes are always about curtailing emotion, success, fighting and sexual competence. Families, schools and peer groups have ways of showing their displeasure to boys who will not be 'proper' men. For many men, however, other men's masculinity looks very unlike theirs. This poses an interesting question: put in criminal justice terms, if norms of masculinity are commonly held constructs pertinent to the study of criminology, why do some men grow up to be law-makers and some law-breakers? Why are there male judges, policemen, probation officers, but also law-breakers and criminals? Although these categories can be demonstrated not to be mutually exclusive, common sense would dictate that many men fall into one category or another.

An answer to this question may be developed from the work of Gramsci (1971), who outlined that there was not one but *many* masculinities. Masculinities may be economically and culturally variable around a series of common threads, with other social factors intervening to influence the interpretation of the themes or their implementation. Hearn and Morgan (1990: 11) comment that this 'concept of hegemonic masculinities addresses itself to those issues pointing to the dominance within society of certain forms of masculinity which are historically conditioned and open to change and challenge. Thus today such a model might be white heterosexist, middle-class, anglophone and so on.'

This perspective would suggest that whilst groups of men may experience subordination or marginalisation as a consequence of sexual preference, ethnicity or class position, the power of the prevailing myths are such that even those subordinated by them adhere to those myths and spend time actively shoring them up or demonstrating how they can buy into them. This is pointed out by Willis (1990) in relation to offenders and by Sallie Westwood (1990) in her study of young black male football clubs. She comments that 'there is a collective mobilisation through football that calls up black masculinities as part of the resistance that black men generate against the racism of society' (Westwood, 1990: 67). Thus masculinity becomes a set of precepts which, if adhered to, confer the reward of being seen to be a man. The individual takes his own particular personal scenarios, and where disadvantage based on other variables denies him opportunity, he will seek out other ways to demonstrate his adherence to the principles and to gain access to the rewards. Thus, in terms of offending, it may be viewed as 'a revenge of subordinate masculinities against police power'

(McGauhey, 1992). Similarly, Jackson (1992) suggests that car theft is an attempt by alienated working-class youth to take the symbols of middle-class, middle-aged power; and Angela Davis (1982) has argued that the working-class man who rapes is being bought off from acknowledging his powerlessness in society. Extending this analysis, it is possible to see offending behaviour as a rational response to the messages of how to construct one's masculinity. In other words, crime is a way of expressing masculinity and behind that emphasising one's gender. It is possible to redefine Brannon and David's (1976) four-way principles in simpler terms and to say that to show you are a man you must show that you:

(a) are strong and tough, lacking sensitivity;
(b) are successful/popular/one of the gang – a real 'lad';
(c) have no feelings, or if you have they must not be shown;
(d) are ready to fight;
(e) regard women as subordinates and objects of gratification.

Interestingly enough the same theme of masculinity which guides men to express their gender seems to be reproduced by the state in its efforts to demonstrate a 'tough' and 'macho' posture in dealing with offenders. As Hudson (1988) suggests, there is a 'paradox' at work: on the one hand, the meaning of male offending is congruent with society's agenda for masculinity; on the other, the state punishes this form of male expression (particularly that by black and working-class men) by even more doses of 'macho' sanctions.

The consequences of masculinity for social work

The usefulness of a masculinity framework for looking at social work practice is that it does not in a sense claim to be exclusive. For example, recent debates on the issue of masculinity have led to alternative interpretations and views that masculinity is not in itself a particularly useful concept in analysing and explaining crime (see, for instance, Cornwall and Lindisfarne, 1994; Messerschmidt, 1993; Newburn and Stanko, 1994). Rather, it allows that other theories of problem causation may have validity and may interact. Thus in the context of offending behaviour, for example, it is apparent that we are dealing with men who, while they are interpreting the codes of masculinity, are interpreting them in the light of poverty, class oppression, inner-city deprivation or damage caused to the person by early and persistent abuse. In this way the constructs of masculinity should be informing the understanding of a range of problems rather than demanding a complete rethink.

This approach does not argue for an abandoning of other anti-oppressive work to concentrate on gender. Patricia Hill Collins (1990) and Angela Davis (1982) have both argued cogently that the denial to black men of the status and achievement conferred in the public arena by masculinity can result in oppressive sexist behaviour in the private domain of the home. As Lynn Segal (1990: 187) comments:

> For the black male underclass, like other men denied the usual confirmations of gender superiority, the only mechanisms of dominance available are frequently the mechanisms of self-destruction – internecine violence, sexual coercion and self-hatred.

In probation terms, no black man is going to explore an analysis of gender and masculinity (which usually appears to mean giving something up) with his usually white probation officer unless he is clear that the officer is willing and able to tackle racism wherever it is found. Our current constructs of masculinity are in any event underpinned by racism, with its implicit devaluation of other family forms and gender roles. Hill Collins (1990) argues, for example, that part of what fuels racism in America has been the fear of acknowledging the success of other forms of family living and child-rearing which are demonstrated in black communities with some success. Hill Collins (see also hooks, 1981) points out that a system where children are the responsibility of all and the property of none has its own checks and balances against abuse and neglect, but also challenges the accepted power structure in white nuclear families.

The challenge to homophobia is also central to the challenge to stereotypes of masculinity since, as Segal (1990: 158) argues, 'homophobia . . . not only keeps all men in line while oppressing gay men; in its contempt for the feminine in men it simultaneously expresses contempt for women'. At the same time, Ford and Robinson (1993) outline how homophobia successfully prevents real discussion of sexual feelings and desires and prevents any in-depth explanations of sexually violent offending, by avoiding any acknowledgement of the role of heterosexism in masculinity.

Will the real men please stand up

Put so starkly, one wonders why an analysis of offending behaviour based on masculinity has not already been proffered and made use of in the criminal justice system. This system remains designed by men, for men, accompanied by a great deal of macho rhetoric. From 'short sharp shock' to 'just deserts' and 'punishment in the community', its philosophies all seem rooted in the value system that runs the successful boys' public schools from which, not perhaps coincidentally, their authors come. The point about this background is that it gives men the tools to make a success of their world, it teaches lack of emotion, despisal of the feminine, how to be a big wheel and a 'lad', and provides a certain licence to 'give 'em hell' in the process (Hudson, 1988). The problem is that these tools require the ready access to privilege and achievement that the products of such schools have. Taught or reinforced to those who are denied that access, they find their fulfilment in all kinds of anti-social and offending behaviour. Two architects may have the same blueprint, but provide them with vastly different materials and the results will be divergent in quality, style and outcomes.

In many respects, one can suggest that the probation service, lacking its own direction, or perhaps suffering from a surfeit of philosophies and directions, has been steadily moving in the same 'masculine' area. It is fashionable to blame its management for bowing to prevailing winds. But they are in many ways, as has been pointed out, only a reflection of the philosophies of their profession. In this profession, a failure to acknowledge the impact of stereo-typical masculinity on male behaviour can lead to a failure to analyse and therefore effectively deal with motivations and conse-quently outcomes. For example, Cordery and Whitehead (1992) examined the nature of interactions between male probation officers and offenders. They found that most of their energies in interview were focused on establishing dominance over the offender and that authority came from their role and from this dominance, not from personality or reason. They also suggested that the efforts of the probation officer to establish dominance merely met with a reaction in the client, who then had to establish his own methods of asserting his authority. They conclude thus:

> . . . it becomes easy to engage in a counter-productive challenging and tackling game which is based on a denial of our own weakness and insecurities. This is meat and drink to men. We . . . learned this game in the playground. (Cordery and Whitehead, 1992: 32)

In fairness to men, there are other factors which impinge on the debate. One of these is the paucity of male role models. Even where the adult male has come to terms with the stereotypes and worked through a new model of how to operate, his opportunities to present this to others are severely limited. Child-care in this society, along with child teaching, is an almost exclusively female activity. 'English fathers', to use Olivia Harris's (1984) phrase, 'are almost arche-typically absent.'

Whether a father is absent in prison, following divorce or as a highly stressed executive working long hours or spending his time in a public house, he is still not there to provide insight and advice to his children. Subject any probation caseload to inspection and you will find an absence of significant, non-abusive fathering and, of equal importance, a lack of significant other males offering time. There is no way of checking that the stereotypes are not real. Others have suggested that two-dimensional television figures or characters may become more real to young boys than their own relatives. In any event the impact of the stereotypes is that these images of real 'manhood' have an impact on men's personalities. As Victor Siedler (1988: 28) writes, 'men learn to pride themselves on the fact that they do not have emotional needs . . . as men we are trapped into feeling that we have to constantly prove our masculinity. We have to be constantly on our guard against others.'

Siedler goes on to suggest that men appear 'not available' in relationships, their energies and thoughts directed elsewhere. Without real experience to challenge the stereotypes, men would be seen to be very vulnerable to them and particularly unable to accept and work with the challenges to them contained in close personal relationships. Thus, they are likely to seek solace in the public world of work, activity and, in certain circumstances, offending. In other words, crime provides for some men the means for showing or expressing their 'norm' of masculinity by illicit activity.

Reinforming the 'search for a floundering purpose'

Accepting the relevance of stereotypes of masculinity to offending behaviour in men does not require a major rethink in practice and methods. Its value lies in its ability to reinform. For example, colleagues running an alcohol course chose to share how they had been set up as men for unwise drinking behaviour by images of what a 'real' man would drink and acting out a male pub culture. They talked about their own experience as people and were rewarded with hard work, honesty and collaboration from the course participants. Perhaps what was taking place here was an honest attempt to establish a mutual understanding rather than attain the hierarchical modes of working quoted earlier by Cordery and Whitehead (1992).

It is often necessary for male professionals to take a lead. In a training session, the present author with a colleague asked a group of male offenders to brainstorm the best and worst things about being a woman and then a man. They provided an in-depth analysis of women's issues, after all most magazines are now permeated with ideas about women's challenge to the stereotype at some level. When it came to looking at men, however, they reached no further than 'birds do your head in'. At one point in fact an interesting discussion took place about the homilies of a local judge who often said that he would take a personal interest in a defendant's further offending and reward it with imprisonment. One group participant commented on how this had stayed in his mind and made him cautious about getting into arguments in public places in case they escalated. Other group members agreed with this point but somehow no analysis of male behaviour came out of the discussion. It was as if the men saw themselves as victims of uncontrollable forces which included their own behaviour. It may be relevant, then, in group-work and individualised work for workers to start naming the social forces, so that they can be identified and worked with. Thus, rather than developing an understanding of masculinity which excuses men's behaviour by allowing them to adopt a victim status, we might develop one which forces them to consider the impact of masculinity on them and their actions. In that way, they may never again view themselves as driven by uncontrollable forces, either biological or environmental. Conversely, by sharing responsibility, one might reduce the problem to a size and shape that can be made manageable and amenable to change. The readiness of probation officers to do this kind of work is not clear, however. As Cordery and Whitehead (1992) note, men must learn how to interact with clients rather than adopting a stylised form of masculine behaviour.

An alternative to the challenging, confronting horn-locking that they described earlier is that men must learn to listen and to share their experiences. Women have been working like this with women clients for years. A recent 'desk-top' inspection in the present author's own team led to a male colleague commenting that there was something happening 'honestly' between women colleagues and women offenders which did not go on between males. Male officers, he felt, did not get close to male offenders, nor share with them openly.

Equally, the knowledge base with which to analyse offending behaviour in relation to masculinity is not always apparent. For example, Spencer's (1993) analysis of probation service reports points out some of the inconsistencies and dilemmas probation officers demonstrate in explaining offending behaviour to the courts. He comments that 'implausibility is most common in reports concerning violence and alcohol-related motoring offences' (Spencer, 1993: 16).

He is inclined to interpret these inconsistencies as arising from a confusion about the appropriateness of community service or probation as a disposal. It is, however, possible to understand the examples he uses as a failure to come to terms with and explain the imperatives of masculinity in driving men to implausible behaviour. It is as if the officer intuitively understands the pressures on the offender, wants to put them forward to the court, but lacks the language to do so. Hence reports may appear as elusive, dismissive or simply covering up.

Such work needs effective supervision and training, but few supervisors or trainers have explored the topic of masculinity for themselves. All services have policies about gender, but these are seen at best as a reminder to explore the needs of women offenders and staff. Rarely is the impact of gender stereotypes or male behaviour explored in case supervision. At recent national workshops run by the present author and a colleague, it was apparent that few staff supervisors were inclined to focus on professional issues. 'Most people's experience', we wrote afterwards, 'was of soldiering on and looking for assistance wherever they could get it' (Buckley and Perry, 1993). Training on issues of gender and masculinity would seem to be a priority need, but one that is not being met. Examples were offered in the above workshop of the increasingly mechanistic nature of some processes now going on in the nature of staff supervision. New demands on seniors and new management styles were not seen to be particularly helpful to practice development.

Tim May (1991) has described the process of social work in the probation service as 'a search for a floundering purpose' and suggested that 'intra-organisational conflict' is one result of this. Another result, he suggests, is openness of the service to central manipulation. May has reviewed the development of probation theory and its impact on one service. What is interesting is to look at the development of that theory in the light of Brannon's four tenets of masculinity: 'no sissy stuff, be a big wheel, be a sturdy oak and give 'em hell'. For all the attempts of the left to view it differently, it remains an occupation which is conducive to such behaviour; probation work becomes the 'big wheel' giving offenders 'hell'. Even the 'professional, objective social work relationship' may be predicated on the notion of the 'sturdy oak'.

Putting theory into practice: reconciling the 'competing modes of working'

In order to regenerate officers' tired challenge to offending behaviour, they need a philosophy which integrates the various methodologies of work and enables them to see themselves as central to that challenge. If they can get that right, then they may be able to demand of themselves and their political leaders the kind of management and support structures they need. So how, in Canton's terms, do they begin to work 'demandingly, creatively and humanely'? How do they, as May challenges, reconcile the 'two competing modes of working' he found in his studies arising from the demands of their political leaders and the ever present needs and demands of offenders?

The answer may be in recognising that they both come from the same root – the demands that stereotypical masculinity makes on men, the elusive promises it offers them, and their various coping strategies. The pressure which makes the Home Secretary promise harsh penalties is the same pressure that makes those he is determined to penalise offend. It is the need to be seen as tough, uncompromising, emotionless; the 'top dog' prepared to 'give 'em hell' in order to win. Caught in the middle of this debate is, as Cordery and Whitehead (1992) remind us, like being between small boys squaring up to each other in the playground.

At the outset, practitioners have to understand masculinity in its various guises and work on it. This does not mean rejecting national standards, or efficiency, or research, but it does argue for a fresh look at what they do with people. In community service, for example, research indicates that the best progress and potential for change is made by offenders who have a choice, who do worthwhile tasks and who have good relationships with their supervisors (McIvor 1992; Vass, 1984). Perhaps they need, therefore, to move away from traditional men's jobs, supervised by men for groups of men, to tasks which allow offenders to explore the sensitive and caring sides of themselves. As an example, we need to stop reinforcing the traditional divide between men's and women's tasks. Amongst a whole country of painting and decorating and gardening groups, we appear, for example, to have no housework groups, although, as Vass (1984) points out, if they exist they are reserved for women. Yet the community is full of people who have all these needs. Perhaps one needs to stop presenting community service, for example, as punishment and tell courts how it can improve a person's self-esteem and self-understanding, hence reduce their propensity to offend. However, even this attempt may come up against offenders' perception of community service as 'punishment and nothing else' (Vass, 1984). This perception is based on restrictions of 'leisure' for no financial gain. In short, the experience of receiving 'punishment' may be one more verification of the masculine slogan 'a man's gotta do, what a man's gotta do' and accept punishment as a man when he is caught. In that sense the issue of punishment and its relation to masculinity requires close inspection and clarification for it may resemble the current rediscovery of 'managerialism', where the classic dictum appears to prevail at all social costs: 'when the going gets tough, the tough get going'. At the same time, one needs to avoid the horn-locking opposition to the best possibilities of national standards. There is evidence that a fast response to failure to turn up for community service gets offenders working and completing with more satisfaction (McIvor, 1992; Nottingham Probation Service, 1993).

Similarly probation orders provide a vehicle for all kinds of work with offenders. The individual relationship needs to focus on challenging the constructs of masculinity whilst encouraging the person. As McGauhey (1992: 66) writes, 'use the tools of the clients' discourse to recognise the oppressive discourse of masculinism which often pervades. Deconstruct the internal logic, expose its flaws. Help clients get beyond it by exploring . . . anti-oppressive ways of doing masculinity'. The task is to enable the offender to see that he is not getting anywhere by doing what 'a man's gotta do'. One needs to address alternative and more subtle ways of doing 'gender' rather than through masculinity.

Supervision also provides access to courses, and course content needs to be carefully evaluated to ensure that challenge is offered to dominant stereotypes. A question needs to be posed in each course context what is it about men, as men, that gets them into this position? What are the values and imperatives given to men by stereotypical masculinity that cross-cut with disadvantage based on race, poverty, lack of opportunity, and so on, which may lead them into drinking, stealing and assaulting people?

Work done with groups of men and women separately indicates just how different these imperatives are for the two genders. Whilst in a group setting, men must be held accountable individually and collectively for their behaviour, they can also be enabled to understand what has been done to them in the name of masculinity. Workers cannot as men (and sometimes women) who are relatively 'powerful' vis-à-vis offenders distance themselves from the society which has advantaged them.

By acknowledging the impact on them, workers may begin to reconcile some of the dilemmas inherent in the conflicting demands, as May (1991) points out, are made on them as workers. Instead of alternating between hostility to the state coupled with compassion for the individual, and hostility to the negative outcomes that offenders have achieved, practitioners can begin, through understanding the constraints of masculinity, to synthesise these elements.

One point of impact that probation officers can have is in the writing of pre-sentence reports, though admittedly within a context of agency policy, relationships with the courts and legal changes.

Spencer (1993), quoted earlier, notes the 'implausibility' in some reports, which, as we have suggested, might arise from a lack of will or ability to interpret masculinity. We have argued elsewhere (see Buckley, 1988; also Hudson, 1988) that probation officers need to be more explicit in pre-sentence reports about the impact of masculinity on offending behaviour. For example, they can point out how prison might reinforce a man's adherence to the norms of alternative masculinity. McGauhey (1992) advises arguing for disposals which involve reparation or conciliation to 'restore greater control over events' (and presumably over masculinity) for both victims and offenders. She sounds a cautionary note that probation officers must not, in the process, allow themselves to provoke the greater scapegoating of white working-class and black men as 'unreconstructed'. This would be easy to do if they ignored the range of oppressions which bear down on individual men and affect the way they interpret masculinity. It would certainly leave the dominant ideologies of masculinity intact and in power.

Nowhere perhaps are the dilemmas of masculinity more acute than in work with sex offenders. Here a genuine attempt is made to focus on the power relationships between offender (male) and victim (usually female), rather than indulge in blaming the victim. In some schemes this has resulted in a complete distancing of the worker from the offender and his offences. The male worker can assuage his anger at himself for his own oppressive behaviour by offering aggressive and determined challenges to the offender, together with monitoring of the offenders' attitudes to sexuality (Perry, 1993).

Failure to acknowledge the ways in which stereotypical masculinity informs all male behaviour, so that it is seen as the norm, leads to half-hearted, inappropriate or unhelpful challenges to aspects of male behaviour. For example, Ford and Robinson (1993: 15) comment that 'the use of acceptable fantasies within this work often focuses at length on adult women, although often pornographic and non-consensual'. The authors are here posing the question whether this is the way to deal with men who may not have acknowledged and who may therefore repress a potential for a gay identity by offending against women. However, if we acknowledge the code of stereotypical masculinity which affects to despise or reject the female whilst valuing men who have sexual prowess, probation officers have to pose the question: is this the way to deal with any men? Practitioners are counselling men who see women and children as sexual objects by providing, through pornography, further evidence that they are just those objects. Furthermore, the worker will corroborate it. Can one logically teach men that women are objects but children are not? Rather, work with sex offenders in a masculinity context, whilst allowing, as Ford and Robinson suggest, for the possibility of gay identity, would explore the offenders' need to abuse power by workers who can acknowledge that they may have done this also in their own contexts.

Working in such ways as these are certainly creative, but they are also demanding. Women officers are victims of sexism in their daily lives and can continue to be discounted victims in work with male offenders who have retreated into what McGauhey (1992) characterises as 'fossilised maleness'. This is seemingly their only way of developing a 'positive identity, if only along the lines of criminal male/outlaw'.

The active challenge of male co-workers is essential, as is appropriate supervision. However, an understanding of stereotypical masculinity also allows that access to its goals is cross-cut by disadvantage based on race, homophobia, class or poverty. Just as male officers have to learn not to ignore their own oppressive behaviour whilst challenging the offenders, so female officers have to acknowledge how much their status may be based on their skin colour or the gender of their partner. The caseworkers of 20 years ago were enjoined in training not to project their feelings onto the offender. Reworking this motif let practitioners project their guilt for their own achievements based on privilege onto the multi-disadvantaged offender.

At the same time, McGauhey (1992) cautions against what she calls the 'men are oppressed too thesis'. As stated earlier, the intelligent use of an analysis of offending behaviour based on stereotypical masculinity should act to prevent the offender from seeing himself as a victim of forces beyond his control and to face him with responsibility for his behaviour, whilst seeking to make the issues manageable and definable. Working with masculinity effectively demands that practitioners call everyone to account for their oppressive behaviour. They must acknowledge that it is where oppressions intersect and conflict with the disadvantages based on one individual removing access to the rewards proffered by status from another that behaviour can exhibit the resolute clinging to the worst excesses of the stereotypes. It is thus no surprise that probation officers often deal with men exhibiting the worst excesses of stereotypical masculine behaviour. Offenders are finding their own ways of being what they have been taught a man should be. Poverty, class disadvantage and in some cases racism have denied them access to more legitimate outlets. Thus, probation officers must work with all the elements in a man's personal scenario if they are to help him unpick the relationship between his concept of masculinity and his offending.

Changing the culture: 'It's not whether you win or lose, but how you place the blame'

Any perusal of television programme, film or daily papers will quickly show that the context of oppressive masculinity is continuously advertised. One only has to watch, for example, the car adverts to see what a successful man is supposed to be: gifted with the benefit of an object which adds to his 'manliness' and symbolises his manhood. Work with the individual offender or groups of offenders has to be seen in that context. Thus, the individual officer needs the support of agency policies and statements.

Probation managers have a responsibility to articulate in policies and in representational forums the premises on which work is based. They have to build on the example of work with women where practitioner-led demands for anti-sexist work has resulted in service policy statements being made to courts, together with improved monitoring and pre-sentence reports, and so forth.

Probation officers are in daily contact with two large organisations: the prison service and the courts. Here they need the support of their managers in reinforcing good practice. The lone court duty officer or the lone pre-sentence report writer can have little impact at times unless the relevant senior or assistant chief probation officer is prepared to offer the firm backing of policy. Unfortunately, the probation management response to increased central pressure and public scapegoating of the service has been, by and large, to suggest that it is officer practice which is responsible for the failings of the criminal justice system. In a sense, here we may see the workings of masculinity writ large – 'you bully me and I'll bully the next person'.

It is perhaps too easy to enter the game of 'it's not whether you win or lose, but how you place the blame'. Both May (1991) and Canton (1993) suggest that a lack of coherent philosophy has left the service open to central government intrusion which has produced this management reaction, and the service needs to understand masculinity if it is to counteract this. In many ways, the system it has bought into offers illusory goals, for example the ability to have an impact on the general level of crime in society (see Chapters 10 and 11 in this volume).

However, as long as the probation service espouses the goals of punishment and retribution it will never be allowed real status in the criminal justice system. The probation service is its conscience, the thorn in its flesh, and however perilous and emasculated a role that seems, it must espouse it wholeheartedly. If probation officers judge themselves in terms of status and acceptability they will fail. They have to bring back to the centre of the debate the sad and deprived reality of offenders' lives, and the extent to which social policies have influenced that. They have a critical campaigning and advocacy role in whatever arenas they find themselves.

Managing with an understanding of stereotypical masculinity means refusing to play 'macho games', supporting and caring for staff, encouraging contributions and hearing what staff have to say. It also involves providing space for staff development and trusting them to use it constructively. It also involves having standards about which organisations probation officers work with in partnership, and how they direct their energies.

Just as one can see offenders searching for ways to show they are men – by stealing the fast cars or consumer goods, or by oppressing women – so one can see probation management and officers searching for ways to show they are 'men' by opting for more control, more packages, more illusions that probation is a hard and punishing option.

If the way to deal with offenders is to get them talking about masculinity and what has been done to them and what they in turn do to others, maybe managers need to start to examine what is happening to them. Just as offenders have to work out how they have been set up by masculinity, perhaps the probation service may need to do so too. Managers in particular may need to talk to each other about how unpleasant their jobs are becoming, even to confess failure and then start to do something about it. A woman assistant chief probation officer once described her first Association of Chief Officers of Probation meeting as having been 'invited into an exclusive boys' club'. Maybe the boys need to break the club down. In order to find the will to do so they need to look at the extent to which stereotypical masculinity and its constraints is preventing them from running effective organisations. Such organisations get the best out of their staff by enabling them to do the job they were trained for: challenging offending behaviour and its causes. Masculinity is given expression through crime. Maybe by dislodging that connection and finding alternative, more subtle and sociable ways of allowing men to 'play gender', the need to turn to crime to demonstrate that they are 'men' may cease to be of relevance. Tackling masculinity may not, of course, solve social problems like crime completely, but can go some way in addressing some of the less understood and less appreciated roots of this problem in social relationships.

References

Bowl, R. (1985) *Changing the Nature of Masculinity*. Norwich: Social Work Monographs, University of East Anglia.

Brannon, R. and David, D. (1976) *The 49% Majority Reading*. Reading, MA: Addison-Wesley.

Buckley, K. (1988) 'Why Dennis the Menace grows up to be Rambo', *Social Work Today*, 28 July: 23.

Buckley, K. (1991) 'An exploration of stereotypes of masculinity and violent behaviour against women'. Unpublished MA Dissertation, University of Loughborough.

Buckley, K. and Perry, E. (1993) 'Supervision staff and sexually violent offenders', *NAPO News*, September: 8–9.

Buckley, K. and Williams, A. (1992) 'Driving with Rambo', *NAPO News*, August: 12–13.

Canton, R. (1993) 'The Criminal Justice Act: trying to make sense of it all', *NAPO News*, October: 7–9.

Cordery, J. and Whitehead, A. (1992) 'Boys don't cry', in P. Senior and D. Woodhill (eds), *Gender, Crime and Probation Practice*. Sheffield: Pavic. pp. 23–34.

Cornwall, A. and Lindisfane, N. (eds) (1994) *Dislocating Masculinity: Comparative Perspectives*. London: Routledge.

Cowburn, M., Wilson, C. and Lowenstein, P. (1992) *Changing Men Pack*. Nottingham: Nottingham Probation Service.

Davis, A. (1982) *Women, Race and Class*. London: Women's Press.

Farrington, D. and Morris, A. (1983) 'Sex sentencing and reconviction', *British Journal of Criminology*, 23 (3): 229–48.

Ford, R. and Robinson, N. (1993) 'Gay men; discrimination within the law and sex offender programmes', in K. Buckley and C. McGauhey (eds), *Sexuality in Youth Work and Probation Practice*. Sheffield: Pavic. pp. 11–20.

Gramsci, A. (1971) *The Prison Notebooks*. London: Lawrence and Wishart.

Greer, G. (1970) *The Female Eunuch*. London: McGibbon and Kee.

Harris, O. (1984) 'Heavenly father', in U. Owen (ed.), *Fathers: Reflections by Daughters*. London: Virago.

Hearn, J. and Morgan, D. (1990) *Men, Masculinities and Social Theory*. London: Unwin Hyman.

Heidensohn, F. (1985) *Women and Crime*. London: Macmillan.

Hill Collins, P. (1990) *Black Feminist Thought*. London: HarperCollins.

hooks, b. (1981) *Ain't I A Woman*. London: Southend Press.

Hudson, A. (1988) 'Boys will be boys: masculinism and the juvenile justice system', *Critical Social Policy*, 7 (21): 30–48.

Jackson, D. (1992) '"You're in someone's car and you're all bubbling": joyriding and masculine desires', *Achilles' Heel*, 13: 8–9.

Kagan, J. and Moss, H.A. (1962) *Birth to Maternity*. New York: Whiley.

Kimmel, M. (1990) 'After fifteen years: the impact of the sociology of masculinity on the masculinity of sociology', in J. Hearn and L. Morgan (eds), *Men, Masculinities and Social Theory*. London: Unwin Hyman. pp. 93–109.

McGauhey, C. (1992) 'Making masculinity explicit in work with male offenders', in P. Senior and D. Woodhill (eds), *Gender, Crime and Probation Practice*. Sheffield: Pavic. pp. 59–69.

McIvor, G. (1992) *Reconviction amongst Offenders Sentenced to Community Service*. Stirling: University of Stirling Social Work Research Centre

May, T. (1991) *Probation: Politics, Policy and Practice*. Milton Keynes: Open University Press.

Messerchmidt, J.W. (1993) *Masculinities and Crime*. Rowman and Littleheld.

Newburn, T. and Stanko, E. (eds) (1994) *Just Boys Doing Business? Men, Masculinity and Crime*. London: Routledge.

Nottinghamshire Probation Service (1993) *Community Service Annual Report*. Nottingham: Nottingham Probation Service.

Perry, E. (1993) 'Male worker and sex offender: congruent behaviour', *Probation Journal*, 40 (3): 140–2.

Segal, L. (1990) *Slow Motion: Changing Masculinities, Changing Men*. London: Virago.

Siedler, V. (1988) 'Fathering authority and masculinity', in R. Chapman and J. Rutherford (eds), *Male Order*. London: Lawrence and Wishart. pp. 272–302.

Smart, C. (1976) *Women, Crime and Criminology*. London: Routledge and Kegan Paul.

Spencer, J. (1993) *Report to Nottinghamshire Probation Service on the Proposals Contained in Pre-sentence Reports*. Unpublished. Manchester. Nottinghamshire Probation Service.

Thomas, A. (1990) 'The significance of gender politics in men's accounts of their gender identity', in J. Hearn and D. Morgan (eds), *Men, Masculinities and Social Theory*. London: Unwin Hyman. pp. 143–60.

Vass, A.A. (1984) *Sentenced to Labour: Close Encounters with a Prison Substitute*. St Ives: Venus Academica.

Vass, A.A. (1996) 'Crime, probation and social work with offenders', in A.A. Vass (ed.), *Social Work Competences: Core Knowledge, Values and Skills*. London: Sage. pp. 132–89.

Westwood, S. (1990) 'Racism, black masculinity and the politics of space', in J. Hearn and D. Morgan (eds), *Men, Masculinities and Social Theory*. London: Unwin Hyman. pp. 55–72.

Willis, P. (1977) *Learning to Labour*. London: Saxon House.

Willis, P. (1990) *Common Culture*. Buckingham: Open University Press.

PART II

CONTEXTS

6

The Role of Probation Committees in Policing the Development of the Probation Service

Simon Holdaway

This chapter is about contemporary change within the probation service of England and Wales and the role of probation committees in making policy. On a broader level, it also has another, more long-standing reference point in sociological and social work research – the development of formal rationality (see Weber, 1976, 1978) as a central feature of modern industrial societies. Bureaucratic structures and formal, rational modes of thought in modern societies have been most fully researched within the manufacturing and financial sectors (Clegg and Dunkerley, 1980). The standardisation of consumer goods within a production-line system of manufacture, based on an intense division of labour, has been identified as the logical outcome of the institutionalisation of formal rationality. Less attention, however, has been given to the ways in which formal rationality has influenced public service institutions in general and criminal justice institutions like the probation service in particular.

The intention is not to engage in a discourse about the validity of formal rationality as a substantive, prescriptive notion. Here, we shall identify and illustrate some limitations of the Home Office view of the probation service. By implication, we will also question some of the assumptions underpinning Central Council for Education and Training in Social Work (CCETSW) Paper 30 and its review because it too is dependent on the idea that it is possible to rationally plan probation and social work training that will somewhat straightforwardly transfer knowledge, skills and competences learned in educational and training settings to the day-to-day routines of the workplace.

This chapter, then, is concerned with one aspect of whether or not the probation service will in the future, and in the light of Home Office reforms, develop as a formal, rational organisation. The focus is on a little-known institution – the probation committee. Although the data analysed here are historical, they are nevertheless directly relevant to the running of the current probation service and the assumptions that underpin Paper 30 and subsequent developments referred to in Chapter 1 in this book.

Particular emphasis will be placed on the role of probation committees in policy development. All the changes proposed assume that the committee and probation boards will provide a strategic policy framework for their area service. Aided by the analysis of data derived from performance indicators, the committee will ensure that their policies are put into practice by the fieldworkers they employ.

The analysis of lengthy, semi-structured interviews with 77 probation committee members and their respective chief probation officers working in five area services will inform the discussion.[1] A central feature of the argument will be that it is necessary to take into account assumptions about the function and purpose of the probation service brought to considerations of policy by the various groups that are party to it. Actors' 'assumptive worlds' intervene in and restructure formal processes of policy-making (Young, 1977).

Ken Young's notion of 'assumptive worlds' has been adapted from the work of the psychiatrist Colin Murray Parkes, especially his use of it in his studies of bereavement. Parkes puts it thus:

> A man is tied to his assumptive world. By learning to recognise and act appropriately within his expectable environment a man makes life space his own . . . the assumptive world not only contains a model of the world as it might be (these models may represent probable situations, ideal situations, or dreaded situations). Models of the world as it might be are used as a rehearsal for actions appropriate to the worlds. (quoted in Young, 1977: 6)

Within the contradictions, complexities and ambiguities that are the daily routine of organisational life, people involved in policy implementation act on the basis of prescriptions, expectations, compatibilities and accommodations that, as far as possible, allow sense to be made of and action to be feasible within their particular world. Young (1977: 1-12) argues that assumptive worlds offer

> the stage directions for environmental response, that is, for the management of demand and dependency; they enable the system controllers, like individuals, to understand the world insofar as possible and to defend it against it insofar as necessary.

Organisations can therefore be conceptualised as multitudes of rationalities (invariably perspectives), vying with and yielding to each other. The assumptive world of probation fieldwork staff may, for example, be rather different from that of senior probation officers, from chief officers, who in turn may view the probation service in a fundamentally different way to their probation committee members, to Home Office officials, and so on. For instance, it is well known that at different levels of the social organisation of work, workers interpret and amend rules and regulations or expectations according to their own 'world view' (see Vass, 1984: 42–58). This places the possibility that diverse rather than uniform understandings of probation work may be sustained within an area service. There cannot be an assumption of a 'top-down' development and implementation of policy where that which is written into policy is more or less put into practice. Area probation services are better understood as loosely coupled rather than tightly bound organisations (Weick, 1969, 1976). The organisational structures of area probation services and related procedures for policy-making are marked by ambiguity and uncertainty as much as by the clarity and security required for the development of formal, rational policy.

Rationality and the Home Office model of implementation

The Home Office paper *Organising Supervision and Punishment in the Community* (Home Office, 1991) may be regarded as the key document about the future governance and management of the probation service, though, as previous chapters in this book have rightly suggested in the light of changes in policy, it is difficult to ascertain with any accuracy the exact nature and purpose of the probation service. None the less, a clear emphasis is placed in the paper on the need for any proposed changes to 'ensure responsiveness to national objectives and standards; clarify accountabilities and responsibilities; and improve the effectiveness of management' (Home Office, 1991: 3). Although the probation service of England and Wales is not a unified, national service directly administered by the Home Office but divided into 56 separate area services, each with its own employing committee (the probation committee), the extent to which the Home Office places a framework of constraint around area policies is considerable. *Organising Supervision and Punishment in the Community*, for example, requires strategic planning by a new probation board in each probation area; the clear management of area services by the chief probation officer, the chief executive of the service; the need for all area staff to work towards agreed, stated objectives, directly related to probation service national aims and objectives; the adoption of national standards of work; the monitoring of policy outcomes through performance indicators; cash limiting of budgets, with responsibility for retention of an area service within budget by its probation board; and the integral role of the probation service within a local and national criminal justice system.

The Home Office definition of policy is one of a prescriptive statement of objectives that managers and fieldwork staff implement, the extent to which they do so being monitored by the analysis of measurable outcomes of their action. The area probation board agrees to policy statements presented by the chief probation officer. Policy is then passed down the organisational hierarchy to managers and on to fieldworkers who implement it. Consistency of policy development and implementation therefore guides the work of all members of the probation service, from top to bottom.

Ideas like these are reflected in the assumptions of training bodies. Once national and local objectives have been defined it is possible to identify cognisant knowledge, skills and competences required by staff. Training curriculars can be constructed on the rational basis of organisational objectives, and so on. This is precisely what CCETSW and the Home Office have set out to achieve in their 'guidance' to training institutions.[2] Ideally, there is a neat fit between the top and bottom of the organisation – policy is put into practice, monitored and, if required, managerial adjustments ensure an ongoing alignment between the two.

Formal rationality therefore structures this process of policy development, implementation, monitoring and the related training needs of probation staff. Indeed, there is a striking symmetry between recent developments in the probation service and Taylor's longer-standing principles of work for industrial production, which are an exemplar of modern, formal rational modes of thought and organisation (Taylor, 1911). These are as follows:

1. Shift all responsibility for the organisation of work from the worker to the manager.
2. Use scientific methods to determine the most efficient way of doing work.
3. Select the best person to perform the job so designed.
4. Train the worker to do the work efficiently.
5. Monitor worker performance to ensure that appropriate work procedures are followed and that appropriate results are achieved.

A perspective like this contrasts sharply with the traditions of probation work. The probation service has based its professional status on social work principles, affording a great deal of discretion to the individual worker, who more or less organised his or her own cases (McWilliams 1987, 1989). A senior probation officer would routinely offer advice and guidance to fieldworkers, but as a supervisory caseworker rather than the manager of a highly structured programme of intervention. Social work ideals still inform the probation service mission but at its core there is now the delivery of a 'package' or 'programme' of intervention, specifically designed to tackle an individual's offending behaviour. A court accepting a sentence that includes a probation provision should be reassured about the various 'components' of the package offered and its adequacy to address the offending behaviour that is being considered. Fieldwork staff are increasingly viewed as managers of probation interventions. This idea of probation officers as managers is quite new, though they have always acted, albeit illegitimately, as 'policy-makers in miniature' (Vass, 1984).

Whilst few probation officers would claim the imprimatur of 'scientific method' for their work, programmatic methods should by now have largely superseded social work meanderings. National standards of work have been introduced and these tend to focus on confronting offenders with the consequences of their offence; their return to court if they are not complying with the conditions of a probation programme; and so on. The discretion of the professional is thereby limited to what are accepted as preferred and effective methods of intervention.

Although many continue to stress the social work base of their training and work, probation officers are increasingly specialists in groupwork with young offenders, sex offenders, motor vehicle offenders, and so the list of offenders expands (Davies et al., 1989). Training for the probation service is also increasingly specialist, somewhat separated from generic social work training, the result of Home Office insistence that the reduction of offending behaviour is the binding task for officers (Nellis, 1992; see also Chapters 1, 10 and 11 in this volume).

The roots of these developments are diverse and complex. At the societal level there is the growth of formal rationality within industrial societies, to which Weber and others have drawn our attention (May, 1994; Weber, 1976, 1978). Within contemporary Britain, and maybe more widely within Europe too, there has been a transfer of management ideologies and techniques from the industrial and financial sectors to the public sector, including criminal justice agencies (Farnham and Horton, 1993). The creation of a market for the trading of criminal justice services and other social provisions has led to local initiatives and a strengthening of the hand of central government. Ironically, the 'framework of market freedom' structured by central government has become one of considerable constraint (Jones, 1993).

At the level of the probation service, there has been a desire to demonstrate 'efficiency and effectiveness' and to challenge the supposed ascendancy of the 'nothing works' doctrine (Martinson, 1974). The 'something' that now works is primarily the addressing of offending behaviour. To this end organisational objectives written into action plans have been developed in all probation areas (Coker, 1988). Cash-limited budgets have been ordered to align with the same objectives (Humphrey and Pease, 1992; Humphrey et al., 1993).

This description of changes affecting the probation service in England and Wales is scene-setting rather than exhaustive. The main point we want to make is that Home Office reforms are intended to reorganise the probation service as a formally rational organisation. The reforms are substantial and firmly embedded in intended policy. Reviewing some of them in relation to the fundamental purpose of the probation service, McWilliams and Pease (1990) have argued that the service has lost a perception of an overarching vision and moral justification for its work, other than one of internal, rational planning for policy development and service delivery, which cannot sustain the appropriate humanistic, rehabilitative purpose it should revive and pursue. Management within the probation service, they argue, is a means searching for an unspecified end.

Whatever the merits of criticism about government and Home Office plans for the probation service, there can be little doubt that systematic policy planning for effective service delivery through rational organisational processes has been and will remain one of their key features. In fact, we know very little about structures for and processes of management within the probation service, not least structures and processes of policy development (Humphrey et al., 1993; May, 1991). Most debates about the future of the probation service have been conducted without the benefit of evidence secured from social science research.

Probation committees

Probation committees are not a well-known institution.[3] Each of the 56 area probation services in England and Wales has a probation committee with a membership of magistrates, elected by local benches. In addition, areas that include a London borough or metropolitan district council within their boundary are required to co-opt a councillor to the committee. Furthermore, all committees may co-opt up to a maximum of one third of its total membership.

Judges serving courts within a probation area are also represented by one or two colleagues who are committee members. Each probation committee therefore has a diverse membership, but, importantly, one dominated by the magistracy. This composition of probation committees, as we will see, has implications for their interpretation of duties and responsibilities defined in *The Probation Rules* (Home Office, 1984a).

Probation Committees are the employer – albeit part-time – of all probation staff. Committee members also have a duty to ensure the efficient running of an area probation service by sanctioning rules and guidance for full-time personnel to follow (Home Office, 1984b). The duties and responsibilities of employers are mostly prescribed by statute; interpretations of efficiency within the context of the work of an area probation service are not.

The emphasis of recent Home Office documents of various kinds has stressed the role of probation committees in the strategic planning of area probation services. Of course, probation committees are now probation boards. Magistrates, therefore, remain as members but as a smaller proportion of the standard membership of 15. All members, however, are appointed because they possess skills and experience of relevance to the work of the probation service. Magistrates will be members, for example, because they have knowledge and experience of relevance to sentencing, court work, and so on, not because they are members of the magistracy per se.

The chief probation officer is also a member of the board, of equal status to all colleagues. The board is the employer of all probation staff but, clearly within the main stream of Home Office rational planning, its primary task is strategic planning. If the proposed reforms of probation committees lead to their intended outcomes, probation board members will work within the framework of the Home Office national plan, agree related objectives for their area service, ensure that resources are available to achieve them, and be sure that performance indicators to monitor policy outcomes are in place. A 'fit' between policy objectives and outcomes, give or take a degree of organisational tolerance, should without doubt strengthen the clarity of function and purpose of the probation service at the national and local levels. It will be an organisation with a formal rational structure, staffed by people who directly manage and implement policy in the field.

This is feasible so long as board members' ideas about the purpose and function of the probation service, and probation officers for that matter (see May, 1991), are consistent with those of the Home Office, chief probation officers, and so on. This point is raised because, during the author's research on probation committees that will be described, it was found that members had a range of views about fundamental objectives of the probation service, which distorted the intended formal and rational policy process, so called.

It was not unusual for committee members to make a distinction between chief officers as 'professionals' and themselves as laypeople having a range of relevant experience, hesitantly related to the governance of an area probation service. As one put it:

> . . . we're laypeople not professionals but we bring together a range of experience, whether it be estate agents concerned with hostels, repairs and their use of money there; whether we are ex-business people with business sense. There are a lot of different qualities that come together in a committee, which the officers can make use of.

As amateurs, committee members said they had to develop proficiency from a position of disadvantage. This view was identified by a member serving in a probation area where considerable responsibility for policy-making was taken by committee members, working in sub-groups with chief officers. This was captured in the following statement by another committee member:

> There are difficulties when there's a load of amateurs. We are all amateurs in that sense and you're faced with management of the service telling you what they've done – pages of financial documents on the financial management of the committee. But having said that there are individuals within the committee who can focus on certain issues of the service and ask relevant questions.

Membership did cohere around one norm – membership of the magistracy. Members attended their probation committee as magistrates rather than people with skills in finance, personnel work, evaluation, and so on. The implication is that a rationality of greater relevance to the magistracy than to Home Office and consonant probation service objectives is in the ascendancy. Formal rationality cannot be assumed as the framework of probation policy determination. A committee member put it thus:

> We are producing the policy more by describing the reactions of magistrates and judges than we are sitting down pouring over figures and saying, 'Well, we have got that much less or that much more.'

Magistrates

During the research interviews committee members were asked what they considered to be the main purposes of the probation service. 'Serving the courts', 'rehabilitating offenders', 'reducing reoffending' and 'providing constructive alternatives to custody' received the most frequent mentions. When answers from sentencer and non-sentencer members of committees were separated, 85 per cent (66) of the former and 45 per cent (11) of the latter group most frequently mentioned 'serving the courts' as the purpose of the probation service.

When asked to rank various probation service tasks in an order of priority, sentencers listed the preparation of court pre-sentence reports as the second most important. The emphasis here was on providing background information about offenders rather than making recommendations for sentencing, which was the business of magistrates. Again, a strong relationship between the probation service and the magistrates' court is evident from these data.

In response to a question about whom they represented on their probation committee, 35 per cent of magistrate members in the sample saw themselves as representatives of their respective benches. A further 30 per cent said they represented the wider magistracy or had a dual responsibility to the bench and the magistracy. Again, this is a partial interpretation of membership because, although election to a committee is from benches in petty sessional areas, members do not have a formal mandate to represent their bench. The committee is responsible for the whole of the work of an area probation service and in law a corporate body in its own right. Views from different benches may at times be pertinent but not an integral part of decision-making about probation area policy.

The magistrates interviewed certainly recognised that the purpose of a probation committee includes a policy-making function, interpreted in various ways. They also recognised their role as the employer of probation staff. The continuing problem they faced, however, was one of integrating these roles within their dominant assumption that the function of an area probation service is to offer a service to the courts.

Members partly resolved this dilemma by placing emphasis on their committee's task of liaison between the probation service and the courts. As an illustration a magistrate stated thus:

> A policy on juvenile justice was recently issued to members of the committee who took it back to their benches and in one or two areas there was distinct unease which was fed back. The policy has now been redrafted and the bench will probably be much happier.

Where specific issues did not figure on the agenda, liaison was sometimes interpreted in a wider sense, as these magistrates explained:

> . . . to help spread the word about the probation service. To sell probation to our colleagues, which is no mean task. There will always be

a tension between sentencers and probation. I think that is the nature of the game but there is also an ignorance and it's that ignorance that I think the committee as a whole and individual members try to break down.

. . . my personal view, I think, is from the role I see myself playing. Profiling the probation service for my local bench. Taking my work from the committee back to the bench and explaining, trying to explain and trying to profile what has been done.

In fact, liaison between the magistracy and the probation service is not part of a probation committee member's role. There is another forum, the probation liaison committee, specifically designed to fulfil this function.[4]

Views like these were expressed frequently and formed part of the 'assumptive world' of the sentencer. The perspective bears some resemblance to what Howard Parker et al., (1989: 116–17), in their research on magistrates' views about sentencing, have called 'the professional ideology of the lay magistrate', which includes 'ideology, attitudes and opinions' associated with work in the courts, and in particular the relationship between the bench and the probation service.

Magistrate committee members have found it difficult to interpret their duty to maintain an efficient area service in a way that broadens out from the specific relationship between the probation service and the courts. Magistrates (and judges) place overriding importance on the probation service as a servant of the court. This is the primary assumption on which their understanding of probation policy is based.

Discrete cases

Chief officers described magistrates' case-by-case approach to sentencing that was carried over to discussions of probation policy. When chief officers were asked about race issues policy, for example, they commented that magistrate members found it particularly difficult to grasp the notion that discrimination can be cumulative, spanning individual decisions to become lodged in organisational procedures that are taken for granted as reasonable and fair. A chief probation officer made the point by stating:

There is resistance, particularly from sentencers on committee who have this judicial framework that deals with each case on its merits. To be able to think in terms of the differential experience of different groups, to be able to make the transition from being judges and magistrates to being employers and policy-makers is actually quite a leap on their part.

For their part, sentencers interpreted a question about the content and extent of race issues policy in their probation service area as one about whether or not they were racially biased when they made sentencing decisions. Race issues were not related to a breadth of probation work but individualised and thereby limited. Within this framework of reference it is easier to discuss policy for work with individual offenders, whose problems form a discrete case, than anti-racism policies, for example, which are in essence more concerned with organisational structures and procedures across a range of work settings.

Rationalising probation

Many features of the probation service are marked by ambiguity and uncertainty. As has been pointed out in previous chapters and will be covered further in other parts of the book, probation work may have a core of tasks, skills and knowledge related to the offering of help, of counselling or addressing the offending behaviour of individuals. The work undertaken by probation officers is nevertheless marked by a diversity that has increased in recent years. Crime prevention, work in prisons, civil work, community service, day centre provision, hostel provision and bail information schemes represent some of the range undertaken.

May (1994; see also Vass, 1988) has highlighted the increasing use of ancillary staff to perform functions previously considered the province of professionally qualified probation officers. Boundaries between core and peripheral skills and knowledge related to the work of specific staff are now blurred. Indeed, the present emphasis on community punishments that involve offenders in highly structured programmes of 'confronting offending behaviour' have at their core a need to follow a training manual. Fieldworkers in these circumstances may feel further de-skilled, not least when comparing their work with the past days of casework.

Any measure of the effectiveness of probation work is contestable. Is it the prevention of reoffending, the adequate provision of help, some demonstrable aspect of rehabilitation, or another phenomenon which may or may not be readily measurable? More fundamentally, is it possible to predict the outcome of any probation interventions with a degree of certainty? Like the work of other human service organisations, probation work is shot through with uncertainty and ambiguity: ambiguity and uncertainty that is rendered manageable for all practical purposes by probation committee members.[5]

Feeling themselves to hold an amateur status within this ambiguous context (and, incidentally, in accord with the notion of being a member of a lay magistracy with an implied amateur status), magistrates justify their membership of probation committees by rationalising the myriad purposes and functions of an area service into a common-sense world with reference points of direct relevance to the bench. The chief probation officers of an area are ascribed a professional status and given an implicit brief to initiate and develop policy. But this status and brief does not amount to a *carte blanche* mandate. Committee members' evaluation of the appropriateness of chief officers' actions is assessed and analysed through the filter of their assumptive world. Some members of committees described this as a type of 'lay monitoring'. A committee chair set the scene by reporting thus:

> I think it is a myth really that the probation committee lays down the policy. It has a supervisory role. It has a typically English sort of role to see that the thing does not go off at a tangent somewhere or go berserk in some direction. It's like a brake on over-enthusiasm . . . because, I mean, the professional has got to get it through 12 to 15 people who don't know what the hell he's talking about . . . a benevolent sort of supervision because the experts are still the service.

Another committee member working in a different probation area clarified this view in this manner:

> A lay monitoring of the process I think is not a bad thing . . . there is a great deal of money involved. One wants to monitor the direction of the service . . . not guidance, because we are laypeople, not professionals.

Faced with ambiguity and uncertainty about their role, probation committee members construct an assumptive world with its own rationality, drawing on the perceived clarity of their magisterial work.

Policy-making

'Who initiates probation area policy?', committee members were asked. 'Who defines the policy you find on your agenda and endorse?' Probation management was seen as the most influential group influencing policy, followed by the Home Office, and then by the probation committee. This makes interesting comparisons with the way in which 'accountability' is understood by probation officers and how they assign importance to the Home Office, probation committee, chief probation officers and other bodies in that order (see Chapter 4 in this volume). Another interesting feature of these data is that they tend to conflict with data from answers to questions about the role of the Home Office in policy development. Here, members gave greater recognition to the ability of the Home Office to use budgetary constraints to influence strongly particular policy decisions. As one member put it:

> They hold the purse strings in as much as they say 'do so much and do this and the other' . . . and we have to work within those constraints. We have to define policy from that.

These and other constraints, however, did not tie committee members to a servile following of Home Office directives. The external environment that impinges upon probation policy-making is an interpreted environment and their actions reflect that meaningful interpretation.

> We do put the Home Office policy into practice if we see it as good for the service and good for the business of the courts. The service is part of the business of the courts and vice versa.

> The Home Office can set national guidelines and standards and they have inspectors. But I don't feel it is right or appropriate that they take all the power centrally, because they don't know the local situation and I think they stifle creativity if they do that. Perhaps their time would be better spent devising proper research in terms of reoffending.

Members therefore certainly perceived themselves to have been involved in policy-making. When asked if this was the case, 66 per cent of our sample said they felt they had been personally involved; 86 per cent said that their committee and its sub-committees had been involved in policy-making. The meaning of this notion of involvement in policy-making, however, was of a discussion and review of documents presented by chief officers. Although area committees were seen as having 'the last word' and able to make amendments to policies placed before them for ratification, senior managers played a more proactive and substantial part in their determination.

This point does not allow the conclusion that probation committees have had no effect on local policy. There were areas of policy – race and equal opportunities, for example – where some committees had taken a strong line of opposition. A magistrate explained this issue thus:

> There are occasions when the service appears to want to do something which your gut reaction says is unreasonable; then you would say, 'Well, look, it's going to be difficult to swing this one with the paying committees, let's tone it down, go for it on a stage by stage basis and so on' . . . there is a monitoring but it's a fairly gentle monitoring and I think that officers, if they use their loaf, know what they can get away with.

It would be surprising if chief officers were not mindful of the likely reactions of their committee to policy proposals. The initiation and development of local probation policy, however, has largely been management-led, which means chief officer-led. This suggests a committee role in which the statutory duty to ensure an efficient probation service in an area is interpreted in terms of committee oversight rather than a more interventionist type of governance. The committee is a 'sounding board' rather than, as David Faulkner, a senior Home Office civil servant urged over a decade ago, a board of directors that has, among other responsibilities, a duty to 'formulate general policy for the conduct of the activities of the enterprise in fulfilment of the objectives defined' (Home Office, 1984b).

An important reason for this level of involvement in policy-making is certainly the amateur status that committee members perceived to be relevant to their work. This leads to a notion of 'lay monitoring' and of the role of the committee in oversight of the service – as reactive rather than proactive; authorising rather than formulating policy; as a sounding board rather than a board of management actively involved in monitoring questions about service performance. Apart, then, from occasional forays leading to a limited revision of a policy, it seems that probation committees have more usually 'fine-tuned' matters placed on their agenda.

Explaining ambiguity

This research leads us to a series of seemingly inconsistent research findings. Committee members articulate a definition of policy they could but do not operationalise in their committee work. They say they have been involved in policy-making but do not describe instances where this has been in evidence to any great extent. They give a priority to service to the courts when they describe the purposes and functions of the probation service and those of a probation committee, which greatly narrows the range of tasks that have been clearly drawn to their attention by the Home Office and other bodies.

We could explain these inconsistencies in terms of a rational model of probation area services as organisations. The magistrates' perspective we have documented and described, so the argument would run, is irrational and should be brought into alignment with the stated objectives of the organisation. This is the intention of the Home Office reforms (Home Office, 1991).

Just how far these proposed changes will lead to a greater involvement of probation committee members in policy-making processes is a matter for debate. A key factor, one that brings the notion of the probation service as a formal rational organisation into doubt, is that within the complexity of probation service purposes and functions committees have interpreted their work through the 'assumptive world of sentencers' (Young, 1977).

Sentencer members thereby 'rationalise' the ambiguity and diversity of area probation services into a taken-for-granted framework of knowledge that makes sense of their probation committee work. Implicit within this analysis is an anthropology that emphasises the reflective attitude of people working in criminal justice institutions. As Weick (1979: 44) puts it;

> The person is not a data collector, is not accumulating replicas of the environment and is not copying outside events. Instead, the person is punctuating and enacting the flow of experience, the results of these activities being retained in a network of causal sequences or causal maps.

When Karl Weick argues that 'the person is enacting and punctuating the flow of experience', he suggests that organisations are best conceptualised as myriad social worlds, at times in tension and at times in harmony with each other (Weick, 1969, 1976). Sentencer members of probation committees enact their environment by stringing together recognisable pieces of information and attributing a causal relationship to them. When a policy issue touches the work of the courts, they recognise and make sense of it as particularly pertinent to their membership of the probation committee. When an issue does not resonate the work of the magistrate in this or a similar way, members find it more difficult to comment on and formulate an appropriate policy.

Chief probation officers made sense of the same stream of information from the Home Office, colleagues and other sources by selecting and coupling rather different 'facts' into a causal sequence. They were much more concerned with the wider role of probation in reducing crime; with the development of policy objectives; and with the monitoring of policy outcomes.

The 'assumptive world of the sentencer' may well be orchestrated by chief officers. While magistrate members of probation committees invest their energies in the relationship between the local area service and the courts, chief officers are relatively free to develop policy as they see fit. The gaze and attention of the majority of their committee is turned away from what they perceive to be and enact as the primary reality of the probation world.[6] It is an example of how, as John Berger (1972) has put it, 'a way of seeing is a way of not seeing'.

The probation committee is loosely coupled to the managerial world of chief officers. The activity and decision-making of the committee does not then wholly depend on the activity and decision-making of chief officers. In loosely coupled organisations a breakdown or gross irrationality in one sector does not necessarily affect other sectors. There is no realignment or evolutionary balancing of the organisational system; no permeation of organisational segments; no functional needs that must be met. The loose coupling of the organisation of an area probation service allows the probation committee to persist – an apparently irrational anomaly within an organisation that is developing formally rational structures.

There is no inevitability of increasing conflict between the new probation boards and chief officers as the Home Office places greater pressure on area services to conform to national standards, cash limits, and so on. The formal, rational basis of Home Office plans for probation boards and area services do not ensure the alignment of organisational structure, policy and, indeed, of fieldwork. Different organisational sectors can remain loosely coupled, even within a rational, corporate strategy of an area service. It is possible for probation boards to continue to govern area probation services within this context and for the 'assumptive world of the sentencer' to remain intact.

There is one, final context for the reform of the probation service. The very government that has tried to control change within the probation service, and other criminal justice institutions for that matter, by the imposition of rational planning can, within its own framework of planning, suddenly become irrational. Well-laid and in many cases sensible plans for reform can be swept aside in the swings and roundabouts of political whim. The probation service was, as the Home Office used to put it, to become the centre stage in the criminal justice system. Since the 1993 Conservative Party conference, however, prison and punitive sentencing has been arbitrarily placed in the ascendancy (see Chapter 8; Dews and Watts, 1995; Home Office, 1995a, 1995b; Home Office et al., 1995). What part the probation service (and probation boards) will play in the future within the criminal justice system is now somewhat speculative.

Notes

1. ESRC Grant 000 23 1183 refers. The author is grateful to the chief officers and probation committee members who participated in the research. Ieuan Miles, Secretary of the Central Probation Committee, was also more than helpful in his support for the project. The project was of two years' duration and involved five probation areas, serving different types of population.

2. This is not to argue that the training of probation officers should not be carefully planned. The point is that these documents are concerned with the logical, rational 'fit' between training programmes, and the implementation of probation service policy, itself an expression of Home Office objectives.

3. Current changes in the probation service have aimed at establishing a new, interim arrangement of a shadow probation board with rather different functions from those of the probation committee. The findings of the present author's research were partly responsible for the establishment of the new probation boards. This renders the research reported here historical but in no way negates the argument about assumptive worlds and processes of policy-making that will be advanced.

4. Under new arrangements there will be a strengthened forum for probation service, court liaison.

5. The point could of course also be made about probation staff of all grades.

6. Chief officers, we suspect, are more concerned with retaining a loose coupling between their own area service and the constraints they perceive the Home Office to place upon them.

References

Berger, J. (1972) *Ways of Seeing*. London: BBC Books.

Clegg, S. and Dunkerley, D. (1980) *Organisation, Class and Control*. London: Routledge.

Coker, J. (1988) *Probation Objectives: a Management View*. Norwich: University of East Anglia.

Davies, M., Boswell, G. and Wright, A. (1989) *Skills, Knowledge and Qualities in Probation Practice*. Research Reports 1–4. Norwich: Social Work Monographs, University of East Anglia.

Dews, V. and Watts, J. (1995) *Review of Probation Officer Recruitment and Qualifying Training* (The Dews Report). London: Home Office.

Farnham, D. and Horton, S. (ed.) (1993) *Managing the New Public Services*. London: Macmillan.

Home Office (1984a) *The Probation Rules*. London: HMSO.

Home Office (1984b) *A View from the Home Office: Address by Mr David Faulkner, Deputy Under-Secretary of State, Home Office*. Annual General Meeting of the Central Council of Probation Committees. London: CCPC.

Home Office (1991) *Organising Supervision and Punishment in the Community: A Decision Document*. London: HMSO.

Home Office (1994) *The Probation Service: Three Year Plan for the Probation Service, 1994–1997*. London: Home Office.

Home Office (1995a) *Strengthening Punishment in the Community: A Consultation Document*. Cmnd 2780. London: HMSO.

Home Office (1995b) *Review of Probation Officer Recruitment and Qualifying Training: Decision Paper by the Home Office*. London: Home Office.

Home Office, Department of Health and Welsh Office (1995) *National Standards for the Supervision of Offenders in the Community*. London: Home Office Probation Training Division.

Humphrey, C.H. and Pease, K. (1992) 'Effectiveness measurement in probation: a view from the troops', *Howard Journal of Criminal Justice*, 31 (1): 31–52.

Humphrey, C.H., Carter, P. and Pease, K. (1993) 'With a little help from their "friends"? *Reflecting on Changing Notions of Accountability in the Probation*

Service'. Research Monograph. University of Manchester: Department of Accounting and Finance.

Jones, C. (1993) 'Auditing criminal justice', *British Journal of Criminology*, 33: 187–202.

McWilliams, W. (1987) 'Probation, pragmatism and policy', *Howard Journal of Criminal Justice*, 26: 97–121.

McWilliams, W. (1989) 'An expressive model for evaluating probation practice', *Howard Journal of Criminal Justice*, 36: 58–64.

McWilliams, W. and Pease, K. (1990) 'Probation practice and an end to punishment', *Howard Journal of Criminal Justice*, 29: 14–24.

Martinson, R. (1974) 'What works? Questions and answers about prison reform', *The Public Interest*, 23: 22–54.

May, T. (1991) *Probation: Politics, Policy and Practice*. Milton Keynes: Open University Press.

May, T. (1994) 'Probation and community sanctions', in M. Maguire, R. Morgan and R. Reiner (eds), *The Oxford Handbook of Criminology*. Oxford: Clarendon Press. pp. 861–88.

Nellis, M. (1992) 'Criminology, crime prevention and the future of probation training', in K. Bottomley, T. Fowles and R. Reiner (eds), *Criminal Justice: Theory and Practice*. London: British Society of Criminology. pp. 135–65.

Parker, H., Sumner, M. and Jarvis, G. (1989) *Unmasking the Magistrates: The 'Custody or Not' Decision in Sentencing Young Offenders*. Milton Keynes: Open University Press.

Taylor, F.W. (1911) *Principles of Scientific Management*. New York: Harper and Row.

Vass. A.A. (1984) *Sentenced to Labour: Close Encounters with a Prison Substitute*. St Ives: Venus Academica.

Vass, A.A. (1988) 'The marginality of community service and the threat of privatisation', *Probation Journal*, 35: 48–51.

Weber, M. (1976) *The Protestant Ethic and the Spirit of Capitalism*. London: Allen Lane.

Weber, M. (1978) *Economy and Society: An Outline of Interpretive Sociology* (2 vols). Berkeley: University of California Press.

Weick, K. (1969) *The Social Psychology of Organising*. Reading, MA: Addison-Wesley.

Weick, K. (1976) 'Educational organisations as loosely coupled systems', *Administrative Science Quarterly*, 21: 1–12.

Weick, J. (1979) 'Cognitive processes in organisations', in *Research in Organisational Behaviour*. CT: JAI Press. pp. 41–74.

Young, K. (1977) 'Values in the policy process', *Policy and Practice*, 5: 1–12.

7

Pre-sentence Reports

David Smith

The term 'pre-sentence reports' (PSRs) became common currency only with the Criminal Justice Act 1991, replacing (in England and Wales) the older designation of 'social inquiry (or enquiry) reports'. While the title is new, the thing itself – a report intended to provide information to help courts decide on the most appropriate sentence – is not, and one aim of this chapter is to place PSRs in their historical context. It is hoped that this will show how changes in thinking about such reports, and in the practice of writing them, have reflected both changes in government policy and, more generally, changed understandings of the nature of crime and criminality, and of how offenders should best be punished or controlled, treated or helped. The first section will discuss the development of PSRs up until the mid-1970s, when, it will be argued, an important change began to appear in conceptions of the purposes and aims of these reports, as a result of some well-founded and some more dubious interpretations of research findings. The next section will review the impact of this change within social work agencies, and the new approach to reports which began to be influential in the early 1980s. The third section shows how these changes at the level of practice both influenced and were influenced by shifts in official policy and legislative developments. The chapter then discusses the current position (as nearly as this can be done within a rapidly changing policy environment), and what we can reasonably say about what counts as good practice in report preparation, writing and presentation. Finally, the chapter offers suggestions for developing good practice not only for reports but also for the involvement of social workers in courts more generally. Throughout, references to 'social workers' include probation officers unless it is necessary to make a distinction; and, except in quotations, the term 'pre-sentence report' (PSR) is used for the sake of clarity – but it should be remembered that this is an anachronism until the discussion reaches 1991, and indeed in Scotland the official title is still 'social inquiry reports'.

The rise and fall of diagnostic optimism

According to McWilliams (1985), PSRs of a kind are almost as old as the probation service itself. A Home Office report of 1910 on the Probation of Offenders Act of 1907 approved the practice of inquiring into the 'character and surroundings' of defendants, and viewed it as the officer's duty to present these in a favourable light. The first PSRs were therefore essentially pleas for mercy and the probation officer laid no claim to scientific expertise or impartiality. Such claims began to appear in the late 1920s, as the probation service, in common with other branches of social work, sought a professional identity, often intimately connected with psychiatry, rather than a sense of mission or vocation. McWilliams (1985: 260–1) argues that 'probation officers' diagnostic thinking was inextricably mingled with their professional aspirations', even though, until 'the re-importation of casework from America' in the 1930s, these would have left the probation officer as a relatively lowly member of a diagnostic team, rather than as the principal diagnostician. The main vehicle for 'social diagnosis', as the influential American writer Mary Richmond called it, was the PSR; and McWilliams (1986) seeks to show, from PSRs of the 1930s to the 1960s, the process by which probation officers moved from presenting courts with essentially layperson, common-sensical accounts of offenders' motives and actions (including the assumption of free will) towards a more deterministic stance in which the language of science, and particularly of Freudian psychology, was used to claim and convey esoteric knowledge and objectivity. McWilliams (1986: 242) sees the 'essence of scientific diagnosis' as 'imputed meaning': that is, the expert, in this case the probation officer, knows better than the objects of the diagnosis what is wrong with them.

Optimism about the possibility of scientific diagnosis of the causes of crime (and how it might be cured) was of course not confined to the probation service. The Inter-departmental Committee which reported on social services in summary courts (Home Office, 1936) seems to have shared it, since it recommended that 'social investigation' should not be confined to cases in which probation was the likely outcome. The Criminal Justice Act 1948, which was the first piece of legislation specifically to recognise PSRs, also took a broad view of the potential value of social diagnosis, stating that, when required, officers could investigate 'the circumstances or home surroundings of any person with a view to assisting the court in determining the most suitable method of dealing with his case' (quoted in Thorpe, 1979: 4). This is a long way from the early special pleading on behalf of defendants who seemed capable of salvation. Official (and academic) optimism continued into the 1960s. One of the most enduringly influential statements on PSRs, the Streatfeild Report (Home Office, 1961), 'appeared at the high tide of rehabilitative optimism' (Raynor et al., 1994). Although the following Morison Report (Home Office, 1962) was more cautious about whether the ailments of offenders could be scientifically diagnosed (or, if they could, whether probation officers were skilled enough to carry out the task), Streatfeild's position remained the more influential, even into the period when, according to McWilliams (1986), confidence in social diagnosis had already begun to wane.

Bottoms and Stelman (1988) show, in the course of a discussion of the Streatfeild Report which does something to redeem it from the blame which it subsequently attracted for misleading the probation service and others about the purpose of PSRs, that it suggested that three kinds of information were relevant to sentencers. In a much-quoted paragraph, these were expressed as follows:

(a) information about the social and domestic background of the offender which is relevant to the court's assessment of his culpability;

(b) information about the offender and his surroundings which is relevant to the court's consideration of how his criminal career might be checked;

(c) an opinion as to the likely effect on the offender's criminal career of probation or some other specified form of sentence. (Home Office, 1961: para. 335)

It is (b) and (c) which reveal the optimism about diagnosis and prognosis which was characteristic not just of the Streatfeild Committee's thinking but also of the contemporary penological climate. In rehabilitating Streatfeild, Bottoms and Stelman (1988: 25) suggest that the essential distinction is between 'backward-looking' and 'forward-looking' considerations, the former relevant to culpability, the latter to an offender's future prospects. They argue that this provided a way of thinking about PSRs which could still be helpful, as long as it was detached from Streatfeild's scientific optimism.

The paragraph quoted above became influential as a succinct and authoritative statement of what a PSR ought to contain. In particular, it encouraged the expression of an opinion by the report writer, not just about probation but about other measures, a view reiterated in Home Office circulars of 1971 and 1974 (Thorpe, 1979). The statement, although this was not Streatfeild's intention, could also be, and was, read as encouraging the inclusion of a great mass of background information on the grounds that some of it would be relevant (Herbert and Mathieson, 1975). In this paragraph

Streatfeild did appear to assume that report writers first knew what information was relevant and secondly were in a position to obtain it (elsewhere it was stressed that the information had to be 'comprehensive and reliable' (Home Office, 1961: para. 292). It is a pity that other paragraphs, more cautiously optimistic and clearer about the irrelevance of some information, were not equally influential. For example, Streatfeild said that in giving an opinion:

> [A probation officer] should confine himself to opinions founded on actual and substantial experience (whether his or that of his colleagues) of the effect of the sentence and should have regard to the results of general research into what sentences achieve as they become available. (Home Office, 1961: para. 342)

Practice experience was to combine with the findings of criminological research on the effectiveness of sentencing, but the (quite correct) implication is that these findings were not yet to hand.

Bottoms and Stelman (1988) cite the following paragraph as evidence that Streatfeild had a sharper sense of what was relevant than the plea for 'comprehensive' information might (and did) suggest:

> Information should not be proliferated for information's sake. It is not simply a matter of providing the court with the fullest possible information about offenders. A mass of background information can be collected with comparative ease, but irrelevant information is not only useless but possibly harmful. There is a risk that it may cloud the issue before the court and induce a cosy feeling in which the absence of really useful information passes unnoticed. The test to be applied is whether the information can help the court to reach a better decision (Home Office, 1961: para. 293).

Notwithstanding this recognition, it remained unclear what the test of relevance should be – what sort of information was to count as helpful.

The cautious optimism of the Streatfeild Report was very much a product of its time. Less typical, if in retrospect more realistic, was the cautious pessimism of the Morison Report (Home Office, 1962), which (unlike Streatfeild) had the probation service as its sole focus. Morison (cited in Thorpe, 1979) made the contrast with Streatfeild explicit: the Report argued that 'even the most experienced probation officer would find difficulty at present' in predicting offenders' suitability for sentences (or 'methods of treatment') other than probation. In paragraph 41, the Morison Report (Home Office, 1962) states further:

. . . probation officers are not now equipped by their experience and research cannot yet equip them to assume a general function of expressing opinions to the courts about the likely effect of sentences . . . we do not see scope at present for more than a very gradual development towards the function that the Streatfeild Committee envisaged.

This was quoted almost as much as the paragraph from Streatfeild which it contradicts, but optimism prevailed over pessimism (this was the 1960s, and the probation service, like other areas of social work, was expanding). The Streatfeild Report can reasonably be regarded as 'for perhaps twenty years the single most influential statement available on the content and purposes of reports' (Raynor et al., 1994: 43). It may be considered as largely responsible for the growth in the use by courts of PSRs in the 1960s and beyond, through Home Office circulars in 1963, 1968 and 1971, which advised courts on the categories of offender on whom a report should be obtained before various decisions were taken (Davies, 1974). However, it was not until 1973, following the Criminal Justice Act 1972, that a PSR was made mandatory, before a community service order could be imposed. As Bottoms and Stelman (1988: 21) remark, Streatfeild continued to have a direct influence on practice guidance until 1983, when it was cited again in a Home Office circular.

As was suggested above, selective reading of the Streatfeild Report encouraged the development of thinking about PSRs which emphasised comprehensiveness at the expense of relevance. In the first half of the 1970s research tended to concentrate on the variability of the information contained in reports, and to argue both for greater standardization and greater inclusiveness (Herbert and Mathieson, 1975; Perry, 1974). In the absence of any consensus on what should count as relevant (the model of scientific treatment failed to specify this), the temptation was to err on the side of caution, and to argue that everything which might conceivably be relevant should be put in. Herbert and Mathieson's (1975: 26–8) recommended list of contents is a good example, although they did add a 'practical note' admitting that most reports would in practice be less comprehensive. These writers were trying to deal with the growing criticism of the 'treatment model' of expert diagnosis by trying to bring reports more into line with what the model seemed to demand – objectivity in the collection of as many 'facts' as possible, and impressively detailed accounts of offenders' backgrounds and histories. But there were difficulties with this approach, both theoretical and practical, which made it impossible to sustain as a viable model for PSR practice.

As Streatfeild had noted, it is not really difficult to accumulate information. The problem was in demonstrating its relevance to the reason the report was being prepared in the first place – the fact that someone had committed an offence. The present author recalls having inklings of this theoretical gap in the early 1970s. Trying to write reports in the style to which the local magistrates seemed accustomed, and which his senior probation officer approved, he would dutifully ask offenders questions about their childhood experiences and upbringing. They were usually cooperative and helpful – after all, the report was more likely to do them good than harm in court – but occasionally someone would say, in effect: 'I'm quite happy to answer these questions, but what have they got to do with my being in trouble?' This was a poser, because the present author had no convincing answer; the best he could manage was that this was the kind of thing the courts expected. This did not seem good enough, and before long the discomfort he felt in the face of this reasonable question was to become more articulate and more widely shared.

Although Perry (1974) could show that the reports he studied were far from the objective scientific diagnoses they purported to be, his solution, as we have seen, was not convincing, for the more comprehensive information he sought could often be readily obtained in a way which avoided the embarrassment of answering the offender's question about relevance: by recycling old records and reports, a practice which had not died out entirely by the late 1980s (Raynor et al., 1994). Further and more serious damage to the diagnostic ideal was done by Davies and Knopf (1973), who showed that the circumstances in which reports were prepared were not conducive to the desired standards of objective scientific assessment. Even supposing that these could be achieved in ideal clinical conditions, they were clearly unachievable when the average length of time spent interviewing a defendant across three probation areas was 42 minutes, and the average time spent on a report in total was just over four and a half hours (including travelling, 'reading, thinking, writing', and attending court). Noting substantial variations in the time spent on reports, Davies and Knopf concluded (1973: 32) that these reflected 'traditional ways of working which are likely to influence all officers moving into the situation'. So much for the post-Streatfeild image of a national body of trained diagnostic experts dispassionately advising sentencers on the basis of criminological knowledge.

PSRs in crisis

By the mid-1970s, then, research was beginning to suggest that all was not well with PSR practice. More than this, it began to call into question the purpose of PSRs: what were they for, and what did they achieve? For example, Davies (1974) reviewed developments since the Streatfeild Report and concluded that there was no evidence that the increased use of reports over the previous decade had produced the outcomes which might have been expected if Streatfeild's aspirations had been well founded. Two developments which ought to have occurred – a reduction in sentencing disparities between courts (cf. Tarling, 1979) and an overall improvement in the quality of sentencing as measured by reconviction rates – had not taken place.

Other work appeared which cast doubt on the nature of the influence of reports on sentencing. The conventional measure of this influence is the 'take up' rate of recommendations (as the 'opinions' encouraged by Streatfeild were generally called), and early research was, on the face of it, generally encouraging, suggesting that around 80 per cent of recommendations were followed (Ford, 1972; Thorpe and Pease, 1976). Closer examination, however, revealed that much of this apparent influence was illusory, since the recommendations that were most likely to be in line with sentences were those which suggested that courts should do what they would have done anyway, without the benefit of a report. Where an influence could be discerned, it was not in the direction that might have been hoped for, by a probation service interested in the humane treatment of offenders and a government interested in reducing the prison population, as the 1972 Criminal Justice Act showed it was. Thorpe and Pease (1976) found that the recommendations most likely to be taken up were those against probation; and Hine et al. (1978) suggested that a recommendation for custody, explicit or otherwise, was a good predictor of a custodial sentence. Slightly later work (Thorpe et al., 1980) on juveniles showed that PSR recommendations for care orders in criminal proceedings were highly influential, even for minor offences, thus contributing to disproportionate and unjust sentencing; and that when options within the care system were supposedly exhausted, reports were likely successfully to recommend penal custody. Local authority social workers were found to be more liable than probation officers to encourage courts in this kind of punitiveness. Their PSRs tended to divert offenders to custody, not from it.

Looking beyond research specifically on PSRs, the picture was no more cheering. In the mid-1970s the grim message that 'nothing worked' began to spread, and be believed, among social workers in criminal justice (Brody, 1976; Lipton et al., 1975; see also Chapters 8 and 12 in this volume). The message was exaggerated in the telling, but from the mid-1970s on it exercised considerable influence on practice and ultimately on policy, including policy on PSRs. The empirical evidence against the treatment model on which reports had been based reinforced growing theoretical objections, rooted in the varieties of criminology which influenced the teaching of sociology – and social work – in Britain from the early 1970s. For example, David Matza (1964, 1969) argued that even offenders whose crimes were not obviously calculated or rationally motivated should be seen as capable of choice: they decided to offend, albeit within a context of pressure and constraint, and logically they could have decided not to. The determinism implicit in the scientific diagnosis of what was wrong with offenders, which in extreme versions literally viewed an offence as the symptom of an illness, was thus powerfully challenged, and the outcome of the struggle was to prove fatal to it.

In the face of these empirical and theoretical developments one response was to argue that there was no justification at all for PSRs (Bean, 1976). In this polemic, PSRs were presented as character assassinations, expressions of moralising judgement unconvincingly disguised by scientific language and pretensions. It was argued that the only justification for reports was in terms of the discredited model of diagnosis and treatment; if the model were abandoned, so, logically, should the reports which it sustained. Another threat to the survival of reports came from the 'back to justice' lobby, which argued for strict proportionality rather than wide discretion in the sentencing of juveniles (Morris et al., 1980). Rightly critical of what naïve welfare-based intervention by social workers had done during the 1970s, these authors advocated a version of 'just deserts' which would have left little or no space for the individualised sentencing which is presupposed by PSRs.

Another response was, however, possible, and emerged both in the sense which practitioners in juvenile justice began to make of PSRs (Thorpe et al., 1980) and in more theoretical proposals for a new rationale for reports and indeed for social work practice in criminal justice (Bottoms and McWilliams, 1979; Raynor, 1980). Although these writers varied in the degree of conviction with which they accepted that nothing worked (or could possibly work), they shared a disenchantment with the medical model of treatment. Central to their arguments was the aim of diversion from custody, and, in the case of juveniles, from care as well. If scientific diagnosis was not a plausible or defensible aim for PSRs, diversion could be. Thus Thorpe et al. (1980) argued for a sensitive strategic awareness of how reports could harm rather than help, through widening the net of formal control or thinning the mesh (increasing the intensity of intervention: see Cohen, 1985), and suggested that a main aim of reports might be to keep young offenders 'down tariff' for as long as possible; when this was no longer possible, reports should argue for supervision in the community whose aims were well defined and relevant to offending.

Raynor (1980), too, argued for greater clarity about the purposes of reports. He suggested that even within a 'just deserts' sentencing framework there should still be room for the individualisation of sentences, no longer on the basis of expertly diagnosed treatment needs but on that of culpability or blameworthiness, and that reports could be the means of giving sentencers the information needed for this kind of moral judgement. Raynor et al. (1994: 45–6) put the argument thus:

> As, in judging people's actions in everyday life, we routinely take account of the circumstances in which they found themselves before coming to a conclusion, so the formal criminal justice system should allow us to consider the circumstances of an offence and whether these count as mitigating or aggravating factors . . . as when, for example, racist provocation is viewed as mitigating the seriousness of an assault. . . . Similarly, evidence of calculation or recklessness of others' welfare may reasonably count as aggravating the seriousness of a given offence.

Raynor thus anticipated the focus on information relevant to offence seriousness which was to become central to the purposes of PSRs following the Criminal Justice Act 1991. But he also argued that reports should be used to explore how offenders might be helped, and that this could lead to a conclusion which would offer, not recommend, an alternative to a 'just deserts' retributive sentence. Report writer and defendant would enter into a form of contract with the court, in which the social worker would commit his or her agency to the provision of specified help and supervision, and the defendant would commit him- or herself to cooperate with what was being offered. Like Thorpe et al. (1980), Raynor saw reports as contributing to better, more focused and more consensual social work practice, as well as having the potential to divert offenders from custody. Reports were conceived as drawing on social work skills and values, and as relevant to social work aims (Bottoms and Stelman, 1988).

PSRs in the 1980s

Two main developments in thinking and policy on PSRs can be traced to this period; and although practice remained variable, in important respects it had an influence on policy. The first is that diversion from custody was increasingly accepted as the main purpose and justification of reports. Secondly, it was argued that this could best be achieved if reports became more focused on the offence and more specific in any offers, proposals or suggestions they made about non-custodial measures. Although the influence of the Streatfeild Report was no longer directly felt, it was as if the parts of it which warned against irrelevance, rather than those which encouraged all-inclusiveness, had been remembered. Commentators who persisted in feeling optimistic that something might work also argued that this greater specificity would improve the quality of social work intervention, and its chances of success (Blagg and Smith, 1989).

Despite this positive outlook, not all were so optimistic. Tutt and Giller (1984), for example, while accepting much of the conceptual basis of Raynor's (1980) argument, were more sceptical about the possible value of social work intervention, and therefore emphasised diversion as the aim of reports. Influenced by the 'nothing works' message, and concentrating on juvenile courts, they suggested that reports should always aim for the 'least restrictive alternative', on the grounds that attempts to provide help were likely to fail, and that the offender would risk a more severe penalty on any subsequent court appearance. PSRs would thus, in effect, become pleas of mitigation, and their purpose would be indistinguishable from that of the defence. Tutt and Giller also argued that reports should consider all questions which might be relevant to sentencing, such as public protection and deterrence, rather than only those within the traditional sphere of a social work agency. As they acknowledged, the kind of reports they advocated would not be social work documents in any useful sense, but legally informed attempts to influence a legal process. Their position was therefore at odds with most thinking about PSRs, but their insistence on minimum intervention as a principle raises an interesting and little explored possibility: that diversion from custody might be more effectively achieved by lengthening the bottom end of the tariff 'ladder' than by trying to persuade courts of the feasibility of non-custodial measures at the top end (which is well known to be difficult: see Vass, 1990).

PSRs as a means of encouraging courts to make less use of custody also featured in Home Office thinking of the time. The *Statement of National Objectives and Priorities* for the probation service (Home Office, 1984), concerned with the effective allocation of resources, suggested specific use of pre-sentence reports by

> . . . concentrating the provision of social inquiry reports on cases where a report is statutorily required, where a probation order is likely to be made, and where the court may be prepared to divert an offender from what would otherwise be a custodial sentence. (Home Office, 1984: section VII)

Reports were thus seen as mainly relevant to mid-tariff offenders, including those for whom the court might consider a custodial sentence appropriate, but might be persuaded to act otherwise. The Home Office had already suggested that an important factor in the persuasiveness of a report might be its degree of specificity. In 1983 the Home Office issued a pair of circulars on reports which both argued in this direction. The first, harking back to Streatfeild, insisted that the content of reports must be clearly relevant, and that sources of information should be clearly stated. The second discussed recommendations in reports, and argued that these were likely to carry more weight if they were specific and focused. It was not enough to say that an offender could benefit from probation; the writer ought to say how this benefit would be brought about. Report writers were being asked to adopt something like the contractual model suggested by Raynor (1980), in the interests of credibility as well as of good, relevant social work practice with offenders. Probation should address issues relevant to whatever problems the offender had which were associated with offending.

It is important to remember that the influence on these developments was not all one way: practice, especially in juvenile justice, was influencing policy as well as being shaped by it (Blagg and Smith, 1989). But one crucial top-down influence was the Criminal Justice Act 1982, which required courts to consider a PSR before imposing a custodial sentence on anyone under the age of 21, unless it considered a report unnecessary. For it to do so, one of three criteria had to be satisfied: that the offence was so serious that a non-custodial sentence could not be justified; that the protection of the public from serious harm demanded a custodial sentence; or that the offender was unable or unwilling to respond to a non-custodial measure. The Act was clear (in section 2) that courts would normally need a report to determine whether any of these criteria were met (Raynor et al., 1994: 46).

The Act thus greatly widened the statutory basis of reports and required a change in report-writing practice, which (in order to give the information needed by the court) would need to focus more narrowly than before on questions related to the offence and to the prospects of success of non-custodial measures. The subsequent legislation, the Criminal Justice Acts of 1988 and 1991, followed and extended the logic of the 1982 Act, the first tightening the criteria for custody and the second extending the requirement to consider a report to all offenders, stressing the seriousness of the offence as the main criterion for sentencing, and substituting refusal of consent for inability or unwillingness to respond to a community penalty.

Both the Home Office and the Department of Health and Social

Security (as it was known then), which was responsible for local authority social work, produced further guidance on PSRs in the 1980s, developing the advice of the earlier circulars and seeking to generalise what was by then recognised as good practice. For juvenile courts, the DHSS (1987) argued, like the Home Office, against the routine preparation of reports on minor offenders and for a more specific focus on offending as the basis of the report. The guidance was specifically critical of the tendency to include in reports details of defendants' family backgrounds which could not be shown to be relevant to their offending. As the Home Office (1986) had done, the DHSS guidance noted the logical nonsense of preparing a report when the defendant denied the offence. This had long caused practitioners discomfort, and properly so; but the impossibility of their position in preparing reports in cases with not guilty pleas only became officially recognised with the expectation that reports should focus on the offence and not on the background factors allegedly relevant to a diagnosis of what was wrong with the defendant (whatever the defendant said).

The third Home Office circular (Home Office, 1986) took a similar line, on the need for selectivity, and for a focus on offending and what might be done about it. PSRs were not to be broad social histories, but to concentrate on the subject's offending history and especially on the current offence. The circular for the first time in official guidance specifically addressed issues of culture and ethnicity thus:

> . . . in considering cases involving members of ethnic minorities it is especially important to bring out any significant aspects of the defendant's social or cultural background which may not otherwise be understood by the court. (Home Office, 1986, para. 11, quoted in Bottoms and Stelman, 1988: 6)

This presupposed that the report writer could recognise such factors and convey their importance and relevance to the court. At least, however, these issues were acknowledged, and the circular's overall argument suggested that they should be included only if they could be shown to be relevant to the court's understanding of the offence and how the defendant had come to commit it.

By the end of the 1980s, then, there was a broad consensus, covering central government officials and many practitioners, including those who had thought about the matter, on the purposes of PSRs and what they should contain. They were to be targeted on relatively serious or persistent offenders (perhaps the most arguable item on the list); they were not to be prepared when the defendant was pleading not guilty; they should be 'offence-focused', helping the court understand the current offence in the context of any offending history; information which could not be shown to be relevant to this should not be there; and any 'recommendations' (or proposals, offers or suggestions) for one sentence over others should be backed by argument and explanation – particularly, when some form of supervision was suggested, of what it would entail, and why it might be helpful or appropriate for the offender. By the end of the 1980s, everyone was claiming to write 'offence-focused' reports. What was actually meant by this varied considerably between agencies, offices and individuals (Raynor et al., 1994), but at least in principle some arguments had been won.

PSRs at the beginning of the 1990s were probably better – more focused, more relevant to their purposes – than 10 years earlier. There was also a heightened sensitivity to the ways in which reports could contribute to, or be used to combat, discriminatory sentencing on the basis of race or gender. The more recent research (Moxon, 1988; Raynor, 1991) showed that at least in Crown Courts there was still little evidence that reports helped to divert offenders from custody; they were, however, influential in changing 'the distribution of non-custodial options', and could show some success in 'making non-custodial disposals available on high-risk young adults' (Raynor, 1991: 299). On the other hand, there was evidence that reports, combined with the strategies of 'system management' developed by practitioners, had made a difference to sentencing in the lower courts, at least with juveniles and to a lesser extent with young adults (Blagg and Smith, 1989; Cavadino and Dignan, 1992), though Vass and Weston (1990) attributed the lack of diversion of offenders to probation day centres to magistrates' refusal to take up recommendations in PSRs. Threatened with extinction in the late 1970s, PSRs had shown a healthy capacity to survive, and the coming legislation was to depend heavily on them if it was to succeed.

PSRs and the 1991 Act: establishing and maintaining good practice

The Criminal Justice Act 1991, as was mentioned above, provided for more extensive use of PSRs by extending the earlier safeguards on the use of custody from young offenders to offenders of any age. The one exception was when the offence was triable only on indictment (that is, only in the Crown Court), when it was open to the judge to decide that a report was unnecessary. The intention, however, was clearly that courts should have a chance to consider a community penalty even in apparently serious cases, and the pre-sentence report, as it was now to be called, was the vehicle through which the relevant information was to be provided. One implication of this was that reports might have to be prepared very quickly, following a finding of guilt in the Crown Court after a not guilty plea. A pilot study was commissioned by the Home Office before the Act was implemented to assess, among other things, the feasibility of producing short-notice reports of reasonable quality (Gelsthorpe and Raynor, 1992). This found, interestingly, that the overall quality of reports prepared at short notice was not significantly worse than that of reports for which the usual length of time – three or four weeks – had been available. Short-notice reports were, however, less likely to go into detail about the facilities that could be made available within a probation order, and the researchers suggested that local arrangements ought to be established to allow for longer adjournments in cases which turned out to be more complex than they appeared at first sight. This is important for anti-discriminatory practice, since black defendants are more likely than whites to plead not guilty at Crown Court, and indeed to be found not guilty (Hood, 1992; Moxon, 1988), and without some agreement allowing more detailed investigation of complex cases their suitability for community penalties could not be properly assessed.

The 1991 Act defined a PSR as a report in writing by a probation officer or local authority social worker, so the short-notice reports were not the same as the 'stand-down' oral reports which courts had occasionally asked for before the Act – a practice understandably disliked by probation officers and social workers. PSRs were to be made 'with a view to assisting the court in determining the most suitable method of dealing with an offender' (section 3 (5) (a)). As well as considering a PSR before making a custodial sentence, courts had to do so before making a probation or supervision order with additional requirements, a combination order or a community service order. Although PSRs were not mandatory before probation or supervision orders with no additional requirements, the training materials produced by the National Association for the Care and Resettlement of Offenders (NACRO) (1992) for the Home Office made clear that it was good practice to obtain them in such cases.

The Act thus widened the range of circumstances in which PSRs should be provided further than any preceding legislation, and defined their nature and purpose more explicitly. PSRs were clearly envisaged as playing an important part in the achievement of the government's explicit aim of ensuring that prison was reserved for the most serious offenders (Home Office, 1990). The importance the Home Office attached to them was highlighted by an unprecedented investment of effort in training and preparation for the Act's implementation in October 1992. In parallel with the production of training materials on various aspects of probation and local authority social work practice under the new Act (NACRO, 1992), the Home Office worked on the production of national standards (Home Office et al., 1992) which were to be binding on local authority social workers as well as probation officers. In line with the development of thinking about reports outlined above, the national standard for PSRs encouraged a focus on the current offence and on information relevant to decisions about sentencing. It proposed a standard pre-printed form for introductory material, identifying the document as a PSR and giving basic information about the offender and the sources drawn upon in preparing the report. This should normally be followed by an account of the current offence(s) and the offender's attitude to it/them; relevant information about the offender, including an assessment of risk in the case of violent or sex offenders; and a conclusion which would include when relevant a proposal for the most suitable community sentence, having regard to the offender's needs, problems and aptitudes as well as to the seriousness of the offence (Home Office et al., 1992).

The national standards acknowledged that in order to produce reports with the information required, especially information relevant to the court's assessment of the seriousness of the offence, social work agencies would need the cooperation of other groups within the criminal justice system, notably the Crown Prosecution Service. Previous arrangements for obtaining details of the prosecution's version of events had been erratic, leading occasionally to the embarrassment of a report which reflected only the offender's understandably played-down account and not the very different view of things taken by the prosecution. The main issue in the part of the national standard which deals with court work is the need to avoid delays in Crown Court, and in particular the need to be ready to prepare short-notice reports when required. It stresses (Home Office et al., 1992: 2) that these arrangements should operate 'on a basis of mutual understanding' between judges and court officials, on the one hand, and probation officers, on the other, and suggests that this should be achieved through negotiation at Crown Court User Groups. Similarly in magistrates' and youth courts, court user groups and liaison meetings provide a forum in which problems can be addressed, for example over access to prosecution files or to defendants remanded in custody. The point is that social workers in criminal justice depend on the cooperation of others in order to do their work effectively (or at all); among the skills relevant to good practice are those of negotiation and articulate advocacy with other professional groups, whose interests will not always coincide with those of social workers.

Another prominent feature of the national standard on PSRs is its insistence on the importance of anti-discriminatory practice. However, this insistence appears to be less prominent in the new national standards as amended in 1995 (Home Office et al., 1995). Early research on the probation service's work with black offenders suggested that they were less likely than whites to be recommended for probation in PSRs (Commission for Racial Equality, 1981), and during the 1980s and early 1990s official, professional and academic concern grew about the overrepresentation of black (especially Afro-Caribbean) people in prison and the possibility that discrimination in criminal justice decision-making contributed to this. While more recent work has not in general found PSRs themselves to be discriminatory (Hood, 1992; Mair, 1986; Moxon, 1988; Waters, 1988) it is still the case that report writers are working within a system which produces racist outcomes, and in which there is evidence of a 'race effect' at the stages of charge, remand and sentencing (Hood, 1992). The 1991 Act's general requirement that courts obtain PSRs before imposing the more serious sentences should have reduced the likelihood that black defendants will be sentenced without a report when convicted after pleading not guilty (Moxon, 1988). However, the Act as subsequently amended widens the scope for judges to sentence without a report should they consider it unnecessary – in practice, in cases where they think a custodial sentence is inevitable. This and other changes to the Act are discussed in the concluding section.

PSR writers therefore have a responsibility to ensure that their reports are sensitive to cultural differences and free of racial stereotyping; a defendant's ethnic background or experience of racism may be relevant to understanding and explaining an offence, but this should not be assumed in advance. Similar considerations apply to reports on female offenders: social workers should not collude with the tendency of the criminal justice system to respond to women as if their offending is necessarily a sign of psychological or social problems. Gelsthorpe (1991) found that despite the awareness of gender issues in criminal justice which developed in social work in the 1980s, reports on women still tended to attribute their offending to personal difficulties, and to emphasise their domestic role and responsibilities, more often than reports on men (see also Chapters 3, 5 and 8 in this book). The 1991 Act aimed to promote an anti-discriminatory approach to decision-making in criminal justice, and the importance of this is stressed throughout the national standards. Anti-discriminatory practice is not merely a product of social work's preoccupation with political correctness, despite what has been suggested by some critics of social work training (see, for instance, Dunant, 1994).

The promotion of anti-discriminatory work is therefore one aim of the quality assurance mechanisms which are insisted on in the national standard for PSRs. Team scrutiny and monitoring of reports on defendants vulnerable to discrimination are now fairly well established as an element of ensuring good practice. Workers who accept this, however, might still balk at the idea that monitoring might provide a means of raising and maintaining the quality of PSRs more generally, and might claim that quality is essentially subjective, a matter of personal preference. The work of Gelsthorpe and Raynor (1992), however, suggests that this is not so, since they found a high level of agreement between their ratings of report quality and those of judges. Analysis of the outcomes of reports rated above and below average (Gelsthorpe et al., 1992) found that this was more than a question of shared aesthetic judgement: reports rated above average were more likely to lead to community penalties, and less likely to lead to custody, than reports rated as poor. On the basis of this, the authors constructed a Quality Assessment Guide (see Raynor et al., 1994) which could be used for team gatekeeping and appraisal of reports. While different versions of this could be and are being employed, some such device seems undeniably important to promote and maintain high standards in PSRs.

Thus, in the context of the 1991 Act, a shared sense emerged of what counted as good practice in PSRs. The good PSR was not, in fact, very different from what would have been a good report before the Act: it would be well presented and free of errors of spelling and grammar; it would make clear the sources of information used, and which it had been possible to verify; it would contain information relevant to offending and to sentencing, and exclude irrelevant information; it would avoid stereotypical or moralistic judgements and language; its conclusions would be specific and clearly argued. The main difference was the post-1991 Act expectation that PSRs should specifically address the issue of offence seriousness and, in reports dealing with sex offences or offences of violence, the risk posed by the offender and the requirements of public protection. In the months following the Act's implementation there were signs that sentencers felt that PSRs were being too specific in their judgements of offence seriousness, and that report writers were encroaching on territory which was properly that of sentencers (Smith, 1994). This was hardly social workers' fault: they had been encouraged to confront the issue of the seriousness of offences, and there is a fine line between assessing seriousness and providing information which allows the court to assess it. The revised guidelines on PSRs (NACRO, 1993) which appeared just over a year after the Act's implementation did, however, place less stress on seriousness and rather more on assessing the offender's suitability for one community penalty rather than another – in which the gravity of the offence was still a factor, but not the only one. This was not all that had changed, in the first year of the Act's operation.

Conclusion: PSRs in a punitive environment

This is not the place to discuss at any length the changes to the 1991 Act which were introduced with what seemed to some surprising haste in 1993, or the further changes in criminal justice policy which were promised for 1994 (for a discussion, see Feaver and Smith, 1994) and which materialised in the Criminal Justice and Public Order Act 1994 (see also Home Office, 1995). But it is important to note those which have had and will have a direct impact on PSR practice. First, the two sections of the Act which were most directly designed to make the seriousness of the current offence (coupled with one other offence if appropriate) the main ground for sentencing decisions were amended by the Criminal Justice Act of 1993 to broaden the range of factors which a court could consider in assessing seriousness. Section 2, as amended, allows the court to combine any number of offences to arrive at a judgement of total seriousness when considering the appropriate length of a custodial sentence; and the amended section 29 allows the court to take into account previous convictions and failure to respond to previous sentences in deciding on seriousness. This directly reverses the sense of the original section 29, and the amended version adds that if an offence was committed while the defendant was on bail the court must treat this as an aggravating factor. Furthermore, a late amendment to the Criminal Justice and Public Order Act of 1994 removes the requirement for Crown Courts to consider a PSR in all but exceptional cases before imposing a custodial sentence.

This last measure was apparently a response to judges' complaints of unnecessary delays in sentencing when a custodial sentence was a foregone conclusion, whatever the PSR might say, and, among other things, it will remove the protection against discriminatory sentencing which the Act originally promised to provide by making PSRs mandatory in Crown Court cases where conviction followed a not guilty plea. All the changes reflect both specific criticisms of the original legislation by members of the judiciary and others, and the willingness of a new ministerial team at the Home Office to respond enthusiastically to them, rather than defending what was claimed as an Act which would establish a new and rational framework for sentencing which would endure into the twenty-first century. In 1993 and 1994 the rhetoric – as well as the practice – of Home Office ministers became explicitly punitive, encouraging (and getting) an increase in custodial sentencing even before the amendments to the 1991 Act took effect (Home Office, 1993; see also Chapter 8 in this volume).

The penological climate is therefore not, at the time of writing, especially healthy for social work with offenders. The features of the 1991 Act which allowed for optimism about the potential for PSRs to have a constructive influence on sentencing are among those which have been changed, and even those who did not welcome the Act at the start, such as the National Association of Probation Officers (NAPO), have belatedly discovered the virtues of its original form. Although it was difficult for a Conservative government to say so explicitly, a major part of the Act's intention was to reduce the use of imprisonment for offenders against property (the great majority, of course, of those who appear in court). Since early 1993, sentencers have been given a different message, summarised by the Home Secretary, Michael Howard, in October of that year, as 'prison works'.

In this context, it is important to retain the sense of purpose, of an advance towards clarity and consensus informed by humane values and concerns, which this chapter has tried to illustrate in its account of the development of thinking and practice in PSRs. Much of the criticism of these reports in the 1970s was justified: they were based on an outmoded and indefensible model of practice, they were often full of irrelevance, they were ineffective. Practitioners themselves took the important first steps towards greater clarity of purpose and more informed and principled practice; legislation and official guidance followed, and affected practice in turn (in line with the account of policy formation by Rock, 1990). As a result, it is possible now, in 1996, to say that we know, in broad terms at least, what a good PSR is like, and what it is for. Apparently negative legislation itself is not an absolute bar to the development of good practice; the first important changes in PSR practice in the late 1970s took place in the context of legislative 'disaster' (Cavadino and Dignan, 1992). The sentencing changes of 1993, although in a direction most social workers would see as wrong, began before the changes in legislation – a paradoxical source of hope, since it shows that sentencing trends are not wholly dependent on the law but, as Chapter 8 argues, rely on a host of factors, not least the role of government in influencing penal trends. But it also shows the limitations and vulnerability of social work's influence. Social workers could do everything right, according to the national standard and the guidance received from training, and still fail to influence sentencing away from custody and towards more humane and constructive responses to offending.

Social workers need more than 'competence' in PSR practice. Of course they need to be competent: they need to be able to write clearly and grammatically, to obtain information and present it coherently and succinctly, to interview people sympathetically, to make rational and empirically informed assessments of risk; they need to be aware of available resources, and to know that some kinds of social work are more likely to be effective than others; they should be able to recognise stereotypical or discriminatory language and concepts, and do something effective about them; they should know the law as much as they need to; and so on; and they must build in some form of quality assurance both to maintain standards and to make quality a collective rather than an individual commitment. They also need to be able to negotiate confidently and professionally with other actors within the criminal justice system; to explain to sentencers what grounds there are for thinking that community penalties may be more effective than custody, as well as more economical and more humane; and to articulate what it is which gives social work a distinctive and important role in the criminal justice process, even – or especially – when to do so entails the possibility of conflict (Blagg et al., 1988).

To do all this requires, as we have consistently argued in this volume, more than 'competence' in carrying out some function without knowing why; it requires a sense of the values and purposes which inform social work in criminal justice, and of the ethical responsibilities social workers bear not only to the offenders with whom they work but also to individual victims and neighbourhoods in fear of crime. It requires that social workers should display the virtues appropriate to their calling (Hugman and Smith, 1995; MacIntyre, 1985), such as courage, honesty, concern for the weak and vulnerable, perseverance in the face of difficulty and disappointment, empirically informed scepticism, self-criticism and a commitment to excellence in practice (see Vass, 1996a, 1996b). As this chapter has tried to show, PSRs have been most effective, and have developed in the most positive directions, when their writers have been not only technically competent but also morally engaged, as the juvenile justice practitioners of the early 1980s were. Their moral commitment to reducing the unjust use of care and custody was also empirically informed; and, now as then, it is this combination of ethical clarity, critical knowledge and practical skill which social workers writing PSRs have to achieve, if social work with offenders is to survive in the present hostile environment.

References

Bean, P. (1976) *Rehabilitation and Deviance*. London: Routledge and Kegan Paul.

Blagg, H. and Smith, D. (1989) *Crime, Penal Policy and Social Work*. Harlow: Longman.

Blagg, H., Pearson, G., Sampson, A., Smith, D. and Stubbs, P. (1988) 'Inter-agency cooperation: rhetoric and reality', in T. Hope and M. Shaw (eds), *Communities and Crime Reduction*. London: HMSO. pp. 204–20.

Bottoms, A.E. and McWilliams, W. (1979) 'A non-treatment paradigm for probation practice', *British Journal of Social Work*, 9 (2): 159–202.

Bottoms, A.E. and Stelman, A. (1988) *Social Inquiry Reports*. Aldershot: Wildwood House.

Brody, S.R. (1976) *The Effectiveness of Sentencing: A Review of the Literature*. Home Office Research Study No. 35. London: HMSO.

Cavadino, M. and Dignan, J. (1992) *The Penal System: An Introduction*. London: Sage.

Cohen, S. (1985) *Visions of Social Control*. Cambridge: Polity Press.

Commission for Racial Equality (1981) *Probation and After-Care in a Multi-racial Society*. London: CRE and West Midlands Probation and After-Care Service.

Davies, M. (1974) 'Social inquiry for the courts', *British Journal of Criminology*, 14 (1): 18–33.

Davies, M. and Knopf, A. (1973) *Social Enquiry Reports and the Probation Service*. Home Office Research Study 18. London: Home Office.

Department of Health and Social Security (1987) *Reports to Courts: Practice Guidance for Social Workers*. London: DHSS.

Dunant, S. (ed.) (1994) *The War of the Words: The Political Correctness Debate*. London: Virago.

Feaver, N. and Smith, D. (1994) 'Editorial introduction', *British Journal of Social Work*, 24 (4): 379–86.

Ford, P. (1972) *Advising Sentencers*. Oxford University Penal Research Unit Occasional Paper No. 5. Oxford: Blackwell.

Gelsthorpe, L.R. (1991) *Race and Gender Considerations in the Preparation and Interpretation of Social Inquiry Reports*. Report to the Home Office Research and Planning Unit.

Gelsthorpe, L.R. and Raynor, P. (1992) 'The quality of reports prepared in the pilot studies', Appendix I in J. Bredar (ed.), *Justice Informed. Vol. II*. London: Vera Institute of Justice.

Gelsthorpe, L.R., Raynor, P. and Tisi, A. (1992) *Quality Assurance in Pre-sentence Reports*. Report to the Home Office Research and Planning Unit.

Herbert, L. and Mathieson, D. (1975) *Reports for Courts*. London: NAPO.

Hine, J., McWilliams, W. and Pease, K. (1978) 'Recommendations, social information and sentencing', *Howard Journal of Penology and Crime Prevention*, 17 (2): 91–100.

Home Office (1936) *Report of the Inter-departmental Committee on the Social Services to the Summary Courts*. Cmnd 5122. London: HMSO.

Home Office (1961) *Report of the Inter-departmental Committee on the Business of the Criminal Courts* (The Streatfeild Report). Cmnd 1289. London: HMSO.

Home Office (1962) *Report of the Departmental Committee on the Probation Service* (The Morison Report). Cmnd 1650. London: HMSO.

Home Office (1984) *Probation Service in England and Wales: Statement of National Objectives and Priorities*. London: Home Office.

Home Office (1986) *Social Inquiry Reports*. Home Office Circular 92/1986. London: Home Office.

Home Office (1990) *Crime, Justice and Protecting the Public: The Government's Proposals for Legislation*. Cmnd 965. London: HMSO.

Home Office (1993) *Monitoring of the Criminal Justice Act 1991: Data from a Special Data Collection Exercise*. Statistical Bulletin 25/93. London: Home Office.

Home Office (1995) *Strengthening Punishment in the Community: A Consultation Document*. Cmnd 2780. London: HMSO.

Home Office, Department of Health and Welsh Office (1992) *National Standards for the Supervision of Offenders in the Community*. London: Home Office Probation Division.

Home Office, Department of Health and Welsh Office (1995) *National Standards for the Supervision of Offenders in the Community*. London: Home Office Probation Training Division.

Hood, R. (1992) *Race and Sentencing: A Study in the Crown Court*. Oxford: Clarendon Press.

Hugman, R. and Smith, D. (eds) (1995) *Ethical Issues in Social Work*. London: Routledge.

Lipton, D., Martinson, R. and Wilks, J. (1975) *The Effectiveness of Correctional Treatment*. New York: Praeger.

MacIntyre, A. (1985) *After Virtue* (2nd edn). London: Duckworth.

McWilliams, W. (1985) 'The mission transformed: professionalisation of probation between the wars', *Howard Journal of Criminal Justice*, 24 (4): 257–74.

McWilliams, W. (1986) 'The English probation service and the diagnostic ideal', *Howard Journal of Criminal Justice*, 25 (4): 241–60.

Mair, G. (1986) 'Ethnic minorities, probation and the magistrates' courts: a pilot study', *British Journal of Criminology*, 26 (2): 147–55.

Matza, D. (1964) *Delinquency and Drift*. New York: John Wiley.

Matza, D. (1969) *Becoming Deviant*. Englewood Cliffs, NJ: Prentice Hall.

Morris, A., Giller, H., Szwed, E. and Geach, H. (1980) *Justice for Children*. London: Macmillan.

Moxon, D. (1988) *Sentencing Practice in the Crown Court*. Home Office Research Study 103. London: HMSO.

NACRO (1992) *Criminal Justice Act 1991 Training Materials Module 3: Practice Issues for the Probation Service*. London: National Association for the Care and Resettlement of Offenders.

NACRO (1993) *Pre-sentence Reports: A Handbook for Probation Officers and Social Workers* (rev. edn). London: National Association for the Care and Resettlement of Offenders.

Perry, F.G. (1974) *Information for the Court*. Cambridge: Cambridge Institute of Criminology.

Raynor, P. (1980) 'Is there any sense in social inquiry reports?', *Probation Journal*, 27 (3): 78–84.

Raynor, P. (1991) 'Sentencing with and without reports: a local study', *Howard Journal of Criminal Justice*, 30 (4): 293–300.

Raynor, P., Smith, D. and Vanstone, M. (1994) *Effective Probation Practice*. BASW Social Work Series. Basingstoke: Macmillan.

Rock, P. (1990) *Helping Victims of Crime: The Home Office and the Rise of Victim Support in England and Wales.* Oxford: Clarendon Press.

Smith, D. (1994) *The Home Office Regional Criminal Justice Conferences May 1990– March 1993.* Liverpool: Home Office Special Conferences Unit.

Tarling, R. (1979) *Sentencing Practice in Magistrates' Courts.* Home Office Research Study 56. London: HMSO.

Thorpe, D.H., Smith, D., Green, C.J. and Paley, J.H. (1980) *Out of Care: The Community Support of Juvenile Offenders.* London: Allen and Unwin.

Thorpe, J. (1979) *Social Inquiry Reports: A Survey.* Home Office Research Study 48. London: HMSO.

Thorpe, J. and Pease, K. (1976) 'The relationship between recommendations made to the court and sentences passed', *British Journal of Criminology,* 12 (3): 230–49.

Tutt, N. and Giller, H. (1984) *Social Inquiry Reports.* Audiotape. Lancaster: Social Information Systems.

Vass, A.A. (1990) *Alternatives to Prison: Punishment, Custody and the Community.* London: Sage.

Vass, A.A. (1996a) 'Crime, probation and social work with offenders', in A.A. Vass (ed.), *Social Work Competences: Core Knowledge, Values and Skills.* London: Sage. pp. 132–89.

Vass, A.A. (1996b) 'Competence in social work and probation practice', in A.A. Vass (ed.), *Social Work Competences: Core Knowledge, Values and Skills.* London: Sage. pp. 190–219.

Vass, A.A. and Weston, A. (1990) 'Probation day centres as an alternative to custody: a "Trojan Horse" examined', *British Journal of Criminology,* 30: 189–206.

Waters, R. (1988) 'Race and the criminal justice process: two empirical studies on social inquiry reports and ethnic minority defendants', *British Journal of Criminology,* 28 (1): 82–94.

8

Community Penalties: The Politics of Punishment

Antony A. Vass

This chapter is about community penalties, that is to say, about attempts to 'punish' offenders in the community instead of sending them to prison. It is not concerned with the legal details or prescriptions about how to implement regulations and requirements (see instead Home Office et al., 1995; Sprack, 1995; Vass, 1996; Ward and Ward, 1993; Wasik, 1993). Rather, it provides a critical review of major issues and concerns about community penalties (see Vass, 1990) and the role of government in shaping penal policy and practice.

Conceptual difficulties

Historically the concept of 'community penalties' has been very problematic. In conceptual terms, community penalties can refer to a wide assortment of tasks, sentences and dispositions. In other words, community penalties can include many diverse activities in the criminal justice system: not just sentencing options following conviction, but also pre-trial decisions and even broader policies of preventing risk groups, such as juveniles, from experiencing formal justice and control. Examples of such community penalties in their wider sense include: fines and fixed penalties; discharge orders; intermediate treatment projects for juveniles; probation orders (with or without conditions or requirements); supervision orders; tracking schemes; tagging; suspended sentences of imprisonment; parole; deferred sentences; compensations orders; binding over; attendance centre orders; community service orders; and combination orders, among others.

All of these, and more, have been variously described as 'community-based penal measures', 'community-based dispositions', 'community care programmes', 'non-custodial penal measures', 'diversionary penal measures' or simply 'diversion from custody', 'decarceration', 'deinstitutionalisation', 'alternatives to prison', 'humane punishment', 'supervision in the community' and 'punishment in the community'. Following the Criminal Justice Act 1991 (see also Home Office et al., 1995) 'community sentences' was also added to the repertoire of terms. These refer to probation, supervision, community service, combination, curfew and attendance centre orders. Curfew orders, though not yet implemented, could in principle be combined with other orders. The 1991 Act includes provisions for the introduction of curfew orders, supported by electronic or other monitoring. The Criminal Justice and Public Order Act 1994 enables the curfew order provisions to be introduced on 'an area by area basis'.

There is not, therefore a single definition of what community penalties are. All such descriptions, irrespective of tone and ambiguity, have been used, at some point, as synonyms or sub-stitutes for each other. In general terms, what they seem to have in common is that they denote almost anything which involves crime prevention, punishment or control *outside* custodial institutions. In short, anything which is conveniently deposited in the 'community' category can be legitimately defined as a 'community penalty'.

The above general and often unclear meaning of community penalties has been one of the main factors which have contributed to the confusion about their exact nature, effectiveness, place in the criminal justice system and role and purpose in relation to prison. This plethora of descriptions and umbrella terms housing many diverse activities in the penal system is problematic both in conceptual as well as practical terms: it means 'all things to all people' and has little value as a heuristic device in understanding their purpose and raison d'être.

In order to avoid confusion and to limit the discussion around specific findings, we treat community penalties as those penalties which are administered following conviction for a criminal offence; and whose availability within a legal framework and use by courts designates them as 'community penalties' whose main purpose is to 'punish' offenders in the community and thus, explicitly or implicitly, keep them out of prison. In this sense, this limited defi-nition of community penalties comes close to the 'community sentences' provided under the Criminal Justice Act 1991, as amended by the Criminal Justice Act 1993, and the national standards of practice for probation services and social services departments in England and Wales (Home Office et al., 1992, 1995).

Each year about 100,000 offenders in England and Wales are given community penalties to be supervised by probation and social services. For adult offenders a range of community penalties are available: probation orders, with or without additional requirements; community service orders; combination orders; and attendance centre orders (for those aged 10–20 years inclusive). All these penalties but with the exception of the attendance centre orders are supervised by the probation service. For younger offenders, those sentenced in the Youth Court, the range of penalties available depends on the age of offenders. Probation orders and community service orders are only available for those aged 16 years. Attendance centre orders can be imposed on anyone aged 10 years or over. Young offenders aged 10 to 17 years can be given a supervision order which may incorporate a variety of specified conditions. Supervision orders can be supervised by the probation service or social services departments.

The Home Office's Green Paper (Home Office, 1995a) proposes to introduce new amendments to current legislation in regard to the availability of community penalties. The government proposes to introduce a single integrated 'community sentence' to replace and incorporate all the current orders available in the adult courts. The main reason offered is that this, with the proposed amendments (for instance, removal of the present requirement that offenders consent to a probation, community service or combination order), will restore the public's confidence in 'tough' and 'harsh' community penalties, and will increase the courts' powers to determine the content, restrictions and compulsions of community penalties in individual cases.

The discussion which follows offers a broad view of the debates about community penalties and incorporates national and international research findings. Although much of the illustrative material which is offered is extracted from findings on community service and probation orders, these illustrations and the discussion in general have wider theoretical and empirical relevance and implications.

The question of effectiveness

The issue of effectiveness is discussed more fully in Chapter 12 (see also Raynor et al., 1994). Here we are more concerned with the debate as it is relevant to community penalties; and with some hidden variables which are at play, albeit not always recognised, and which affect the perceived outcomes of intervention and supervision.

It is difficult to make accurate judgements about the effectiveness of any penal measure, particularly when the arguments are linked to crime reduction and recidivism. One should refrain from making empirical statements such as the one made by Michael Howard, the Home Secretary, that 'prison works'. The available evidence is, at best, inconclusive and, at worst, riddled with methodological flaws. Thus, for example, the statement that 'prison works' is sharply contradicted by research conducted by the Home Office research unit itself (Lloyd et al., 1994). The study shows that reconviction rates among 65,624 offenders who left prison in 1987 are much higher than previously thought. The study found that reconviction rates over a four-year period were particularly high. Adult males showed a 57 per cent reconviction rate within two years, rising to 68 per cent within four years. Women offenders showed a reconviction rate of 40 per cent within two years and 48 per cent within four years. Results were even worse for young offenders. For those under 21, 71 per cent were convicted of new offences within two years of leaving a custodial establishment, and this rose to 82 per cent within four years. Even more serious, 92 per cent of those in the age group 15 to 16 who had served time in a youth custody centre had been reconvicted within just two years. Similar findings, though marginally better, were reported in regard to community penalties and the mere interpretation of statistics led to a fresh round of accusations and counter-accusations about the futility of prisons or community penalties, depending on one's political and ideological leanings (see, for example, Fletcher, 1995; Harding, 1995; Somerville, 1995; Statham, 1995). Thus, for example, the Chief Probation Officer of Inner London Probation Service defended the success record of the probation service and pointed out that things had moved on since 1987, the year from which the data for the report were drawn (Harding, 1995). The Labour Party's prisons spokeswoman, Joan Ruddock, flatly denied that 'prison works' and criticised the Home Secretary for his support for harsher penalties and a return to high levels of imprisonment. The Prison Reform Trust called the Home Secretary's claim a 'lie' and argued that prison does not work, 'especially when it is borne in mind that less than 2 per cent of crimes end with a criminal conviction. It is probable that an even higher proportion [of those released] committed criminal acts' (quoted in Travis, 1994d).

In the face of such arguments and the evident contradiction between the Home Secretary's assertion that 'prison works' and his own Home Office research unit which finds that it does not, the conclusion that can be reached is, simply, that it all depends on the perspective adopted by an observer in defining and interpreting the data. In other words, what someone means and how she or he defines 'effectiveness', or 'success', or simply claims that 'something works' or 'does not work' is crucial in understanding debates about the effects of penal measures. For example, it is interesting that the above contrasting claims by different parts of the Home Office led to yet another Home Office spokesperson to 'put the record straight': he refuted the 'idea that the [Home Office research] study challenged the Home Secretary's prison works philosophy'. He put it down to a misunderstanding and explained that 'Mr Howard had made clear he believed prison did indeed work in stopping offenders committing crimes *while they were in prison* (quoted in Travis, 1994d; emphasis added). In short, according to the new official version, when the Home Secretary referred to the claim that 'prison works', he was making a direct and clear statement about incapacitation. If offenders are given their just deserts and kept in prison, society is saved from further crimes.

However, even this qualification has serious flaws. For even in prison, offenders are capable of committing offences. The use of illicit drugs and other offences are a regular feature of prison life. Judge Stephen Tumin, the government's Chief Inspector of Prisons, has consistently called for action to deal with the problem (Travis, 1994e; see also, Burrell, 1994; Mills, 1995). His last report on Styal prison in Cheshire claims that 80 per cent of the women there were taking hard drugs. In finding that over a hundred of them shared needles for injecting heroin, cocaine and crack, he recommended a policy of a needle exchange scheme to prevent the spread of serious illnesses such as AIDS and hepatitis B (quoted in Mills, 1995). The government aims to start tests in all 133 prisons to determine the extent of the problem. The first official figures of drug-testing problems in seven prisons revealed that most prisoners who tested positive were taking cannabis and a minority were found to be taking heroin, cocaine and tranquillisers (Mills, 1995).

From another perspective, incapacitation often provides limited and temporary indemnity against crime in the community: sooner or later, most prisoners are released back to the community. What these simple illustrations demonstrate is that one should treat such claims that something works or does not work with considerable scepticism, for the so-called 'facts' do not speak for themselves. They need to be interpreted, and those interpretations are a function of the perspectives and the ideological views held by the interpreters. As there are competing perspectives, it is inevitable that the outcome of any debate or points of view will have to be considered carefully and with considerable caution.

Notwithstanding the above cautionary tale, the Home Office's findings that, given the high recidivism rates recorded, prison (and community penalties alike) 'may not work' is not new. Various attempts to review research studies on the rehabilitative effect of penal measures in general share a common characteristic. They claim that very little, if anything, works (for example, Brody, 1976; Home Office, 1975; Home Office, 1986; Lipton et al., 1975). For instance, the Home Office review of the criminal justice system in 1976 (Home Office, 1977) stated that there was not enough evidence to justify claims that anything works. The Home Office went further 10 years later (Home Office, 1986) to state unequivocally that increased use and terms of imprisonment have no real effect on crime rates as regards deterrence or recidivism. It added that the same applied to community penalties.

A specific illustration of this expressed pessimism about the effectiveness of penal sanctions is the case of the community service order. The early Home Office studies (Pease et al., 1975, 1977) were not particularly positive about the rehabilitative aspects of the order. The research team concluded that the 'data did not show that community service had a stabilising effect on the criminal careers of the offenders studied' (Pease et al., 1977: 23). Similar concerns have been raised by other studies (Thorvaldson, 1978; Vass, 1984; Young, 1979), though comparisons should be viewed with considerable care. Each study's research theme, focus and scope is different and may not therefore make comparisons reliable. None the less, more recent studies in England and Wales (Hoggarth, 1991; Lloyd et al., 1994) and Scotland (McIvor, 1992) continue to address similar concerns. For example, McIvor (1992, 1993) argues that the community service order leads to positive effects on recipients, the community, the penal system and specifically on offenders, in that 'three quarters of a sample of offenders who completed their community service orders in work teams believed that they had gained, in various ways, from the experience' (McIvor, 1993: 400). However, she also finds that over 75 per cent of offenders were reconvicted and nearly a quarter were imprisoned in the three years after being sentenced to community service. A third of the offenders were reconvicted while serving under an order (McIvor, 1992). These findings do not provide evidence that community service is any more or less effective than prison in reducing recidivism and question the main purpose of the community service order in aiming to 're-integrate the offender into the community' (Home Office et al., 1992: 67). Similar findings have been reported in the United States (Berg and Feeley, 1990; McDonald, 1986; Schneider, 1986). For example, McDonald (1986: 186) writes that 'community service is not a cure for crime, at least in the population of recidivist offenders (mostly thieves) that the New York courts sentenced to the Vera Institute's project. Approximately 40 to 50 percent of those in our sample were rearrested within six months of having been sentenced'.

The public and private domain of community penalties

The concern that community penalties do not seem to have any discernible effect on recidivism rates has a fairly long history.

Various debates raged in the 1970s, particularly in the United States, as to whether any real positive differences can be identified between custodial and community penalties (cf. Empey and Erickson, 1972; Gibbons, 1970; Grygier et al., 1970; Lerman, 1975; Moos, 1975; Palmer, 1971, 1973; Sarason, 1974; Scull, 1984; Taggart, 1972). Similarly, a study in England by Phillpotts and Lancucki (1979) which considered the reconvictions of a sample of 5,000 offenders concluded that results were not encouraging for any particular type of sentence. They argued that although offenders given custodial sentences appear to have higher reconviction rates than those given suspended sentences or probation or supervision orders, the latter do worse in comparison to a fine or discharge order. This pessimism was somewhat confirmed by the 'nothing works' perspective, which was successfully popularised by Martinson (1972, 1974). Martinson (1979) later retracted some of his original statements and agreed that different sentences may suit different types of offenders and that one cannot therefore generalise that 'nothing works'. However, his argument that 'nothing works'; that no particular penal measure (custodial or community-based) has any appreciable effect on recidivism; and that correctional programmes of all sorts are a waste of taxpayers' money, created widespread pessimism about the capacity of community penalties to offer a more positive and effective approach to custodial sentences.

Recidivism as a measure for counting success or failure has serious limitations and usually matters relevant to the question are often left untouched. For instance, recidivism is not just a function of committing new offences. There is a difference between re-offending and recidivism. The first may take place without the offender being found out or apprehended or reported. The second is more of a 'bureaucratic' decision taken by supervising or prose-cuting officers to treat the commission of a new offence as a failure. The way in which they act or react to identified infractions of the rules is a material source of influence on whether an offender will be processed through the courts as a recidivist or whether he or she will be shielded by those supervisors or law enforcers from a re-exposure to the criminal justice system. For example, offenders on probation or community service may appear to be doing slightly better in terms of reconviction rates than offenders given custodial sentences, but that difference may not mean fewer offences. Such community penalties may do better not necessarily because those offenders commit fewer offences after conviction and sentence, but because they may, as they are now known to welfare agencies, receive preferential treatment. Technical or other more serious infractions of the law may not be reported and attempts may be made by supervising officers to deal with the new infractions through internal, administrative or informal sanctions as opposed to external, legal and formal penalties (cf. Day, 1981; Fielding, 1984, 1986; Lawson, 1978; McIvor, 1992; Vass, 1980, 1984, 1990).

In terms of community service, for instance, McIvor (1992), although supportive of the practice, provides findings which support previous research and views about the suspect nature of 'outcomes' (that is to say, the emphasis on pure arithmetical comparisons, successful completion rates or reconviction rates) and the inherent risks of not taking into account the *process* (cf. Smith, 1987; Vass, 1984, 1988, 1990) of administering and enforcing community penalties. Thus in McIvor's research, although reconviction rates are high, successful community service order completion rates are also very high. However, closer examination reveals that the process is marred by many absences and breach proceedings. As in England and Wales, the administration and enforcement of community service in Scotland is an extended 'process of negotiation and tolerance' (Vass, 1980, 1984, 1990: 115–31). Breach of requirements and the prosecution of defaulters is not a rigid or smooth affair as laid down by the law and national standards. Discretion and negotiation become important aspects of those social encounters between offenders and supervising officers. What emerges from McIvor's study is that following the Criminal Justice Act 1991 and the introduction of national standards (Home Office et al., 1992, 1995) the above negotiable outcomes may have been reduced, and thus under current orders there may be more emphasis on prosecuting offenders who violate the terms of their sentences than has been reported in previous studies. However, despite this increased activity in formally charging offenders with new offences, the main theme raised by previous studies was still evident in McIvor's study: that had officers applied the law in a rigid and inflexible manner the completion rates and thus reconviction rates for such offenders would have been higher. In short, supervising officers are capable of determining 'outcomes' by either shielding offenders from further formal penal sanctions (thus increasing the arithmetical outcomes of 'success') or uncovering and reporting their infractions (thus increasing the arithmetical outcomes of 'failure'). Success or failure (apparent recidivism) can be controlled by officials.

What concerns us here in treating something as a 'success' or 'failure' are the mechanics of law enforcement and what role they play in the process (cf. Vass, 1984: 42–58; 1990: 52–9, 115–31). The problem can be summarised in a few words: policy intentions are one thing, practice, interpretation of those intentions and enforcement are another. Supervising officers have a 'bag of tricks' which can help them cope with pressures as well as apply their own 'world views' in dealing with offenders. In so doing, they form policy on the spot and become policy-makers in miniature; they deviate from the rules and control situations according to their own ends. Usually, those ends relate to a discernible goal: a positive and successful portrayal of their practices and the effectiveness of their work. This is a social characteristic of organisational structures first noted in research on 'middle managers' (cf. Roethlisberger, 1945). Subsequently, research in other diverse areas and organisations (see Vass 1984: 42–58 for a detailed summary of these studies) has consistently shown that where rules and regulations inform social relations, participants are actively involved in negotiating and accommodating rule-breaking. This is done via selective enforcement that defines which offences can be ignored; which can be treated in an informal and lenient manner; and which necessitate or warrant drastic responses through the activation of formal sanctions. What is common to all these research studies (see also Chapter 6 in this volume) is the consistent finding that systems of control expedite, evade, routinise, alter and distort. Through these interpretations, adjustments, negotiations, decisions and actions, supervising officers determine the shape and character of relationships, and their outcomes (Vass, 1984, 1986, 1990; Vass and Menzies, 1989).

Recognition of the effects of those relationships and the role supervising officers play in colouring outcomes prompted Bottomley and Pease (1986: 107) to write that the assumed success of community penalties is 'open to doubt, given the confusion and active trickery which often attend the imposition of serious non-custodial penalties'. This recognition (though for the wrong reasons – see Vass, 1990: 163–85) led to the government's attempt to structure and tighten up those relationships by prescribing how they should operate (Home Office et al., 1992, 1995).

Even when the relevance of outcomes is taken for granted without questioning how they are achieved and under what circumstances, the evidence remains contradictory and is subject to different interpretations. Thus Sheppard (1980) found that 67–71 per cent of those completing two-year probation orders were reconvicted within five years, but it is difficult to measure the significance or relevance of such a broad finding. There is some evidence available that individual penal sanctions appear to work differently with different types of offenders and, therefore, whereas they can be effective with some offenders, may not be so with others. This was recognised and acknowledged by the Home Office study into reconviction rates (Lloyd et al., 1994) by stating that recidivism provides only a partial answer and that national averages mask the fact that some programmes work better than others. Walker (1985), for example, in considering various findings, suggests that for some offenders at various stages in their criminal career different sentences may have different effects. Thus, probation orders appear to be more effective in controlling recidivism if they are used for offenders with previous convictions – particularly between two and four – although once again why that should be so is not clear from the evidence (Walker, 1983). As Bottomley and Pease (1986: 164) state, in our ignorance, we suffer a sort of 'penal agnosticism'. They suggest that we tend to look at all prisons, probation officers, community penalties, and so forth, as having the same effect or lack of effect on people, when in fact they may not. In order to avoid distorted perceptions of the effects of penal measures, including community penalties, they call for more 'differentiation among sanctions in the same nominal category'.

Community Penalties as a Trojan horse: the dispersal of discipline thesis

In the previous sections we examined a number of contentious issues which relate to prisons and community penalties. In general, claims about the desirability of community penalties are found to be lacking in clarity, depth and conviction. In particular, the creation of new sanctions and the expansion of community penalties since the 1970s (see McMahon, 1992; Vass, 1990; Young, 1979, for an historical account of community penal measures) has taken place amid hopes that they would reduce the role of prisons and engineer a more humane and cheaper approach to containing offenders in the community. However, critics have marshalled claims and 'facts' which sharply contradict those hopes: the development and expansion of community penalties does not automatically lead to a reduction in costs, and there are questions about their effectiveness (as has already been discussed) in controlling crime. More serious than those problems, however, is the criticism that the creation of community penalties does not automatically or necessarily lead to a decrease in the use of imprisonment (Harris, 1985). In fact, it has been argued that through such a policy of offering and expanding community penalties, prisons remain unaffected and overcrowded but at the same time new forms of overcrowding are introduced in the form of 'overcrowded' community penalties (Vass, 1986: 103). Bottoms (1987), in a review of penal developments in England, concluded in pessimistic terms. Although he identified some minor achievements and successes in the use of community penalties, he wrote that the 'English experience offers no support at all to the optimistic suggestion sometimes made in the past, namely that the progressive adoption of various measures to limit prison use would, in a gradual way, erode the central importance of the prison in modern penality' (Bottoms, 1987: 177). His conclusion was that those who wish to reduce the prison population should stop wasting their time in pursuing further initiatives and expanding community penalties, for 'alternatives all too often turn out not to be real alternatives, but ways of buttressing the social institutions to which an alternative is sought (in this case, the prison)' (Bottoms, 1987: 198).

MacMahon (1990: 122) suggests that in general the 'conventional wisdom of the critical literature on community corrections' is that community penalties are synonymous with the expansion of penal controls (cf. Austin and Krisberg, 1981; Chan and Ericson, 1981; Cohen, 1979, 1985; Garland, 1985; Hudson, 1984; Hylton, 1981a, 1981b, 1982; Lerman, 1975; Lowman et al., 1987; Mathiesen, 1974; Matthews, 1979; McCullagh, 1988; Rothman, 1974; Scull, 1984; Vass, 1982, 1986; Vass and Menzies, 1989; Warren, 1981, among others).

Despite the diversity of perspectives adopted and emphases placed on issues under consideration, the criticisms relate to the same theme: the 'dispersal of discipline thesis' (cf. Rodger, 1988). This theme, in its broader conception, suggests that community penalties are not substitutes for imprisonment. They fail to divert offenders from imprisonment and, on the contrary, they appear to expand the means or forms of punishment. They are not as humane as they are supposed to be because they 'disguise coercion, increasing invisible discretion' (Cohen 1985: 38). Community penalties are advocated in response to government and overall political expediency – ideological or financial – to demonstrate political will, satisfy the prevailing 'fashion' of law and order, or demonstrate stringency in fiscal policy. In effect, as they do nothing, or little, to challenge the prison's hegemony, it is business as usual, that is to say, more expansion of the means of control and more discipline. As Austin and Krisberg (1981: 188–9) put it, '"Widening the net" describes the nightmare of the benevolent state gone haywire' (see also Chan and Ericson, 1981; Lowman et al., 1987; Scull, 1984; Van Dusen, 1981).

This view that community penalties are another convenient means of extending the process of control, enlarging itself, becoming more intrusive and capturing more and varied groups of people in its meshes, is well captured by Cohen (1985), who likens community penalties, and what he calls attempts to 'destructure' prison establishments, to a Trojan horse. Community penalties are thus a monster in disguise (cf. Vass, 1990: 77–114; Vass and Weston,

1990). He argues that community penalties have merely left us with 'wider, stronger and different nets' (Cohen, 1985: 38). In a nutshell, community penalties do three things: they *widen* the net of surveillance and control; they make that net *denser*; and they produce and reproduce *new and different* nets which are added to the original ones.

As has already been referred to, findings claiming that community penalties do not act as real alternatives to incarceration and that they tend to widen the net of sanctions without any real benefits have been reported in a number of countries. Other than criticisms expressed in England (for example, Bottoms, 1987; Hudson, 1984; Pratt, 1986; Vass, 1984, 1986), serious concerns have also been raised at different times and in different states: Tasmania, Australia, New Zealand (cf. Hopkins et al., 1977; Varne, 1976); Canada (for example, Chan and Ericson, 1981; Hylton, 1981a, 1981b; Solicitor General Canada, 1982; Menzies and Vass, 1989; Vass and Menzies 1989); the United States (cf. Callison, 1983; Clear and O'Leary, 1983; del Carmen and Trook-White, 1986; Doig, 1983; Lerman, 1982; Nimmer, 1974; Rutherford and McDermott, 1976; Scull, 1984); and the Netherlands (Junger-Tas, 1986).

The impression given by these findings is that although there appears to be a general acceptance of the moral that community penalties may be one way of alleviating overcrowded prisons, in reality that view finds little support and it is argued that 'the movement to use alternatives has never taken hold on a serious scale, and those incursions that have been made have often produced ambiguous results' (Mullen, 1985: 40); and that merely expanding community penalties does not lead to an automatic or corresponding depletion of the prison establishment (Harris, 1985: 154). In a sense, as far as the argument goes, it all comes down to political expediency. Community penalties are introduced to avert more serious crises in prisons, or show that something is done to satisfy the law and order lobby, or because they give the impression that central government is active in expanding the availability of penal sanctions for the benefit of courts in their efforts to punish and deter. This is a view – about creating new means of control in response to 'crises' in the state – which historically has consistently been advanced in justification for the development and emergence of new penal sanctions (cf. Vass, 1990). The net effect of this reactive approach to political expediency is to lead to new and varied community penalties while maintaining a high prison population. Pease and Young (1993: appendix 5), in an original and ambitious cross-cultural study of prison rates and custodial sanctions involving 23 different jurisdictions, appear to confirm this view, and report that the availability of community penalties is directly linked to higher prison populations. They suggest that although some people may be diverted from short sentences of imprisonment, community penalties have little practical effect in reducing high prison populations.

A competing perspective: community penalties as an effective and constructive alternative to prison

The main problem with studies which purport to argue or demonstrate that community penalties are not effective in offering an alternative to crowded prisons is that they are by and large based on impression. Where findings are based on empirical work, such work is found lacking in methodological or interpretative terms. Although the criticisms levelled against community penalties are useful in guiding attention to discrepancies between intent and actual practice, they focus too much on the negative aspects while ignoring the more positive aspects of such penal measures. The spectre of net widening as a primarily negative development may be valid to a point in demonstrating where policy can go wrong, but it fails to recognise that some community penalties for some types of offenders under certain conditions may actually be successful in keeping some offenders out of prison (cf. McIvor, 1993; McMahon, 1990, 1992; Matthews, 1987; Raynor, 1988; Vass, 1990; Vass and Weston, 1990).

According to McConville (1988), there are a number of community penalties which have a 'decade of solid success behind them and are increasingly earning public and judicial respect'. McConville's claim refers, of course, to the work of the National Center on Institutions and Alternatives and The Sentencing Project (TSP) in the United States, which have developed refined approaches to diverting offenders from prison sentences to community penalties. These approaches involve packages of 'individual sentencing schemes' which try to fit the punishment to the crime, the offender, the victim and society. Judges, in other words, are presented with a package of community penalties which takes account of deterrence, retribution and restitution. These schemes' potential or usefulness may be restricted to some offenders, in some circumstances, in some courts and in a social and political context which allows close cooperation between probation service, police, courts and other community agencies (see also Musheno, 1982; Quay and Love, 1977; Rutherford, 1986). They do demonstrate though that at least at the local level they are capable of keeping some people, for some time, out of prison.

There is a tendency in the literature on community penalties to over-generalise, or, as Matthews (1987) puts it, to 'globalise' findings from very specific and often idiosyncratic experiences, studies or contexts to wider concerns. Such 'globalism' is expressed without much concern that such a 'blurring of the categories of analysis and lumping together of diverse groups into an undifferentiated whole' (Matthews, 1987: 42) can be a serious distortion of reality. For there are exceptions to the rule that community penalties merely expand the system without any real benefit. In the first place, a lot of activity in diverting offenders from custody often remains far removed from popular awareness; there are many small, local projects which may be successful in diverting, but because they remain unknown and unpublicised, they do not appear to have any obvious and direct effect on the prison population. There is some evidence which shows that some local projects and types of community penalties do appear to be quite successful in keeping some offenders out of prisons for some of the time (see, for example, Children's Society Advisory Committee, 1988; Longley, 1985; Mair et al., 1994; Parker et al., 1987; Pitts, 1988: 74–82; Raynor, 1988; Rhys et al., 1989; Rutherford, 1986; C. Smith et al., 1972; D. Smith et al., 1984; Vanstone, 1993; Vass and Weston, 1990). In the second place, community penalties may appear to fail because they are usually targeted by courts at the wrong offenders – those who may not be at risk of imprisonment anyway. More seriously, where they are targeted at offenders who are at risk of imprisonment, those offenders are normally diverted from short-term prison sentences which, by implication, may have little impact on crowding and the size of the prison population (cf. Bottomley and Pease 1986: 107; Fitzmaurice and Pease, 1982).

However, the above criticism, that the problem of overcrowding in England and Wales has much to do with prisoners serving long sentences, has been challenged on the ground that evidence from Germany (Graham, 1990) and comparative analysis of imprison-ment rates in England and Wales and Australia (Walker et al., 1990) suggests that the higher prison population in England and Wales is due to the greater number of people received into prison, not length of sentence. The implicit assumption is, therefore, that efforts to divert all types of offenders from custody by the use of community penalties is a worthy means of checking prison populations.

Other than the above concerns which are not adequately addressed, the 'dispersal of discipline' thesis and the idea that alternatives widen the net may be confusing mere expansion of penal sanctions with surveillance and control. The thesis assumes that as the system expands, inevitably more people are or ought to be caught up in its meshes. Although it is true that there has been an expansion of penal sanctions in most Western states, and that the '"carceral" society has taken quite substantial hold' (Downes, 1988: 64), it does not follow that more people are actually caught up in the expanded net. Indeed, that assumption still remains to be demonstrated. Furthermore, as Downes (1986: 111) suggests, trends in informal controls are completely ignored, and while formal controls may be expanding, they 'may be makeshifts for net reductions' elsewhere.

Despite much rhetoric about the failures of community penalties, we still know very little about what exactly those penalties are and how they are administered; what the real effects of such measures are on the criminal justice process and those who experience them; and what their true relationship is to imprisonment. This relationship is not always quantifiable (cf. Smith 1987; Vass 1988) or a simple mathematical calculation. The critics tend to look at quantity – that is to say, whether alternatives reduce or do not reduce imprisonment. However, such an assumed relationship, even in studies which appear to offer correlational evidence (Hylton, 1981b), is very dubious, for it may rest on very crude and simplistic assumptions about the variables measured. Correlational evidence may imply a relationship but does not confirm the existence of an association, for too much is left to chance and too little taken into account. For example, when outcomes are considered in this restrictive style of interpretation, even what is presented as a watertight conclusion, such as that advanced by Hylton (1981b), begins to look insecure.

Hylton's work has been consistently cited by critics as an empirical verification of the proposition that community penalties widen the net of social control without reducing the prison population. Briefly, Hylton analysed data from the Canadian province of Saskatchewan which referred to custodial institutions and methods of supervision in the community (probation, community training residences and the community service programme for fine defaulters – known as the Fine Option Program). He found that the rate per 100,000 population under supervision (including custodial establishments) increased from approximately 84 in 1962 to approximately 322 in 1979. This constituted a rise of 283 per cent in 18 years. Hylton then looked at admissions to custodial establishments by relating them to admissions to probation and community service for fine defaulters. The analysis showed that the relationship between increases in community penalties and increases in admissions to custodial establishments (thus an increase in the social control and surveillance in the system) was statistically significant. He reported that the number of admissions per 100,000 population to all types of supervision rose from about 480 in 1962 to 1337 in 1979, a rise of 179 per cent (Hylton, 1981b: 22, Table 3). He concluded, 'There can be little question that the expanded use of community programs in Saskatchewan provided the means by which the correctional system expanded' (Hylton, 1981b: 22).

However, in a scathing attack, McMahon (1992) offers new and devastating evidence that Hylton not only ignored vital data in his analysis but also his calculations and therefore conclusions were far from accurate. In effect, McMahon challenges the conclusion that community penalties in Saskatchewan failed to reduce the prison population, and comments that if the evidence is looked at more carefully there is every reason to believe that community penalties actually work in diverting offenders from custody. Nevertheless, even McMahon's thorough analysis and convincing counter-arguments in favour of community penalties must be treated with caution. For instance, the claim that the Fine Option Program has been effective in diverting offenders from prison to community penalties must be seen in the context of Saskatchewan. It cannot be readily accepted and applied outside that context. For in England and Wales, there is still strong evidence that the fine, used for the vast majority of convicted persons (for instance in 1992, 78 per cent of 1.52 million offenders sentenced by the courts were fined) plays a significant role in keeping the daily prison population high. During 1993, the number of people incarcerated for fine default ($n = 22,754$) rose by 17 per cent on the previous year, and since 1990 the figure has risen by 36 per cent (Fletcher, 1994: 10–11). The most worrying aspect of this increase in the rate of imprisonment for fine default is that '[m]ost people are gaoled because of culpable neglect, often where the offence was itself non-imprisonable' (Fletcher, 1994: 11).

The above contradictions in the evidence and interpretations offered should demonstrate that comparisons between prison population statistics and community penalties and the conclusions drawn from such assumed connections are riddled with difficulties and are thus suspect. The assumed association between a rising prison population or the rate of imprisonment and an expanding system of community penalties ignores a host of intervening variables which could, if taken into account, nullify that association, or, if not nullify it, challenge it and throw it into disrepute. Such factors include changes in policing tactics, legislation, sentencing practices, length of prison sentences, enforcement issues, the differential nature of supervision and intervention, social characteristics of offenders (for instance, the ratio of men and women in prison and ethnic origin of offenders), differences between types of community penalties, changes in attitudes and penal policy, among many others. What this means is that before concluding that something is a failure, it is important that one recognises that there may be other factors at play which may determine changes in the prison population. For instance, as has been argued about probation day centres (Vass and Weston, 1990), day centres were not allowed to act as full alternatives to custody because the courts discounted a priori the possibility of community penalties for 'deep end' offenders. The study pointed out that courts may themselves divert offenders from community penalties to prison establishments rather than vice versa (Vass and Weston, 1990: 200). In short, the decisions of the courts and the policy followed may have a significant influence on the way in which community penalties are administered and how they relate to other sanctions including custody.

The social problem of government

The point made above is particularly relevant to the effects of penal policy and decisions by policy-makers, namely government. A good illustration are the sentencing trends in England and Wales. Following the implementation of the Criminal Justice Act 1991 on 1 October 1992 and its emphasis on community penalties, there was a fall in the prison population of nearly 3,000 from 45,835 at the end of September to 43,064 at the end of December 1992. According to analysis provided by the National Association for the Care and Resettlement of Offenders (NACRO), this drop could not be explained by seasonal or other factors, including a reduction in the number of offenders coming before the courts. According to NACRO, 'The evidence indicates that the Act produced a real reduction in the court's use of custody' (Cavadino, 1993: 1). In other words, a combination of government initiatives in penal policy to upgrade the relevance of community penalties, changing attitudes about the relevance of the prison as a last resort, the development of guidelines to courts and practitioners, and a new awareness by practitioners about the purpose of the Act led to a concerted action in reducing the prison population.

However, from January 1993 onwards a sudden shift first in government thinking (the rediscovery that 'prison works'), and then in penal policy, through amendments to legislation masterminded by the new Home Secretary, Michael Howard, at the height of an intensive media campaign about crime and the ineffectiveness of community 'soft options', led to significant changes in practice. It led to a new penal 'climate' in which 'sentencing and remand decisions were made, and there was a sharp increase in the prison population' (Cavadino, 1993: 5) accompanied by a simultaneous increase in the use of community penalties. Between January and February 1993 there was an increase of imprisonment of 4 per cent for all Crown Courts in England and Wales and a simultaneous increase in the use of probation orders, community service orders and supervision orders. In fact, by 15 October 1994, the number of prisoners in England and Wales had reached more than 50,000, the highest since 1988, and 9,500 higher than at the beginning of 1993.

In the two years since Michael Howard has been in office, the 'tough' talk and 'tough' measures have greatly accelerated under the Conservatives. They have introduced new criminal justice acts (for example, the Criminal Justice Act 1993 and Criminal Justice and Public Order Act 1994); they have reintroduced a previously abortive experiment to use electronic monitoring of offenders (tagging) despite mounting costs and poor reliability (Campbell, 1995b; Travis, 1995c); they have declared that 'prison works'; that a 'get a job or go to jail' new tough style policy in dealing with persistent offenders should be implemented to stamp out crime and idleness; that further probation and bail hostels should be axed to save taxpayers' money; that, in general, offenders should be given a 'cold wet shock' by 'tough and demanding' community penalties which will leave offenders 'wet, tired and hungry'; that the government will stamp out illegal immigrants and toughen immigration laws (Travis, 1994c, 1995d); that new penal measures will be introduced to 'revive ailing police faith in justice' (Campbell, 1995a; Zander, 1995); that tough measures against young 'thugs' will be introduced based on 'US-style military discipline in pilot "shock incarceration boot camp" regimes' (Freedland, 1995; Travis, 1995e); that new legislation will be introduced to redefine the purpose and type of community penalties on offer 'in order to give courts more choice' (Home Office, 1995a); that new amendments to the national standards guidelines were necessary to restore confidence about the toughness of community penalties (Home Office et al., 1995); and last, but not least, that new reforms to change the ethos of probation training to move it away from social work and allow on-the-job training to attract more 'ex-army types' as new recruits and thus 'toughen up' its purpose and image are being considered (Dews and Watts, 1995; Home Office, 1995b, 1995c).

The practical outcome of that flurry of activity is depressing. The prison population reached such heights in 1994 that an 'emergency programme to provide an additional 2,000 places in house blocks at [the 133] existing jails is under way' (*Times*, 1994; Travis, 1994c). Remand prisoners are experiencing longer delays in being processed by courts than ever before and the cost of the delays is put at £20 million a year. Figures from the Lord Chancellor's department show that the number of defendants in prison awaiting Crown Court trial for longer than the statutory 16-week limit rose from 4,200 in 1991 to 6,100 in 1994 (Travis, 1995c). This represents a 45 per cent increase in less than three years. Similarly, prison suicide rates continue to remain high, with a group of board visitors demanding an inquiry (Travis, 1995b). In the same vein, prison riots have risen sharply, showing a 284 per cent increase from 1985 (n = 38) to 1994 (n = 146). In 1989/90 there were 67 recorded prison disturbances. By 1993/4 the number increased to 146, a 118 per cent rise (Travis, 1995a).

On 16 March 1995, the prison population broke existing records for England and Wales when it reached 51,243, amidst warnings from penal reform groups, professional associations and agencies, including the Prison Governors' Association, that the prison system cannot cope with this sort of pressure. The Penal Affairs Consortium considered the 'shameful figure' to be the result of ill-informed government policies (Travis, 1995f). On 16 August 1995, the number of offenders given immediate custody for all offences increased to 68,500. This was also accompanied by a simultaneous increase of 12 per cent in the number of offenders given community penalties (Campbell, 1995c). *The Guardian* (1995) newspaper took up the issue thus:

Probation is still seen as a soft option. Who says so? Michael Howard in his green paper published yesterday. Is this surprising? Hardly. Ever since he arrived at the Home Office Michael Howard has played a one note tune: the value of prison. Everything was going to be solved by prisons: juvenile delinquency, rising crime, rising violent crime. All manner of experienced advisers told him to cool it – his researchers, policy-makers, police officers and even the courts. But he would not be diverted. Within two years the prison population has increased by 10,000. There are now 51,000 inmates at a cost of £437 per prisoner per week. . . . Could he possibly be on the point of conversion? Alas no. Instead of spelling out the values of community penalties – which cost only £25 a week – Mr Howard talked the tired rhetoric that has been trotted out by successive Tory ministers for the last 16 years. . . . Mr Howard's new package will replace the current range of community orders – probation, community service, and supervision orders – with a single integrated sentence. He claimed this would give courts more say about supervision. Tosh. All the proposed new powers for the courts are available already. . . . So why produce another new green paper? Because Mr Howard has to look busy. . . . Perhaps the Home Secretary should have [listened] to Lord Justice Rose . . . urging ministers to stop tampering with the law. In the 60 years up to 1985, there were only six criminal justice acts. Since 1986 there have been six more – one every 18 months. Now another one is promised. The Americans have a phrase for it: wheel spinning.

Conclusion: Government as a subject of inquiry

There is an ongoing debate about the role and purpose of community penalties in the criminal justice process. The debate is
marred by the confusion surrounding the concept itself. That is to
say, 'community penalties' encompass diverse sentences and
dispositions and may mean different things to different people. It
is an area which has been consistently misused and abused by a
variety of political interests.

The criticisms levelled against community penalties – namely that
they make things worse; that they succeed in expanding surveillance
and control; that they are complementary sanctions to prison; and,
in general, that they do more harm than good – have yet to be
demonstrated. Equally, community penalties are enmeshed in
rhetoric and occasional fantasy about their assumed achievements.
Again, these claims do not always stand up to serious scrutiny.
Despite the existence of an extensive and considerable amount of
research in the area, we remain ignorant of the broader effects –
positive or negative – of these penal measures on criminal justice
and the wider social structure. In addition to what has already been
covered, there are also other wider concerns arising from the use of
community penalties which ought to receive closer attention (see
Vass, 1990, for a broader view). One such other area of concern is
whether the administration and enforcement of such penalties
perpetuates social divisions in society in the form of 'class', 'age',
'gender' and 'race'. Although there are exceptions to the rule, by
and large those who are given community penalties are often young,
white and unemployed male offenders. The evidence for this
observation is far from clear-cut. But serious thought must be given
to the possibility that many offenders who run the risk of imprisonment are excluded from community penalties on grounds of class,
age, gender and race (see, for example, Crow 1987; Dominelli, 1984;
Hoggarth, 1991; Hudson, 1989, 1993; Inner London Probation
Service, 1989; McIvor, 1992; Mair, 1986; Mair et al., 1994;
NACRO, 1988; Parker et al., 1987; Pease et al., 1977; Vass, 1984;
Vass and Menzies, 1989; Vass and Weston, 1990; Young, 1979).

In sum, there is much more to be learned about the use of
community penalties. However, as has been argued elsewhere (Vass,
1990: 183), even though improvements in the administration and
enforcement of community penalties can be achieved, they alone
cannot be expected to resolve the prison crisis, which is a policy
crisis. As others have also argued (cf. Downes, 1988; Graham, 1990;
Rutherford, 1986) prison populations 'represent the end-product of
highly complex social and judicial processes . . . fluctuations in

prison populations . . . are the products of a wide range of judicial, penal, social, and economic variables, and to isolate the influential factors underpinning any particular trend is no simple task' (Graham, 1990: 151). Whether community penalties are increased or decreased in quantity, whether they keep people out of prison or whether they contribute to the prison population or widen the net of surveillance and social control, or whether they play any significant part in the overall social structure of a society, it is a matter which cannot be settled by resort to simple explanations. There is, though, a clear interplay between policy (legislation and government activity), decision-making processes (courts), other practice-related activities (police, probation officers) and a shared as well as diverse 'world view' of crime and punishment. This interplay takes place within particular social contexts at particular times in a penal system's 'career'. It is propagated by alliances among self-styled experts, media, practitioners, policy-makers and politicians which express concern about the desirability or futility of imprisonment and alternative methods of sanctioning offenders. Community penalties, their nature, type and raison d'être, are but only one effect of those social factors and as such they are only a small part in a much bigger and very complex network of social relationships.

When put in a historical context, the above illustration from recent experiences in penal policy reveals that the nucleus of this network of social relationships is, we suggest, *the activities and policies of the government of the day*. Time and again, ministerial theology – dogma and arrogance – has created the social conditions and a perverse penal climate which propagate new and irrational decisions and irrational practice. The recent fiascos in criminal justice policies and the collapse of a coherent and rational approach to prisons and community penalties (but see Vass, 1990, for this recurring crisis) has little to do with prison governors, prison officers, probation officers, police or even courts, as has been argued thus far. For example, serious commentators (see, for instance, Ashworth, 1983; Bottomley, 1986; Box, 1987; Downes, 1988; Rutherford, 1984) have consistently argued and called for a way of structuring sentencing practices. That is to say, they regard the judiciary and magistracy to be the stumbling block in attempts to bring about a coherent and meaningful criminal justice policy. However, we believe that the problem lies elsewhere: it lies in the corridors of government and particularly ministerial and prime ministerial power, where decisions are taken based on ideological grounds and often in circumstances which defy reason and facts. The last few years should give ample evidence to social observers that an irresponsible government by irresponsible people has the capacity to generate irresponsible policies for an irresponsible society. It is this irresponsible attitude to social and penal affairs and the resultant irrational decision-making processes which have historically, and more so in the last few years, bedevilled criminal justice and led to the current mess.

It is time that criminologists and penal reformers add government to their list of variables that make up the 'social problem' of prisons and in general the machinery of discipline and punishment which includes community penalties. Students of socio-legal and political behaviour ought to rethink afresh the part played by government in constructing and deconstructing penal discourse. The 'social problem' of government has hitherto remained unnoticed and uninvestigated. It is now ripe, as a major concern, for inspection and analysis. It ought to become a legitimate target for investigative social scientists. Without this analysis of the part played by government in guiding and affecting practice, the debate about prisons and community penalties will remain at best incomplete, and at worst misplaced. Although political theorists have long discussed the role of government in defining or characterising the type of society one lives in, such analysis has not been extended to penal policy and practice in a proper and systematic way. It is perplexing that such an omission has been allowed by contemporary criminology to remain outside its major concerns. As a 'science of society' it ought to encompass and critically assess and evaluate the 'science of government' and how it defines, affects and effects socio-legal and other social relationships in the criminal justice system.

References

Ashworth, A. (1983) *Sentencing and Penal Policy*. London: Weidenfeld and Nicolson.

Austin, J. and Krisberg, B. (1981) 'Wider, stronger and different nets: the dialectics of criminal justice reform', *Journal of Research in Crime and Delinquency*, 18: 165–96.

Berg, R. and Feeley, M.M. (1990) *An Evaluation of the Community Service Order Program in the US District Court for the Northern District of California*. Berkeley: University of California Center for the Study of Law and Society.

Bottomley, A.K. (1986) 'Blue-prints for criminal justice: reflections on a policy plan for the Netherlands', *Howard Journal of Criminal Justice*, 25: 199–215.

Bottomley, A.K. and Pease, K. (1986) *Crime and Punishment: Interpreting the Data*. Milton Keynes: Open University Press.

Bottoms, A.E. (1987) 'Limiting prison use: experience in England and Wales', *Howard Journal of Criminal Justice*, 26: 177–202.

Box, S. (1987) *Recession, Crime and Punishment*. London: Macmillan.

Brody, S.R. (1976) *The Effectiveness of Sentencing: A Review of the Literature*. Home Office Research Study 35. London: HMSO.

Burrell, I. (1994) 'Prisoners earn £100,000 a year from heroin syndicates', *The Times*, 6 November.

Callison, H.G. (1983) *Introduction to Community-Based Corrections.* New York: McGraw-Hill.

Campbell, D. (1995a) 'Howard acts to revive ailing police faith in justice', *The Guardian,* 13 March.

Campbell, D. (1995b) 'Alarm bells as first "tagged" offender is arrested again', *The Guardian,* 17 August.

Campbell, D. (1995c) 'Alarm at rise in number sent to prison', *The Guardian,* 16 August.

Cavadino, P. (1993) *The Criminal Justice Act 1991: Its Impact on Sentencing: A Summary of Available Research Findings and Statistical Data* (Brief paper), December, London: NACRO.

Chan, J. and Ericson, R.V. (1981) *Decarceration and the Economy of Penal Reform.* Research Report, Toronto: Centre of Criminology, University of Toronto.

Children's Society Advisory Committee (1988) *Penal Custody for Juveniles: The Line of Least Resistance.* London: The Children's Society.

Clear, T.R. and O'Leary, V. (1983) *Controlling the Offender in the Community.* Lexington, MA: Lexington Books.

Cohen, S. (1979) 'The punitive city: notes on the dispersal of social control', *Contemporary Crises,* 3: 339–69.

Cohen, S. (1985) *Visions of Social Control: Crime, Punishment and Classification.* Cambridge: Polity Press.

Crow, I. (1987) 'Black people and criminal justice in the UK', *Howard Journal of Criminal Justice,* 26: 303–14.

Day, P. (1981) *Social Work and Social Control.* London: Tavistock.

del Carmen, R.V. and Trook-White, E. (1986) *Liability Issues in Community Service Sanctions.* US Department of Justice: National Institute of Corrections.

Dews, V. and Watts, J. (1995) *Review of Probation Officer Recruitment and Qualifying Training* (The Dews Report). London: Home Office.

Doig, J.W. (ed.) (1983) *Community Corrections: Ideas and Realities.* Lexington, MA: Lexington Books.

Dominelli, L. (1984) 'Differential justice: domestic labour, community service and female offenders', *Probation Journal,* 31: 100–3.

Downes, D. (1986) Review of '*Visions of Social Control: Crime, Punishment and Classification*', *Howard Journal of Criminal Justice,* 25: 309–11.

Downes, D. (1988) *Contrasts in Tolerance: Post-war Penal Policy in the Netherlands and England and Wales.* Oxford: Clarendon Press.

Empey, L.T. and Erickson, M.L. (1972) *The Provo Experiment: Evaluating Community Control of Delinquency.* Lexington, MA: Lexington Books.

Fielding, N. (1984) *Probation Practice: Client Support under Social Control.* Aldershot: Gower.

Fielding, N. (1986) 'Social control and the community', *Howard Journal of Criminal Justice,* 25: 172–89.

Fitzmaurice, C. and Pease, K. (1982) 'Prison sentences and population: a comparison of some European countries', *Justice of the Peace,* 18: 575–9.

Fletcher, H. (1994) 'Fines, default, and debtors' gaol', *NAPO News,* 61: 10–11.

Fletcher, H. (1995) 'Letters to the editor', *The Guardian,* 14 February.

Freedland, J. (1995) 'Pain not gain in the camps of correction – Michael Howard is ill-advised to nick a US idea for the latest in short sharp shock', *The Guardian,* 7 February.

Garland, D. (1985) *Punishment and Welfare: A History of Penal Strategies.* Aldershot: Gower.

Gibbons, D. (1970) 'Differential treatment of delinquents and interpersonal majority levels theory: a critique', *Social Service Review*, 44: 23–33.

Graham, J. (1990) 'Decarceration in the Federal Republic of Germany: how practitioners are succeeding where policy-makers have failed', *British Journal of Criminology*, 30: 150–70.

Grygier, T., Nease, B. and Anderson, C.S. (1970) 'An exploratory study of halfway houses', *Crime and Delinquency*, 16: 280–91.

Guardian, The (1995) Comment: 'Mr Howard papers over cracks', *The Guardian*, 16 March.

Harding, J. (1995) 'Letters to the editor', *The Guardian*, 14 February.

Harris, K.M. (1985) 'Reducing prison crowding and nonprison penalties', *Annals of the American Academy of Political and Social Science*, 478: 150–60.

Hoggarth, E.A. (1991) *Selection for Community Service Orders.* Aldershot: Avebury.

Home Office (1977) *Review of Criminal Justice Policy 1976.* London: HMSO.

Home Office (1986) *Sentence of the Court: A Handbook for Courts on the Treatment of Offenders* (2nd edn). London: HMSO.

Home Office (1995a) *Strengthening Punishment in the Community: A Consultation Document.* Cmnd 2780. London: HMSO.

Home Office (1995b) *Review of Probation Officer Recruitment and Qualifying Training: Discussion Paper by the Home Office.* London: Home Office.

Home Office (1995c) *Review of Probation Officer Recruitment and Qualifying Training: Decision Paper by the Home Office.* London: Home Office.

Home Office, Department of Health and Welsh Office (1992) *National Standards for the Supervision of Offenders in the Community.* London: Home Office Probation Service Division.

Home Office, Department of Health and Welsh Office (1995) *National Standards for the Supervision of Offenders in the Community.* London: Home Office Probation Division.

Hopkins, A., Schick, A. and White, S. (1977) 'A prison for the Australian capital territory?', *Australian & New Zealand Journal of Criminology*, 10: 205–15.

Hudson, B.A. (1984) 'The rising use of imprisonment: the impact of "decarceration" politics', *Critical Social Policy*, (Winter): 46–58.

Hudson, B.A. (1989) 'Discrimination and disparity: the influence of race on sentencing', *New Community*, 16: 23–34.

Hudson, B.A. (1993) *Penal Policy and Social Justice.* London: Macmillan.

Hylton, J. (1981a) *Reintegrating the Offender: Assessing the Impact of Community Corrections.* Washington, DC: University Press of America.

Hylton, J. (1981b) 'The growth of punishment: imprisonment and community corrections in Canada', *Crime and Social Justice*, Summer: 18–28.

Hylton, J. (1982) 'Rhetoric and reality: a critical appraisal of community correctional programs', *Crime and Delinquency*, 28: 341–73.

Inner London Probation Service (1989) *The Sherborne House Day Centre.* London: Research and Intelligence Unit.

Junger-Tas, J. (1986) 'Community service in the Netherlands', *Community Service Newsletter*, Part I, 13: 4–10; Part II, 14: 2–5.

Lawson, C. (1978) *The Probation Officer as Prosecutor: A Study of Proceedings for Breach of Requirements in Probation.* Cambridge: Cambridge Institute of Criminology.

Lerman, P. (1975) *Community Treatment and Social Control: A Critical Analysis of Juvenile Correctional Policy*. Chicago: University of Chicago Press.

Lerman, P. (1982) *Deinstitutionalization and the Welfare State*. New Jersey: Rutgers University Press.

Lipton, D., Martinson, R. and Wilks, J. (1975) *Effectiveness of Correctional Treatment: A Survey of Treatment Evaluation Studies*. Springfield, IL: Praeger.

Lloyd, C., Mair, G. and Hough, M. (1994) *Explaining Reconviction Rates: A Critical Analysis*. Home Office Research Study 136. London: HMSO.

Longley, R. (1985) 'Halving the custody rate', *Community Care*, 5: 17–19.

Lowman, J., Menzies, R.J. and Palys, T.S. (eds) (1987) *Transcarceration: Essays in the Sociology of Social Control*. Aldershot: Gower.

McConville, S. (1988) 'When punishment breaks out of gaol', *The Guardian*, 24 August.

McCullagh, C. (1988) 'A crisis in the penal system? The case of the Republic of Ireland', in M. Tomlinson, T. Varley and C. McCullagh (eds), *Whose Law and Order? Aspects of Crime and Social Control in Irish Society*. Belfast: Queen's University Bookshop. pp. 155–66.

McDonald, D.C. (1986) *Punishment without Walls: Community Service Sentences in New York City*. New Jersey: Rutgers University Press.

McIvor, G. (1992) *Sentence to Serve*. Aldershot: Avebury.

McIvor, G. (1993) 'Community service by offenders: how much does the community benefit?', *Social Work Practice*, 3: 385–403.

McMahon, M.W. (1990) '"Net-widening": vagaries in the use of a concept', *British Journal of Criminology*, 30: 121–49.

McMahon, M.W. (1992) *The Persistent Prison? Rethinking Decarceration and Penal Reform*. London: University of Toronto Press.

Mair, G. (1986) 'Ethnic minorities, probation and the magistrates' courts: a pilot study', *British Journal of Criminology*, 26: 144–55.

Mair, G., Lloyd, C., Nee, C. and Sibbitt, R. (1994) *Intensive Probation in England and Wales: An Evaluation*. Home Office Research Study 133. London: HMSO.

Martinson, R. (1972) 'The paradox of reform', *New Republic*, 166 (14): 23–5; 166 (15): 13–15; 166 (16): 17–19; 166 (17): 21–3.

Martinson, R. (1974) 'What works? Questions and answers about prison reform', *The Public Interest*, Spring, No. 35: 22–54.

Martinson, R. (1979) 'New findings, new views: a note of caution regarding sentencing reform', *Helbstra Law Review*, 7 (2): 243 ff.

Mathiesen, T. (1974) *The Politics of Abolition*. London: Martin Robertson.

Matthews, R. (1979) 'Decarceration and the fiscal crisis', in B. Fine, R. Kinsey, J. Lea, S. Picciotto and J. Young (eds), *Capitalism and the Rule of Law*. London: Hutchinson.

Matthews, R. (1987) 'Decarceration and social control: fantasies and realities', *International Journal of the Sociology of Law*, 15: 39–60.

Menzies, K. and Vass, A.A. (1989) 'The impact of historical, legal and administrative differences on a sanction: community service orders in England and Ontario', *Howard Journal of Criminal Justice*, 28: 204–17.

Mills, H. (1995) 'Half of prisons take drugs', *The Independent*, 22 March.

Moos, R.H. (1975) *Evaluating Correctional and Community Settings*. New York: John Wiley.

Mullen, J. (1985) 'Prison crowding and the evolution of public policy', *Annals of the American Academy of Political and Social Science*, 478: 31–46.

Musheno, M. (1982) 'Criminal diversion and social control', *Social Science Quarterly*, 63: 280–92.

NACRO (1988) *Some Facts and Findings about Black People in the Criminal Justice System* (June). London: National Association for the Care and Resettlement of Offenders.

Nimmer, R.T. (1974) *Diversion: The Search for Alternative Forms of Prosecution.* Chicago: American Bar Association.

Palmer, T.B. (1971) 'California's community treatment program for delinquent adolescents', *Journal of Research and Delinquency*, 8: 74–92.

Palmer, T.B. (1973) 'Matching worker and client in corrections', *Social Work*, 18: 95–103.

Parker, H., Jarvis, G. and Sumner, M. (1987) 'Under new orders: the rehabilitations of social work with young offenders', *British Journal of Social Work*, 17: 21–43.

Pease, K.G. and Young, W. (1993) *Cross-cultural Prison Rates: A Comparative Study of Custodial Sanctions.* Unpublished report. Swindon: ESRC.

Pease, K., Durking, P., Earnshaw, I., Payne, D. and Thorpe, J. (1975), *Community Service Orders.* Home Office Research Study 29. London: HMSO.

Pease, K., Billingham, S. and Earnshaw, I. (1977) *Community Service Assessed in 1976.* Home Office Research Study 39. London: HMSO.

Phillpotts, G.J.O. and Lancucki, L.B. (1979) *Previous Convictions, Sentence and Reconviction.* Home Office Research Study 53. London: HMSO.

Pitts, J. (1988) *The Politics of Juvenile Çrime.* London: Sage.

Pratt, J. (1986) 'Diversion from the Juvenile Court', *British Journal of Criminology*, 26: 212–33.

Quay, H. and Love, C. (1977) 'The effect of juvenile diversion programs or rearrests', *Criminal Justice and Behavior*, 4: 377–96.

Raynor, P. (1988) *Probation as an Alternative to Custody: A Case Study.* Aldershot: Gower.

Raynor, P., Smith, D. and Vanstone, M. (1994) *Effective Probation Practice.* BASW Social Work Series. Basingstoke: Macmillan.

Rhys, M., Faulder, P., Hogarth, L., Parker, I., Ruff, C., Turner, J. and Green, A. (1989) *Demonstration Unit: Phase Two 1985–1988.* London: Inner London Probation Service.

Rodger, J.J. (1988) 'Social work as social control re-examined: beyond the dispersal of discipline thesis', *Sociology*, 22: 563–81.

Roethlisberger, F.J. (1945) 'The foreman: master and victim of "double talk"', *Harvard Business Review*, XXIII (3): 285–94.

Rothman, D. (1974) 'Prisons and the failure model', *Nation*, 21: 641–50.

Rutherford, A. (1984) *Prisons and the Process of Justice: The Reductionist Challenge.* London: Heinemann.

Rutherford, A. (1986) *Growing Out of Crime: Society and Young People in Trouble.* Harmondsworth: Penguin.

Rutherford, A. and McDermott, R. (1976) *Juvenile Diversion.* Washington, DC: National Institute of Law Enforcement and Criminal Justice.

Sarason, S.B. (1974) *The Psychological Sense of Community: Prospects for a Community Psychology.* San Francisco: Jossey-Bass.

Schneider, A.L. (1986) 'Restitution and recidivism rates for young offenders: results from four experimental studies', *Criminology*, 24: 533–62.

Scull, A.T. (1984) *Decarceration, Community Treatment and the Deviant: A Radical View* (2nd edn). Cambridge: Basil Blackwell/Polity Press.

Sheppard, B. (1980) 'Research into aspects of probation', *Home Office Research Bulletin No. 19*. London: Home Office.

Smith, C., Farrant, M. and Marchant, H. (1972) *The Windcroft Youth Project*. London: Tavistock Publications.

Smith, D. (1987) 'The limits of positivism in social work research', *British Journal of Social Work*, 17: 401–11.

Smith, D., Sheppard, B., Mair, G. and Williams, K. (1984) *Reducing the Prison Population: An Exploratory Study in Hampshire*. Research and Planning Unit Paper 23. London: Home Office.

Solicitor General Canada (1982) *International Conference on Alternatives to Imprisonment Report, Toronto, June 8–11, 1980*. Ottawa: Communications Division Solicitor General Canada.

Somerville, M. (1995) 'Letters to the editor', *The Guardian*, 14 February.

Sprack, J. (1995) *Emins on Criminal Procedure* (6th edn). London: Blackstone Press.

Statham, R. (1995) 'Letters to the editor', *The Guardian*, 14 February.

Taggart, R. (1972) *The Prison Unemployment: Manpower Prisons for Offenders*. London: Johns Hopkins University Press.

Thorvaldson, S.A. (1978) 'The effects of community service on the attitudes of offenders'. Unpublished PhD thesis, University of Cambridge.

Times, The (1994) 'Prison numbers soar', 15 October.

Travis, A. (1994a) 'Study puts lie to Howard claim that "prison works"', *The Guardian*, 24 June.

Travis, A. (1994b) 'Prison offences surge 13pc', *The Guardian*, 4 October.

Travis, A. (1994c) 'Offenders to get a cold wet shock', *The Guardian*, 13 October.

Travis, A. (1995a) 'Prison riots increase fourfold in 10 years', *The Guardian*, 25 January.

Travis, A. (1995b) 'Jail suicides inquiry call', *The Guardian*, 8 March.

Travis, A. (1995c) 'Remand delays "costing £20m"', *The Guardian*, 13 March.

Travis, A. (1995d) 'Howard promises tough immigration bill', *The Guardian*, 14 March.

Travis, A. (1995e) 'Howard picks site for first boot camp', *The Guardian*, 14 March.

Travis, A. (1995f) 'Howard under fire as jail total hits record 51,243', *The Guardian*, 17 March.

Van Dusen (1981) 'Net widening and relabeling: some consequences of deinstitutionalization', *American Behavioural Scientist*, 24: 801–10.

Vanstone, M. (1993) 'A "missed opportunity" re-assessed: the influence of the day training centre experiment on the criminal justice system and probation policy and practice', *British Journal of Social Work*, 23: 213–29.

Varne, S. (1976) 'Saturday work: a real alternative?', *Australian & New Zealand Journal of Criminology*, 9: 95–108.

Vass, A.A. (1980) 'Law enforcement in community service: probation, defence or prosecution?', *Probation Journal*, 27: 114–17.

Vass, A.A. (1982) 'The probation service in a state of turmoil', *Justice of the Peace*, 146: 788–93.

Vass, A.A. (1984) *Sentenced to Labour: Close Encounters with a Prison Substitute*. St Ives: Venus Academica.

Vass, A.A. (1986) 'Community service: areas of concern and suggestions for change', *Howard Journal of Criminal Justice*, 25: 100-11.

Vass, A.A. (1988) 'The effectiveness of social work intervention', *Eklogy*, 79: 180–94.

Vass, A.A. (1990) *Alternatives to Prison: Punishment, Custody and the Community*. London: Sage.

Vass, A.A. (1996) 'Crime prevention and social work with offenders', in A.A. Vass (ed.), *Social Work Competences: Core Knowledge, Values and Skills*. London: Sage. pp. 132–89

Vass, A.A. and Menzies, K. (1989) 'The community service order as a public and private enterprise: a comparative account of practices in England and Ontario, Canada', *British Journal of Criminology*, 29: 255–72.

Vass, A.A. and Weston, A. (1990) 'Probation day centres as an alternative to custody: a "Trojan horse" examined', *British Journal of Criminology*, 30: 189–206.

Walker, J., Collier, P. and Tarling, R. (1990) 'Why are prison rates in England and Wales higher than in Australia?', *British Journal of Criminology*, 30: 24–35.

Walker, N. (1983) 'The effectiveness of probation', *Probation Journal*, 30: 99–103.

Walker, N. (1985) *Sentencing: Theory, Law and Practice*. London: Butterworth.

Ward, R. and Ward, S. (1993) *Community Sentences: Law and Practice*. London: Blackstone Press.

Warren, C. (1981) 'New forms of social control: the myth of deinstitutionalization', *American Behavioral Scientist*, 24: 724–40.

Wasik, M. (1993) *Emins on Sentencing* (2nd edn). London: Blackstone Press.

Young, W. (1979) *Community Service Orders: The Development and Use of a New Penal Measure*. London: Heinemann.

Zander, M. (1995) 'Not guilty as charged', *The Guardian*, 13 March.

9

The Transition from Prison to Community

Brian Williams

The previous three chapters tackled the role of probation committees, pre-sentence reports and community penalties. This chapter will review legal and other changes which have affected probation officers' work with people in prison over recent years, and consider the implications of some of the further amendments to the law and to probation practice currently being discussed.

The overall argument will be that the emphasis of probation work with prisoners has changed in recent years, although this has received little attention due to the rapid and confusing changes in the overall sentencing framework. The notion of throughcare (the idea that prisoners should receive a social work service from their first remand until well after their release) has received stronger official blessing than in the past, but supervision of ex-prisoners has been increasingly bureaucratised. Treating prisoners, many of whom have a suspicion of social workers and probation officers – and indeed of all authority figures – in this bureaucratic way is particularly counter-productive. Those most likely to benefit from purposeful probation work are among the potential clients most in danger of being neglected.

At a time of financial constraints, throughcare for its own sake is being questioned by politicians and service managers more than ever, but the group of clients who are subject to compulsory post-release supervision has been redefined and resources have been diverted towards such supervision. Meanwhile, the programme of contracting-out the running of some prisons and some of the services in state prisons has continued apace, with considerable implications for regimes and for prisons' accountability.

Probation officers find themselves confronted by new national standards and a 'national framework' policy on throughcare. They also have a rising number of prisoners on their caseloads, with the number of black inmates increasing disproportionately, and have to deal with a prison system which is under increasing pressure. At times, it can be a struggle simply keeping up with prisoners' whereabouts. Some of the satisfaction of the work is threatened by greater emphasis on getting clients through supervision periods without breaching national standards, combined with reduced discretion on whether to offer assistance to short-term prisoners. Some probation services and Scottish social work departments have responded to the growing caseloads by introducing specialisation, and staff are bound to wonder whether this is simply a strategy for constraining the growth in the resources devoted to work with prisoners, or whether it enables them to offer a more professional service.

While the politicians encourage sentencers to overcrowd prisons, prison and probation officers begin to question whether the 'national framework' really means anything: can it ever be delivered in practice when prisons are full to overflowing? Inevitably, a degree of cynicism starts to creep in. On the other hand, an academic debate about 'what works' with offenders has led to some optimism about the prospect of working with offenders towards changing their behaviour, including that of some of those in custody.

These changes form the context within which work with prisoners nowadays has to be understood. The remainder of the chapter will look at a number of these areas in greater detail:

(a) legal changes to throughcare and their implications for relationships with clients;
(b) the implications of privatisation (the pace of which is likely to accelerate in the coming years);
(c) anti-discriminatory probation work with prisoners; and
(d) effective engagement with prisoners.

Compulsory after-care

The Criminal Justice Act 1991 and the White Paper *Custody, Care and Justice* (Home Office, 1991) published the same year changed the emphasis of social workers and probation officers' work with prisoners. A prison sentence no longer finishes upon release, but is served partly in custody and partly in the community – an approach which had its intellectual origins in the Carlisle Report on parole, but which was given considerably wider application in the 1991 Act (Sanders and Senior, 1993). Supervision thus becomes, in effect, part of the punishment rather than offering help with resettlement for its own sake.

The goal of work with prisoners is officially defined as 'helping prisoners prepare for law-abiding lives in the community, and supervising them after release' (Home Office, 1994: 4): note that 'help' does not appear to figure in the post-release period. Many probation officers have taken these changes philosophically, accepting that their help was always received with ambivalence, and deciding that they can live with an official formulation of the task which uses the rhetoric of punishment without significantly altering the nature of their day-to-day work with clients. National standards, although burdensome, can be applied flexibly. Indeed the through-care standards, in their 1992 version (Home Office et al., 1992), explicitly encouraged this. This discretion remains in the generally much less flexible 1995 version (Home Office et al., 1995). Nevertheless, the change is significant, particularly in the context of more punitive sentencing.

In practice, however, those working with prisoners have continued to form professional relationships by using traditional social work skills and applying long-established values. Effective work with prisoners and ex-prisoners is difficult and demanding, and the phrase 'supervising them after release' does not do it justice. A purely supervisory response is rarely appropriate, and the context statement which follows the bald statement of the 'goal' of work with prisoners in the three-year plan for the probation service implicitly acknowledges this when it mentions the increase in the number of 'individuals reluctant to engage in supervision' (Home Office, 1994: 22).

Qualities and skills needed for effective work

So how does one supervise a reluctant ex-prisoner? It is not simply a matter of putting the client through the hoops erected by national standards – indeed, part of the trick of effective work is surely to play these requirements down in practice, having made them clear to the client at the outset of the supervision period. In order to work constructively with someone who has served a prison sentence, some kind of understanding has to be reached as to the goals of the contact. This is made more difficult by the 1991 Act's extension of compulsory supervision (to all adults serving 12 months and over, and to all young offenders for at least three months after release), in that these categories will include many perfectly self-sufficient people who see no need for a probation officer or social worker. All but the most challenging prisoners will, however, accept an honest account by the supervising officer of what is involved.

Those who have been in the job for 10 years or more will remember the lengthy post-release supervision periods required of Borstal inmates. The breach requirements then were much less severe than under national standards, but many staff developed strategies for getting clients through the supervision period. These

included trying to form helpful relationships before release, supporting families during the custodial part of the sentence, being open
about the reasons for insisting on maintaining contact after release
(for example, admitting that the primary aim of supervision is
surveillance, whether or not one is happy about this, and that one's
aim as supervisor is mainly to get people through it without the
harmful consequences of prosecution for breach), and being flexible
about the use of breach powers.

These strategies flow from the application of social work values;
respect for persons, openness, responsiveness to need, mediation.
The supervisor of a released prisoner should have shown respect for
the individual in the pre-release period by negotiating the content of
the supervision plan during a visit rather than simply trying to
impose a particular strategy (Coker and Martin, 1985; Kingston,
1979; Williams, 1991, 1995a), and by establishing at an early stage
what kind of contact was needed with family and friends (Monger et
al., 1981; Wilson-Croome, 1992). The requirements of supervision
should have been made explicit at this stage, and opportunities
taken to discuss the client's (and the supervisor's) feelings about
them and the associated sanctions. A probation officer is more than
an official enforcing national standards: part of the role is to
mediate between the rules and the client (Williams, 1992). Where a
constructive relationship has been formed, clients are more likely to
accept that the worker is interested in protecting them from the
consequences of breach, and in helping them and their families
where this has been negotiated as part of the work.

This suggests that the skills and values required for effective work
with prisoners are broadly similar to those involved in any kind of
social work. While this is true, this area of work also demands some
additional skills and effort.

The offenders are particularly likely to be angry and bitter
(although many are not). Visits and interviews will thus need more
preparation and thought than many other routine social work
activities, and it is particularly important in working with people
rendered powerless by confinement to ensure that any undertakings
given by the worker are honoured – and promptly. Prisoners'
perception of the passage of time alters, and most people working
with them will have experienced irritation at being reminded about a
task they have already begun or completed. When agreeing to carry
out a task or make an enquiry on an offender's behalf, workers
should indicate how long it is likely to take – and get in touch with
them, giving reasons, if it takes longer.

Prisoners often feel that matters are being taken out of their
hands, and that action is not being taken promptly enough to meet

their needs. Staff have to accept that these feelings arise from the experience of imprisonment, which infantilises and demeans people, and that clients' complaints or anxious enquiries arise from an attempt to maintain their dignity and their involvement in solving their own problems. It is pointless to give vent to irritation when needlessly reminded of what has to be done. The work arising from a prison visit has to be given priority, because otherwise the prisoner frets and generates more work by asking what progress has been made. By way of preparation for working with prisoners, probation officers can usefully do some reading and use creative imagination: how would I cope with being in prison? What kind of strategies are open to prisoners? How would it feel having to depend on officials for news of family and friends? How would I pass the time? The literature – both autobiographical and fictional – is particularly useful in this respect (Carlen, 1985; Hercules, 1989; Padel and Stevenson, 1988; see also Williams, 1991: Chapter 2).

In working with prisoners, it is more than usually important to keep them informed. Their imprisonment systematically deprives them of information and often provides an environment for mis-information to be generated. One of the ways in which probation officers can distinguish themselves from other functionaries is by acting upon this understanding, and making efforts to keep prisoners up-to-date with the progress of their requests.

Work with prisoners also requires up-to-date knowledge. Staff have to understand the prison system, early release arrangements and sentence planning. They need local knowledge too: what goes on in particular prisons, how visits are organised and financed, welfare and other facilities, community resources. This may seem obvious, but many staff lose credibility in prisoners' eyes by not having this kind of information.

Similarly, it is particularly important in working with prisoners to be prepared at times to act as the grit in the penal machinery: if an offender is being treated unjustly, a probation officer must be willing and able to act as advocate where appropriate. Field probation officers are in a strong position to help offenders pursue complaints, and they need to be familiar with the relevant procedures (Loucks and Plotnikoff, 1993; Prison Service, 1991) and organisations.

The literature on social work with prisoners constantly refers to the need for improved liaison between the different professions and departments responsible for such work. Although many of the tasks involved will be tedious or distasteful, the liaison role falls par-ticularly upon field probation officers. If they are to act as the humane face of a largely inhumane and uncaring prison system, they have to take these jobs on, and they need to be persistent in dealing with the prison and other bureaucracies (such as the employment and benefits agencies outside, the parole and medical services in prisons, and so on). The danger is that, as probation work itself is increasingly bureaucratised, it will become more difficult for probation officers to claim with any plausibility that they stand for human, and humane, values. It is crucial that probation officers defend their values in this field of work, and practise them (Williams, 1995a).

One reaction to the increased pressure of work and the bureaucratic constraints imposed in recent years has been for probation officers to find mechanistic ways of seeming to give a personal service. Thus, in a team where most throughcare cases were not actually allocated, there was an arrangement for its duty officer to send birthday cards to the prisoners (Rogers, 1992). Elsewhere, probation officers promised to visit prisoners but never got around to it, or made 'half-hearted offers of help on release' (Williams, 1992: 268). This is clearly contrary to probation values of respecting individuals' differences and needs, and of personal service in general.

Anti-discriminatory throughcare work

The issue of anti-discriminatory practice runs throughout this volume and its relevance at various levels (issues, contexts and outcomes) has been clearly stated. Although the issue is far more complex than it is often assumed and, as has been pointed out in other parts of this volume, the evidence is far from clear, this is a matter which raises concerns. The criminalisation of black people by the police and politicians has intensified since 1981 (Gordon, 1988; Hudson, 1993; Jefferson, 1993; Smith, 1994), leading to increased suspicion by black people of white criminal justice professionals (Ballard, 1989; NACRO, 1991; Pinder, 1982, 1984).

Unfortunately, many white probation officers have responded in a confused and unhelpful way, and there is some evidence that their work with black defendants has become stilted and unimaginative because of their fear of making mistakes or giving offence. In the crucial area of preparing court reports, they have failed to make credible arguments on behalf of black clients (Denney, 1992; Green, 1987; Voakes and Fowler, 1989; Whitehouse, 1983; see also Chapter 7 in this volume). This has compounded the distrust of white professionals felt by many black people, and means that white professional workers have some extra work to do in gaining the trust of black prisoners.

Anti-racist practice is simply good practice. But the justified anger of black clients towards what appears to be a systematically discriminatory system cannot be ignored, and is not surmounted easily in practice. Colour-blind service may inevitably be racist in its effects, and extra time and effort will be needed by white workers in forming appropriate professional relationships with black clients (Celnick, 1993; Denney, 1992; Green, 1987; Williams, 1991) and with black community groups (Denney, 1992; Kett et al., 1992; Mavunga, 1993; NACRO, 1991).

Similarly, Irish people and travellers have been criminalised – and for a much longer period (Cheney, 1993b; Jefferson, 1993; Murphy, 1994), and under the Criminal Justice and Public Order Act 1994 they face even harsher treatment. Workers need to be aware of and sensitive to this history and its everyday implications for practice, particularly where bail and pre-sentence reports proposals, family visits and parole are concerned.

Angry offenders are hard to deal with, and offenders in prison are easily neglected. Supervision of main grade probation officers' work needs to be sensitive to these dynamics – although, in practice, professional supervision has become increasingly mechanistic and over-preoccupied with statistical monitoring and national standards (McWilliams, 1992). Probation officers also need to monitor their own practice: if, as argued above, extra attention should be given to the cases of black prisoners and members of other oppressed groups, this will be reflected in the level of contact maintained before their release. Prison-based probation officers can take responsibility for monitoring colleagues' parole reports, keeping incident books recording racist behaviour towards clients in the prison and services' responses to these, and examining the implications of black offenders' needs for sentence planning and post-release work (Rogers, 1992). Some areas have altered their throughcare policies in response to research findings about discriminatory provision (for example, Essex Probation Service, 1994).

Resource-conscious service managers will have to be challenged if they place difficulties in the way of professional and anti-racist throughcare practice, and section 95 of the Criminal Justice Act 1991 gives at least rhetorical support to such a strategy. There is anecdotal evidence that black ex-prisoners are less likely than whites to take up voluntary after-care (Celnick, 1993), and the reasons for this need to be brought out into the open (a process being undertaken at present by the Nottingham Black Initiative: NACRO 1991).

Angry offenders in prison will generally not be treated with understanding: uniformed staff are quick to resort to stereotypical thinking about black people being arrogant and having 'chips on their shoulders'. There is some evidence that this is reflected in discriminatory application of disciplinary rules, although more research is needed (Genders and Player, 1989). This is only one reason for prison-based staff to be proactive and become fully involved in implementing the prison service's race relations policies at local level: although it has taken some years to develop, the system of Race Relations Management Teams has considerable potential for positive change. It represents great progress, as does the supporting *Race Relations Manual*, despite its continuing preoccupation with the supposed dangers of 'domination or taking over of particular facilities' by particular ethnic groups (Prison Service, 1991: 52).

Field probation officers can also organise, in conjunction with community groups, to improve the support provided to black prisoners. Recent initiatives in Sheffield, Huddersfield, Luton and Nottingham, setting up support groups for black prisoners from particular localities and researching their situation, are encouraging signs that this is being taken seriously (NACRO, 1991; South Yorkshire Probation Service, undated).

Field probation teams in inner-city areas may feel that they are offering an appropriate throughcare service, but black community groups and individual offenders have sometimes challenged this perception. Probation officers have not always understood or met black offenders' needs, partly due to restrictive allocation procedures and high caseloads, although throughcare policies recently adopted by some probation areas offer 'potential for pro-active, planned involvement rather than re-active, crisis work' (Rogers, 1992: 29).

Similarly, there is a role for probation staff in publicising and monitoring the less well-known arrangements for safeguarding the interests of foreign prisoners and providing interpreters for those who do not speak English. In some areas, probation staff have taken important steps to improve the service provided to prisoners from abroad in recent years (Abernethy and Hammond, 1992; Inner London Probation Service, 1993; Towl, 1993), and prison officers have also addressed similar issues (Cheney, 1993a).

If probation services seriously intend to make anti-racist work with prisoners a priority, this will involve decisions about resourcing. In a time of financial restrictions, something else may have to go. At team level, this is likely to involve careful consideration of local priorities. In prisons, it may mean spending less effort on servicing other aspects of the regime (Kett et al., 1992), which in the long term may have an important symbolic function: spending time on improving race relations and giving up traditional routines where probation officers' likely impact is limited will certainly arouse comment.

Women prisoners also require a different kind of attention from the probation service. Much of what has been said above, of course, concerns them – not least because over a quarter of women prisoners are black, a significant proportion from overseas.

Women are often imprisoned for different reasons to those applying to men, and mainly for shorter periods. This is likely to have important implications for throughcare.

Women's offences are mostly non-violent and property-related, and many women prisoners are still serving very short sentences for fine default (Carlen, 1983, 1990; Carlen and Worrall, 1987). Because there are so few of them, women prisoners are more likely than men to be held in institutions far from their home areas. As Heidensohn (1987: 12) puts it, 'Criminal justice agencies seem always to have found women a problem because there were so few of them. (There is a certain irony in this.)'

The implications of the Woolf Report (Woolf, 1991) for women are ambiguous. Women's groups and penal reform groups are clear that Woolf's recommendations must not be used as a justification for holding more women within men's prisons as at Durham. Rather, there should be greater and more consistent use of home leave and extended family visits.

Women are also often held in more secure prisons than merited by their offending, because there are only two or three women deemed to need very high security conditions at any one time, but a whole establishment is maintained to provide such conditions. The sort of throughcare assistance most women are likely to need is much more short-term and focused than traditionally offered to male prisoners. Offenders need swift allocation to a probation officer, who should quickly be in touch with them and, where appropriate, with social workers and housing departments.

Bail assistance is clearly a priority, given the characteristics of the women's prison population already mentioned. The Probation Inspectorate has drawn attention to the probation service's failure to prioritise this area of work sufficiently by stating that 'there is potential for greater use of bail which in turn can lead to [greater willingness by courts to consider] community-based disposals' (quoted in NACRO, 1992: 2).

Regimes in women's prisons are even more infantilising than in men's. Pollock-Byrne and Jocelyn (1990: 102) suggest that 'training tends to be solely in the "domestic arts", reinforcing the idea that the women imprisoned have violated social rather than legal norms'. This results from a history of paternalism which has been very slow to change over time (Heidensohn, 1994; Williams, 1995b; Zedner, 1991).

Perhaps not surprisingly, this is a real threat to women prisoners' self-esteem. Their responses to imprisonment are different from men's, and this needs to be taken into account in working with them. Like men serving longer sentences, some women withdraw into themselves, and some mutilate themselves (Eaton, 1993). Others react defiantly to being treated like children, and this can have severe consequences. The disciplinary system magnifies trivial challenges disproportionately, and the paternalistic ethos leads to over-reliance on medical solutions and psychiatric explanations of difficult behaviour (Eaton, 1993; Stevenson, 1989).

The risk of suicide has to be recognised, and probation officers have a role to play in ensuring that it is taken seriously. Indeed, some attempted suicides seem to have related to depression about outside events with which field probation officers might have been able to assist. Easier access to outside agencies including probation is one of the necessary improvements identified by research on self-harm by prisoners (Liebling, 1994).

Throughcare has to be not only more focused, but also more challenging where women offenders are involved: challenging offenders if necessary but also the regimes and their assumptions. Again, there is a range of community groups ready and willing to assist, although this may sometimes need to be arranged covertly and most of the groups – particularly the independent ones – are in London. Surprisingly little has been written about probation work with women prisoners, probably because there has not been much of it, and it will be important to defend the resources necessary for voluntary throughcare of women prisoners where they want such assistance. What literature there is suggests that this work is both necessary and in demand (Carlen, 1990; Eaton, 1993; Peckham, 1985) as long as it is provided in sensitive and unpatronising ways.

Where women prisoners have young children, they are likely to need help in maintaining contact and, indeed, in retaining parental rights. There is mounting evidence of the distress suffered by prisoners' children, and of women prisoners' concern to avoid losing their children (Shaw, 1992). Probation officers have tended to focus on helping women released from prison with practical tasks at the expense of ensuring that they are aware of their rights where children in local authority accommodation are concerned (Woodrow, 1992). One key area for field probation officers' work with women prisoners is in ensuring, and where necessary facilitating, contact between women and their children who are in local authority care (NAPO, 1990).

Group work with sentenced prisoners is also important, and recent innovations have included groups for first-time women prisoners, women far from home (mainly foreign prisoners) and abused women (Towl, 1993).

Under the Criminal Justice Act 1991, however, voluntary work with short-sentence prisoners was further downgraded, and many areas have decided to restrict access by prisoners to the services of probation officers. Some areas have gone so far as to ban the allocation of fine defaulters to probation officers (Inner London Probation Service, 1993), and many have procedures for referring anyone on automatic unconditional release (AUR) who seems interested in after-care direct to voluntary agencies such as the Society of Voluntary Associates. Most areas' throughcare policies are written in gender-neutral language without any specific references to women. This is likely to be criticised by the Probation Inspectorate if its future reports reflect the spirit of section 95 (Player, 1994), but it is hardly a surprise that the probation service makes cuts when opportunities arise, in the context of diminishing real budgets.

Unfortunately, cuts in this area are likely to prove short-sighted. Short-sentence prisoners who receive no help in resettlement are highly likely to reoffend. The cuts also take no account of the misery endured by children whose parents are imprisoned – and it is predominantly women prisoners who tend to lose their children while they are inside – or of the needs of such children and their mothers (White, 1989; Woodrow, 1992).

Sexual orientation is rarely raised as an issue where throughcare is concerned, but it is clear that gay prisoners experience particular discrimination (NAPO, 1990; Preece, 1993), and the assisted prison visits scheme does not even apply to their families. The service offered by probation officers is unlikely to be ideal: stereotyping begins with the assumption that the norm is to be white, male and heterosexual.

Probation officers working with gay and lesbian prisoners need to be open to discussion of clients' sexual orientation and of the ways in which the criminal justice system pathologises it. This is likely to necessitate challenges to the assumptions and behaviour of other staff – and a willingness to examine their own. Once again, staff should be informed about outside groups which are willing to assist gay and lesbian prisoners, and should facilitate their access to them (see Preece, 1993).

In view of the legal and institutional discrimination gay and lesbian prisoners are likely to face, records and reports should not contain probation officers' assessments of offenders' sexual orientation, unless this has been fully discussed.

Prisoners who are HIV positive also continue to suffer discrimination, although some of the worst excesses have been stopped, including segregation and the use of 'viral infectivity restrictions' (which both lasted into the early 1990s until condemned in the Woolf Report). Such prisoners need additional support (Richards, 1986; Thomas and Costigan, 1992) and this is increasingly being provided by community groups. These are no longer all London-based, and they have negotiated much greater access to prisoners than was previously allowed. The prison health service seems belatedly to have realised that this can only be beneficial (Ralli, 1994).

Contracting-out

Privatisation is a controversial and emotive topic, and the intro-duction of private security companies into the penal system has been particularly so. There was a wide consensus against the contracting-out of prisons on political and moral grounds: it was argued that making a profit from punishment is unacceptable, and that only the state should be empowered to administer punishment. The govern-ment initially accepted the force of this argument by limiting the exercise to remand prisons, on the grounds that the inmates were not sentenced and not there for punishment (as well as a more pragmatic reason: the remand system was under particular pressure). The government's view was that it should retain the monopoly of post-sentence imprisonment.

It has been argued that the experiment with contracting out first one, and later many more, remand prisons was rigged and bound to succeed. Be this as it may, the relative success of the pilot project at the Wolds made it much easier for the programme to succeed. To be sure, Group 4 became something of a laughing-stock and was ridiculed during the early days of the Wolds, and its record was attacked from all sides. There were many serious mistakes, and the prison recruited inexperienced staff who were placed at risk, as were inmates, one of whom died in transit. The inquest jury decided that his death was due to a lack of care by the company's staff (Nathan, 1994).

The real test of the success of a privately run prison, however, is its regime. In this respect, Group 4 had a good deal to be proud of. Early accounts – including the official inspection report – emphasised some serious failings (Chief Inspector of Prisons, 1993; Prison Reform Trust, 1993), but it rapidly became clear that prisoners found the regime humane and far from degrading. Indeed, those with experience of the state system were initially baffled by the polite and respectful staff (Navin, 1994), and visiting professionals were impressed by the 'can-do' attitudes of management and custodial workers (Bean, 1992). The prison clearly had better industrial relations than most, and traditional demarcations between custodial and professional staff were eroded, although this has been disputed (Prison Reform Trust, 1993).

Aspects of the state system were, however, reproduced in some avoidable ways. Prisoners were given far more time out of their cells, but not enough activities were provided and the Chief Inspector of Prisons described the regime as one of 'corrupting lethargy' (Campling, 1994). Alcohol and drug misuse were commonplace, and staff appeared to ignore or fail to notice inmates smoking cannabis. There have also been disturbances at the Wolds, although the full story of these has yet to be told, raising the possibility that the original criticisms levelled against the private sector as lacking accountability (see, for instance, Vass and Menzies, 1989) may hold true.

It has been suggested that the large-scale extension of contracting-out to sentenced prisoners will expose the inability of private companies to cope with the most challenging inmates. This may prove to be the case. The Home Secretary, Michael Howard, has taken powers to transfer prison officers to work in privatised prisons if the need arises (Prison Reform Trust, 1994). The issue of accountability for punishing offenders, which the government at first avoided by the appointment of a Home Office 'controller' in private remand prisons to chair adjudications and monitor the firms' compliance with their contracts, will also be posed more acutely where large numbers of sentenced prisoners are concerned.

Ironically, one of the arguments advanced by proponents of private prisons was that accountability would be increased by the existence of a detailed contract stipulating what was expected. If the contractor failed to comply, penalties could be enforced by the government, including ultimately a refusal to renew the contract (Hutto, 1989; Shaw, 1990). This reasoning did not fully account for the politics of the situation: a government ideologically committed to privatisation was unlikely to engage in public denunciation of its pilot project in the prison field. Much of the argument, at the Wolds and previously, was shrouded in secrecy, justified by the government on the grounds of commercial confidentiality (Shaw, 1990). In the event, Group 4 seems to have got away with failing to fulfil its contract in certain respects, at least for a time. As the Chief Inspector drily noted, the contract failed to require the contractor to help inmates lead useful lives, and certain initial specifications were not enforced. For example, the prison was slow to set up a bail information scheme or a proper library (Prison Reform Trust, 1993), and financial monitoring was lax: 'a service was being paid for [which] was being monitored only superficially' (Chief Inspector of Prisons, 1993: 1.49).

The specification document for the Wolds required Group 4 to set up anti-discriminatory training for custody staff, and this has been done to the minimum level required (eight hours' training). No black staff have been appointed to posts at the prison, although nearly 10 per cent of inmates are black (Prison Reform Trust, 1993).

An argument never advanced by the government, but one well known to influence its thinking, was that 'privatisation is, and has been, a stick with which to beat the Prison Officers' Association' (Shaw, 1990). The POA has bitterly opposed contracting-out, along with most other public sector unions with members working in prisons, but its influence has undoubtedly been reduced – and many in the penal system have quietly welcomed this – by the end of its monopoly. Apart from profit, this opportunity to end trade union monopolies is clearly a major attraction of contracting-out from the government's point of view (Ascher, 1987).

In the long term, it is the politically motivated extension of the practice of privatisation which will have a major impact upon the criminal justice system, rather than arguments about the principle. As those on both sides have pointed out, there is nothing new or inherently dishonourable about private sector involvement in the penal system (Hutto, 1989; Ryan and Ward, 1989; see also Lilly, 1992). The polarised argument about whether public or private provision is morally superior has obscured some issues quite unhelpfully (Ascher, 1987; Culpitt, 1992). If the staffing and management of remand prisons is taken as a case study, it would be hard to sustain the argument that state provision cannot be improved upon by giving a private provider a clean slate. On the other hand, if the contracting-out of hospital cleaning or prison education or community penalties were taken as case studies (see Ascher, 1987; Vass and Menzies, 1989; Williams, 1993), it would be easy to argue that ideologically driven, unnecessary change can cause considerable damage.

The implications for other aspects of the criminal justice system are as yet unclear, but the farcical example of the private sector's venture into the education of prisoners suggests that contracting-out will be introduced hastily and indiscriminately and the impact upon services could be profound. This is because, 'For market economists, privatisation is a means to an end: greater competition leading to greater efficiency. For the present government privatisation has tended to become an end in itself, the product of the belief that ownership is the key variable in economic performance' (Wilding, 1990: 18).

There is no aspect of the public sector which is immune from privatisation in its various forms, and there is a powerful multinational lobby which is becoming increasingly influential upon criminal justice policy (Lilly, 1992). It is therefore important that probation officers and other public servants learn the lessons of the early experiments rather than engaging in sterile disputation about the abstract merits and demerits of contracting-out. The government has made it clear, not least by going ahead with an extended privatisation programme before the results of the so-called 'experiment' at the Wolds were available, that it is committed to this policy.

Sentence planning and partnership

All prisoners serving sentences of over 12 months are involved in the sentence planning and 'compacts' systems recommended in the Woolf Report. The early experience of the system has not been encouraging. Sampson (1994: 19) writes:

> . . . it is depressing to see the paucity of information being provided to mandatory lifers by the Home Office even under the new, more 'open' lifer procedures forced upon it by the Law Lords. The Woolf system, for all its advantages, is hugely bureaucratic.

This is clearly not what is needed. There is a great deal of work to be done by the probation service in order to ensure that the potential for improvement of throughcare which was contained in the Woolf Report is not lost (Roy, 1993; see also Chapter 10 in this volume). The jettisoning of the Woolf agenda by politicians who claim that 'prison works' need not prevent the amelioration of some of the most damaging consequences of imprisonment, and sentence planning offers an opportunity for genuine partnership between probation and prison staff in improving regimes.

Conclusion

It is impossible to isolate the impact of probation work with prisoners from the other, mostly harmful, influences on their lives and behaviour. Recent writings on probation officers' work with prisoners has tended to stress damage-limitation rather than rehabilitation (Raban, 1987; Williams, 1991). This may seem unambitious, but it is perhaps more realistic than the earlier tendency to make grand but hollow claims. One thing seems clear: the 'national framework' for throughcare is unlikely to be a high priority of prisons struggling to maintain order because of pressure of numbers. Throughcare itself can only 'work' when the prison system is relatively stable, and current policies present considerable difficulties.

Acknowledgement

The author is grateful to Chris Tchaikovsky for her comments on an earlier version of this chapter.

References

Abernethy, R. and Hammond, N. (1992) *Drug Couriers: A Role for the Probation Service*. London: Middlesex Area Probation Service.

Ascher, K. (1987) *The Politics of Privatisation*. London: Macmillan.

Ballard, R. (1989) 'Social work with black people: what's the difference?', in C. Rojek, E. Peacock and S. Collins (eds), *The Haunt of Misery: Critical Essays in Social Work and Helping*. London: Routledge. pp. 123–47.

Bean, J.P. (1992) 'A private sort of place', *New Law Journal*, 20 November: 1610.

Campling, J. (1994) 'Social policy digest', *Journal of Social Policy*, 23 (2): 255.

Carlen, P. (1983) *Women's Imprisonment: A Study in Social Control*. London: Routledge and Kegan Paul.

Carlen, P. (1985) *Criminal Women: Autobiographical Accounts*. Cambridge: Polity.

Carlen, P. (1990) *Alternatives to Women's Imprisonment*. Milton Keynes: Open University Press.

Carlen, P. and Worrall, A. (eds) (1987) *Gender, Crime and Justice*. Milton Keynes: Open University Press.

Celnick, A. (1993) 'Race and rehabilitation', in L.R. Gelsthorpe (ed.), *Minority Ethnic Groups in the Criminal Justice System*. Cropwood Conference Series 2. Cambridge: Institute of Criminology. pp. 114–31.

Cheney, D. (1993a) 'Progress on race equality', *Prison Report*, 23: 4.

Cheney, D. (1993b) *Into the Dark Tunnel*. London: Prison Reform Trust.

Chief Inspector of Prisons (1993) *Inspection Report: The Wolds*. London: Home Office.

Coker, J.B. and Martin, J.P. (1985) *Licensed to Live*. Oxford: Basil Blackwell.

Culpitt, I. (1992) *Welfare and Citizenship: Beyond the Crisis of the Welfare State?* London: Sage.

Denney, D. (1992) *Racism and Anti-racism in Probation*. London: Routledge.

Eaton, M. (1993) *Women after Prison*. Buckingham: Open University Press.

Essex Probation Service (1994) Letter to the author from John Budd, Assistant Chief Probation Officer, 25 February, quoting draft policy document.

Genders, E. and Player, E. (1989) *Race Relations in Prisons*. Oxford: Clarendon.

Gordon, P. (1988) 'Black people and the criminal law: rhetoric and reality', *International Journal of the Sociology of Law*, 16: 295–313.

Green, R. (1987) 'Racism and the offender: a probation response', in J. Harding (ed.), *Probation and the Community: A Practice and Policy Reader*. London: Tavistock. pp. 180–93.

Heidensohn, F. (1987) 'Women, crime and justice', in NAPO (ed.), *Access to Justice:*

Race, Class and Gender. London: National Association of Probation Officers. pp. 11–13.

Heidensohn, F. (1994) 'Gender and Crime', in M. Maguire, R. Morgan and R. Reiner (eds), *The Oxford Handbook of Criminology.* Oxford: Clarendon Press. pp. 997–1040.

Hercules, T. (1989) *Labelled a Black Villain.* London: Fourth Estate.

Home Office (1991) *Custody, Care and Justice.* London: HMSO.

Home Office (1994) *The Probation Service: Three Year Plan for the Probation Service, 1994–1997.* London: Home Office.

Home Office, Department of Health and Welsh Office (1992) *National Standards for the Supervision of Offenders in the Community.* London: Home Office Probation Division.

Home Office, Department of Health and Welsh Office (1995) *National Standards for the Supervision of Offenders in the Community.* London: Home Office Probation Division.

Hudson, B.A. (1993) *Penal Policy and Social Justice.* London: Macmillan.

Hutto, T.D. (1989) 'Public agencies and private companies – partners for progress', in M. Farrell (ed.), *Punishment for Profit?* London: Institute for the Study and Treatment of Delinquency. pp. 19–24.

Inner London Probation Service (1993) *Adult Through and After-Care Handbook: Supervision Before and After Release from Custody.* London: ILPS.

Jefferson, T. (1993) 'The racism of criminalisation: policing and the reproduction of the criminal other', in L.R. Gelsthorpe (ed.), *Minority Ethnic Groups in the Criminal Justice System.* Cropwood Conference Series 21. Cambridge: Institute of Criminology. pp. 26–40.

Kett, J. et al. (1992) *Managing and Developing Anti-racist Practice within Probation: A Resource Pack for Action.* St Helens: Merseyside Probation Service.

Kingston, R. (1979) 'Through-care: the client's point of view', *Probation Journal*, 26 (2): 38–43.

Liebling, A. (1994) 'Suicide amongst women prisoners', *Howard Journal of Criminal Justice*, 33 (1): 1–9.

Lilly, J.R. (1992) 'Towards an international perspective on privatization in corrections', *Howard Journal of Criminal Justice*, 31 (3): 174–91.

Loucks, N. and Plotnikoff, J. (1993) *Prison Rules: A Working Guide.* London: Prison Reform Trust.

McWilliams, B. (1992) 'The rise and development of management thought in the English probation system', in R. Statham and P. Whitehead (eds), *Managing the Probation Service: Issues for the 1990s.* Harlow: Longman. pp. 3–29.

Mavunga, K.P. (1993) 'Probation: a basically racist service', in L.R. Gelsthorpe (ed.), *Minority Ethnic Groups in the Criminal Justice System.* Cropwood Conference Series 21. Cambridge: Institute of Criminology. pp. 73–95.

Monger, M., Pendleton, J. and Roberts, J. (1981) *Throughcare with Prisoners' Families.* Nottingham: University of Nottingham Department of Social Administration and Social Work.

Murphy, P. (1994) 'The invisible minority: Irish offenders and the English criminal justice system', *Probation Journal*, 41 (1): 2–7.

NACRO (1991) *Black Communities and the Probation Service: Working Together for Change.* London: National Association for the Care and Resettlement of Offenders.

NACRO (1992) *Women and Criminal Justice: Some Facts and Figures.* Briefing 91. London: National Association for the Care and Resettlement of Offenders.

NAPO (1990) *Working with Women: An Anti-sexist Approach.* Professional Committee paper 41/90. London: National Association of Probation Officers.

Nathan, S. (1994) 'Privatisation factfile 5', *Prison Report*, 26: 13–16.

Navin, John (1994) 'The Wolds, Britain's first private prison: an inmate's view'. Unpublished entry for Prison Reform Trust Research Prize.

Padel, U. and Stevenson, P. (1988) *Insiders.* London: Virago.

Peckham, A. (1985) *A Woman in Custody.* London: Fontana.

Pinder, R. (1982) 'On what grounds? Negotiating justice with black clients', *Probation Journal*, 29 (1): 19–23.

Pinder, R. (1984) *Probation and Ethnic Diversity.* Leeds: University of Leeds Applied Anthropology Group.

Player, E. (1994) 'Women's prisons after Woolf', in E. Player and M. Jenkins (eds), *Prisons after Woolf: Reform through Riot.* London: Routledge. pp. 203–28.

Pollock-Byrne and Jocelyn, M. (1990) *Women, Prison and Crime.* Pacific Grove, CA: Brooks/Cole.

Preece, A. (1993) 'Being gay in prison', *Probation Journal*, 40 (2): 85–7.

Prison Reform Trust (1993) *Wolds Remand Prison – Contracting-out: A First Year Report.* London: Prison Reform Trust.

Prison Reform Trust (1994) 'Editorial', *Prison Report*, 26: 3.

Prison Service (1991) *Race Relations Manual.* London: Home Office.

Raban, T. (1987) 'Removed from the community: prisoners and the probation service', in J. Harding (ed.), *Probation and the Community.* London: Tavistock. pp. 83–99.

Ralli, R. (1994) 'Health care in prison', in E. Player and M. Jenkins (eds), *Prisons after Woolf: Reform through Riot.* London: Routledge. pp. 125–42.

Richards, T. (1986) 'Don't tell me on a Friday', *British Medical Journal*, 18 (2): 162–9.

Rogers, P. (1992) *Unbarred? Throughcare in Practice.* Birmingham: West Midlands Probation Service.

Roy, E. (1993) 'Partnership in throughcare', *Prison Service Journal*, 91: 14–16.

Ryan, M. and Ward, T. (1989) *Privatisation and the Penal System.* Milton Keynes: Open University Press.

Sampson, A. (1994) 'Drowning in paper', *Prison Report*, 26: 18–19.

Sanders, A. and Senior, P. (1993) *Jarvis's Probation Service Manual, Vol. 2.* Sheffield: Pavic.

Shaw, R. (ed.) (1992) *Prisoners' Children: What are the Issues?* London: Routledge.

Shaw, S. (1990) 'Privatising prison services', in R. Parry (ed.), *Privatisation: Research Highlights in Social Work, Vol. 18.* London: Jessica Kingsley. pp. 117–26.

Smith, D.J. (1994) 'Race, crime and criminal justice', in M. Maguire, R. Morgan and R. Reiner (eds), *The Oxford Handbook of Criminology.* Oxford: Clarendon Press. pp. 1041–118.

South Yorkshire Probation Service (n.d.) *Probation, Race and Anti-Racism.* Sheffield: South Yorkshire Probation Service.

Stevenson, P. (1989) 'Women in special hospitals', *Open Mind*, 41: 14–16.

Thomas, P.A. and Costigan, R.S. (1992) 'Health care or punishment? Prisoners with HIV/AIDS', *Howard Journal of Criminal Justice*, 31 (4): 321–36.

Towl, G. (1993) 'Groupwork in prisons', *Probation Journal*, 40 (4): 208–9.

Vass, A.A. and Menzies, K. (1989) 'The community service order as a public and private enterprise: a comparative account in England and Ontario, Canada', *British Journal of Criminology*, 29: 255–72.

Voakes, R. and Fowler, Q. (1989) *Sentencing, Race and Social Enquiry Reports.* Bradford: West Yorkshire Probation Service.

White, S. (1989) 'Mothers in custody and the punishment of children', *Probation Journal*, 36 (3) (September): 106–9.

Whitehouse, P. (1983) 'Race, bias and social enquiry reports', *Probation Journal*, 30 (2): 43–9.

Wilding, P. (1990) 'Privatisation: an introduction and a critique', in R. Parry (ed.), *Privatisation: Research Highlights in Social Work, Vol. 18.* London: Jessica Kingsley. pp. 18–31.

Williams, B. (1991) *Work with Prisoners.* Birmingham: Venture.

Williams, B. (1992) 'Caring professionals or street-level bureaucrats? The case of probation officers' work with prisoners', *Howard Journal of Criminal Justice*, 31 (4): 263–75.

Williams, B. (1993) 'What is happening to prison education?' *Prison Writing*, 1 (2): 40–56.

Williams, B. (ed.) (1995a) *Probation Values.* Birmingham: Venture Press.

Williams, B. (1995b) 'Social work with prisoners: from missionary zeal to street-level bureaucracy', in P. Pettit and J. Schwieso (eds), *Aspects of the History of British Social Work.* Reading: University of Reading. pp. 21–65.

Wilson-Croome, L. (1992) 'Prisoners' families: should the probation service have a role?', in R. Shaw (ed.), *Prisoners' Children: What are the Issues?* London: Routledge. pp. 161–9.

Woodrow, J. (1992) 'Mothers inside, children outside: what happens to the dependent children of female inmates?', in R. Shaw (ed.), *Prisoners' Children: What are the Issues?* London: Routledge. pp. 29–40.

Woolf, H. (1991) *Prison Disturbances April 1990: Report of an Inquiry by the Rt Honorable Lord Justice Woolf* (The Woolf Report). Cmnd 1456. London: HMSO.

Zedner, L. (1991) *Women, Crime and Custody in Victorian England.* Oxford: Oxford University Press.

PART III

OUTCOMES

10

New Partnerships in Work with Offenders and Crime Prevention Work

Bob Broad

In this chapter the background to post-1990s partnership proposals in work with offenders will be reviewed, describing both community partnership and service partnership types. The government initiatives and forums to promote the sorts of partnerships introduced in the Criminal Justice Act 1991 will then be examined. It will be argued that the scope for new strategic partnerships beyond the immediate situational (one-to-one) or service provision level, though welcomed, appear very limited, and virtually non-existent. It is further argued that despite creative local partnerships emerging, the absence of any larger-scale and strategic local partnerships about work with offenders and crime prevention already represents a lost opportunity for greater things. After an analysis of the policy and meaning of partnerships, and drawing on direct practical experiences of negotiating partnerships, the chapter will end with an examination of issues unresolved at this early stage.

Potentially partnerships in crime prevention work and work with offenders could involve local community groups, voluntary organisations, church group volunteers, the probation service, the police and many others meeting locally and setting objectives together. Potentially funding could be drawn from the £7,160 million total expenditure on the criminal justice system, as at 1990–1 (Home Office, 1992c: Annexe A). The national probation expenditure for that year, £304 million, represents just 4 per cent of the total criminal justice budget. Partnerships developed from the locality could use funding in creative ways to respond to locally determined problems and solutions. They could draw on that vast amount currently spent on the criminal justice system as a whole. Such a partnership between different groups would require a considerable shift in the distribution of power regarding ideas, funding and services. In this scenario, whatever the emerging policies might be and whatever the level of interest in such a venture, it is virtually inevitable that frustrated citizens and cash-strapped local voluntary and community groups would have different strategic priorities than those currently set by probation services. It would also feed into the debate, not uncommon for local police forces, of the extent to which *they will allow* others to influence their local strategic goals. For the emerging world of new probation partnerships described in this chapter it will be argued that the Home Office and probation services, understandably, are taking the lead in limiting the scope and size of partnerships, useful though these might be.

Perspectives on partnership

In its general usage the term 'partnership' can mean different things. First, as in the guidance to the Children Act 1989, partnership is used to denote a different sort of social work approach. This is one in which planning, consultation and decision-making processes are widened to include, as a matter of course, significant people in the immediate service user's, or client's, life (Department of Health, 1991). The scope for an 'honest partnership' will depend on the extent to which power differentials exist in, or impact on, the face-to-face working relationship. But where statutory powers and funding questions are not involved, status differentials are negligible, resources and information can be shared and race and gender and disability differentials are not an issue, more genuinely equitable, or at least fairer, partnerships are possible. The opposite is also true. So without these and other criteria being met there is likely to be dishonesty about the capacity of, for example, a social worker and client to work or be in partnership on a particular problem. Whilst there is not a consensus on what partnership means, in the Children Act 1989 guidance notes it is the expectation to move clients' views, interests and networks more centre-stage which appears to receive virtually unanimous support.

A second type of partnership relevant to this chapter concerns shared agreements and common understandings about different agencies working together. In this chapter's context, partnerships will most likely involve the probation service and an independent agency delivering a previously agreed service, probably, but not necessarily, involving payment. In the Home Office's partnership decision document (1992a: 2) the term 'partnership'

. . . is intended to include all projects which involve organisations with differing goals and traditions, linking to work together. It includes work done under competitive contract for a probation, as well as jointly planned projects.

The pursuit of partnerships between agencies in working with offenders, and crime prevention work, acknowledges the subject's multi-faceted and complex nature. The same is true of at least two other problematic social problem areas, namely working with drug problems and child abuse problems. In the sense of different agencies working closely together to agreed aims, partnerships involving probation are not new. What is new, essentially, with the passing of the Criminal Justice Act 1991, and the publication of *Partnership in Dealing with Offenders in the Community: A Decision Document* (Home Office, 1992a), is the more formal basis for partnerships.

In the absence of any official explanations about why partnerships and why partnerships now, it is necessary to examine the broader context. Within that context can be identified ideological, financial, strategic, pragmatic and historical strands. By 'ideological' is meant the current administration's programme of, some would say, ideological obsession with, dismantling the welfare state and pursuing a competitive business approach and efficiency drives across the various social care sectors. In the criminal justice field there are already private sector initiatives in the prison service, and prison escort services and crime prevention schemes. Of the 60 or so partnership initiatives listed in the Association of Chief Officers of Probation *Partnership* publication (ACOP, 1993), just one commercial company, the Gracewell Clinic (which was publicly funded in the past), a residential centre for treating sex offenders, is listed as being involved in supervision work. With the introduction of the NHS and Community Care Act 1990, and other purchaser provider developments in social services, education and elsewhere, contracting and partnerships with private companies is expanding. Additionally, as with the Gracewell Clinic, previously publicly funded services to all will become more focused and available only to purchasers, like private business.

The second ideological strand is concerned with the government seeking to further marginalise trade unions (this would include the National Association of Probation Officers – NAPO), and limit their capacity to negotiate national agreements and working agreements. In that sense NAPO's fears of a gradual privatisation of some traditional probation work areas are well grounded. However, there is also a wide measure of agreement by NAPO and the voluntary sector about the professional principles of partnership (NAPO, 1993).

The next explanation for partnership relates to the saving of money for the government. With policies of reduced taxes and expenditure, and increased competition and unemployment, there is always money to be saved, or so it seems, through compulsory competitive tendering. More controversially, work that is not contracted out to the less qualified and trained workforces operating in some parts of the independent sector is likely to attract lower costs. The financial gain of partnership can be quite considerable, especially with small voluntary organisations with minimal overheads.

The strategic explanation is that for a variety of reasons it was seen as politically expedient by the Home Office and the Probation Division to introduce these plans at a time when they were under pressure to change, to prioritise punishment in the community, to be more effective and efficient, and to direct probation services to do the same (see the Audit Commission, 1989). There is also the sense in which this policy, any social policy, contains an element of pragmatism. Why the term 'around 5 per cent'? Why choose the particular framework for implementation it has chosen? Why the timescale it has adopted? The last reason, which is historical, denotes the important long-standing relationships that have existed between the Home Office, the probation service and the voluntary sector.[1]

Background to the new partnerships

Since 1990 the emergence of the term 'partnership', at least in official literature, is increasingly being regarded as a descriptive term to denote a more formalised business-like relationship between probation services and the independent sectors. The term 'independent' is used to describe both the voluntary sector and private sector. Of course there is at least one more sector, the informal sector, involving families, friends, neighbours and good citizens, in effect the unpaid carers. This group, essentially volunteers, is not acknowledged by the Home Office as a separate group with its own identity or identities. Or perhaps it is assumed that when volunteers do become involved in criminal justice work, at least in terms of partnerships, it will be as a contributor to a voluntary organisation or indeed even to the probation service itself. Also in the past partnerships have embraced at least two quite separate forms. The first concerns agencies working together in a formal or informal way to provide a service for offenders in the community; this can be called a servicing partnership. The second concerns agencies working together more broadly in the crime prevention or to a lesser extent community work spheres; this can be described as community partnership.

At least since 1963, when probation services took over the responsibility for supervising all after-care work from the voluntary sector, the Home Office has regarded the community as a resource principally for the probation service in overseeing and helping offenders settle or resettle into their localities. Then the community was taken to mean volunteers as well as voluntary organisations. The community has *always* been primarily regarded by probation as another potential service provider, usually for specialist services. Although this designated role for the community may appear satisfactory and desirable, it is and always has been a very limited and servicing role. As Haxby (1978: 187) has noted, traditionally the probation service was one which acted *for* the community without acting *with* it. Nevertheless, the Home Office, probation services and the voluntary sector have an established record of working together especially in the areas of provision of accommodation and juvenile offenders' initiatives and education and training developments. Although generally they are more the responsibility of social services, work with juvenile offenders has involved and continues to involve probation services. The DHSS LAC 83(3) initiative introduced in January 1983 resulted in £15 million in grant aid to voluntary bodies to develop intermediate treatment facilities. This policy was set against a background of a government's criminal justice policy seeking effective alternatives to custody through strengthened supervision orders. Since that time the long-standing and substantial accommodation scheme grants for voluntary organisations, as well as smaller supervision grants and grants to national voluntaries such as the National Association of Victim Support Schemes and the National Association for the Care and Resettlement of Offenders (NACRO) (Home Office, 1993c), have continued.

Community partnerships

By 1984, when the local probation services were required by government to draw up prioritised statements of local priorities (or SLOPS) alongside statements of national priorities (SNOPS), 'other work in the wide community' (despite its unclear meaning) was listed as a new national probation priority. This was placed alongside a greater priority for probation to be given to crime prevention work.

That call in the Home Office's SNOPS paper (Home Office, 1984) for widening the probation service's role to incorporate inter-agency cooperation and crime prevention (and confirming existing interests in Victim Support schemes) was repeated in subsequent Home Office papers, especially *Criminal Justice: A Working Paper* (Home Office, 1986). However, as the author has discussed elsewhere (Broad, 1991: 32–49), subsequent debates about the broader role of the probation service in the community focused increasingly on crime prevention work with other agencies. Yet a questionnaire survey of one large urban probation service about community involvement or partnerships portrayed probation staff primarily being involved in probation service working with agencies to service adult offenders' perceived social needs and not servicing localities' broader needs as a whole. In that survey (discussed in Broad, 1991: 38–45), involvement with voluntary housing and hostels was by far the largest of what was then called 'probation service community involvement'. In that area, as with less prioritised areas such as drug projects or motor projects, probation staff served variously on voluntary organisations' management committees, seconded staff or provided grant aid. In that survey, just 2.5 per cent of all probation officers' potential working week was found to involve work in community partnerships, outside the immediate servicing of offenders' needs. In effect that survey confirmed a resistance on the part of probation to community partnerships, and confusion as to what such partnerships, other than those which served offenders' needs, might or could be.

Servicing partnerships

A central theme of the White Paper *Crime, Justice and Protecting the Public* (Home Office, 1990a) was the reduction of the unnecessary use of imprisonment. Subsequently the Green Paper *Supervision and Punishment in the Community* (Home Office, 1990b) argued that the probation service should regard itself less as an exclusive service provider and more as managers of supervision programmes. By the time the discussion document *Partnership in Dealing with Offenders in the Community* was published (Home Office, 1990c), a much clearer policy emphasis was emerging. In that document reference is also made to the purchaser/provider development elsewhere in local authority social service departments (Department of Health, 1990) and value for money developments (Audit Commission, 1989). In the partnership discussion paper then (Home Office, 1990c), there was a much greater emphasis than hitherto on developing partnerships with the independent sector.

Seven areas of potential partnership work were identified in that paper: crime prevention; providing services for those cautioned and charged; accommodation and support for people on bail; activities forming part of supervision programmes especially for young adult offenders; work with prisoners before and after release; support for victims of crime; and conciliation work. None of these were new areas of work for partnerships but hopes were raised that they would expand further. Underpinning partnership proposals is an assumption that in time local probation services, decreasingly in discussion with the Home Office, will identify, fund and service local needs. It is very apparent that probation services are expected to lead on establishing partnership plans and that these will continue to be focused on dealing with offenders. Devolved partnerships seem the order of the day. Indeed in many ways much of the subsequent discussion about partnerships in working with offenders seems to indicate that it will involve little more than probation areas being responsible for administration functions, previously the responsibility of the Home Office. However, as we will see, it is slightly more than that, yet whether it is a complete change of direction or change of emphasis remains open to debate.

The publication *Partnership in Dealing with Offenders in the Community: A Decision Document* (Home Office, 1992a) contained a number of important points. The three essential elements of the partnership policy outlined there can be summarised as: (1) joint agreements between agencies underlying partnerships; (2) each probation area to work with a range of independent organisations; and (3) 'around 5 per cent' of the revenue budget of each probation service to be allocated to partnership schemes. The legislative context for this devolution is section 97 of the Criminal Justice Act 1991 which provides for an addition to schedule 3 to the powers of the Criminal Courts Act 1973. The key feature of that section of the Criminal Justice Act 1991 is the power to enable local probation committees to make direct payments to other organisations for certain work. The subsequent decision document (Home Office, 1992a) stated that the policy framework for implementation will involve more locally based decision-making (led by probation services), a national advisory forum (subsequently called the National Partnership Forum) and a progressive devolution of control of funds. Probation services are required to produce three-year partnership plans for 1994–7 and presumably after that period.

Another probation document, *The Probation Service: Three Year Plan for the Probation Service, 1993–1996* (Home Office, 1992b), lists 11 goals, with 'crime prevention' elevated to top position, reflecting one of the government's own key criminal justice priorities. The partnership goal, tenth in the list, is described as 'promoting community involvement, voluntary effort and partnership in work with offenders' (Home Office, 1992b: 28). Subsequently there have been a plethora of Home Office documents, letters and circulars (including Home Office, 1993a, 1993b, 1993c, 1993d, 1993e, 1993f, 1994a) to take things further forward, but within a very short timescale, leaving minimum scope for consultation. The proposals for probation services not to serve on local partners' management committees (Home Office, 1993f) also represents a shift towards a contracting-out approach based on a total separation of administrative arrangements. One probation circular (Home Office, 1993d) describes the powers for probation services to make payments for wider purposes than the Supervision Grants scheme. That scheme, it will be recalled, was established centrally in the early 1990s for voluntary organisations in conjunction with local probation services, and/or social services, to apply to the Home Office for short-term project funding (for example, two years' funding for a bail support worker). The management of hostels, originally via the Probation Accommodation Grants Scheme, is also to be devolved, but how and to what effect is unclear at this stage.

Transitional arrangements concerning the devolution of supervision grants were introduced for 1993–4 with area partnership plans being required and coming on stream for the present to 1997. For the transitional year 1993–4 a number of areas had not spent their allocated budget in partnerships (Home Office, 1994b). It is also apparent that at the National Partnership Forum there are many more Home Office-funded probation voices than voluntary sector voices (the ratio is about 13:6 depending on how one calculates it). This forum and the direction of its discussion lends weight to the view that partnerships in probation are driven by dominant probation interests. ACOP's (1993) publication states that partnership initiatives should 'promote the achievement of probation services' objectives'. These are listed in order as preventing re-offending, reintegrating offenders into the community, protecting the public and working with families in distress. A new government-funded organisation (DIVERT) following the disbanding of the Intermediate Treatment Fund (which distributed the LAC 83 funds) also has the task of promoting and directing partnerships. There is, then, some considerable effort going into implementing and controlling the nature and scope of partnerships.

It is also abundantly clear from direct experience and from reading through various partnership documents that the whole devolution process has been rushed through, often in an uncoordinated way. The pressure to submit 1994–7 probation partnership plans to tight deadlines and with overall probation budgets not always finalised much in advance of them, combined with other factors, has sometimes led to forms of consultation which are consultation in name only. Furthermore, with all players being coy about information, costs, needs and plans, there remain a number of outstanding questions rather than answers at this stage. How will probation services publicise their partnership proposals and to what extent have voluntary organisations already been consulted about them? How can voluntary organisations, especially the smaller ones and black voluntary organisations in the criminal justice system, ensure their voices are heard and acted on in partnerships?

Once partnership schemes are established, the question of who is responsible for monitoring what is not totally clear. The National Partnership Forum has been finding it extremely difficult to reach agreement on this issue. Indeed it seems there has been a tendency, at central government levels, for the more senior partners, that is, the probation service in most partnerships, to wish to monitor the 'junior partner', that is, the voluntary or, indeed, the independent sector's performance. This debate at the National Partnership Forum goes right to the heart of the matter about the organisational relationships and value issues involved in partnerships. A service contracted-out by probation surely should expect to monitor its provider's performance. Yet at a time when partnerships in one area are contractual arrangements in another and informal cooperation (in non-financial terms) elsewhere, it is difficult to produce a universal monitoring formula for different purposes from a central advisory group. One's impression of local and central discussions about partnership is of probation services with the power afforded the purchaser moving at a slower pace and adopting a more limited view of partnership eligibility than some voices in the independent sector. It is increasingly likely that informal agreements, partnerships even, could form between providers to set standards and costs, despite the trend towards competition not cooperation.

Training implications

What are the training issues in relation to developing and sustaining partnerships in criminal justice work with offenders in the community, and to what extent does the current version of the Central Council for Education and Training in Social Work (CCETSW) Paper 30 meet them at the point of qualification?[2] The answer to these questions depends on the levels at which partnerships operate, namely the individual case level, the systematic service provision level or the strategic service planning level. At the first level CCETSW requirements for qualifying social workers to 'assess needs, strengths, situations, risks, skills in using resources' and 'plan appropriate action' (CCETSW, 1991: 2.35, 2.41 and 2.42; see also amended requirements, CCETSW, 1995) are especially relevant and useful. What requires even more recognition than is contained in that paper is the importance attached to making comprehensive assessments. After all, if qualifying probation officers are to develop more of a partnership approach, rather than a single-agency focus and approach, to service assessments and delivery, they will need to further develop their capacities to make social as well as offending assessments.

At the second service provision level of partnerships, the one the Home Office is focusing on, different sets of skills, beyond CCETSW's qualifying core competencies, are required. Predominantly these are in the NHS and Community Care Act 1990 requirements of assessing existing and future group needs, and devising and producing a budget to meet them. In respect of assessing group need, one example would be to assess the existing and projected local youth court remand population, when considering introducing or strengthening a remand management programme, including bail support, as one distinctive element. Ways of assessing need and costs in meeting them, and generally a greater awareness of purchaser/provider issues, need much greater recognition in CCETSW's Paper 30 (CCETSW, 1991, 1995).

Ongoing training will also be required in more detailed budgeting, business management, information technology and monitoring skills. In Kay's National Partnership Forum discussion document *Secondary Performance Indicators – Partnership* (Kay, 1993: 3), apart from bail support, examples at this service provision level include housing, mental health problems and services for sex offenders. Finally, so far as training is concerned, the third strategic planning level, the one that provides the greatest challenge to probation services, but could produce the highest dividend, requires advanced business and management skills at the post-qualifying level.

What sort of partnerships are most likely?

The majority of offenders referred to probation have complex and disproportionate levels of deprivation that far outstrip the capacity of the probation service, or indeed any other single agency, to tackle. More help for offenders from others, therefore, is desirable to meet these needs. The issue is whether there is a case for the total needs of offenders to be assessed jointly or separately, involving a social care agency alongside probation to ensure the 'corrective agenda' does not dominate. Indeed there are already probation services which have taken steps in this direction (admittedly at the pre-sentence assessment stage rather than service provision stage) with, in some cases, educational, drugs or training assessments being made by other agencies.

The sharing out of tasks either that *cannot* be done by probation alone because of acknowledged expertise elsewhere (for example, drug advice services, psychiatric services, housing advice) or *cannot be done well* by probation because of lack of time outside the 'community penalties brief' of supervision (perhaps the provision of welfare rights advice, even counselling) seems likely to benefit the service user. Yet acknowledging that all relationships and institutions operate from established power bases, partnerships will require major shifts in the culture of some probation areas towards that of purchasers, brokers, fixers and monitors rather than that of direct service providers. In many areas none of this is new – what *is* novel is the fact that local services will have greater responsibility, including direct responsibility for the partnership budget. This is likely to be accompanied by greater financial caution and service accountability, whether the partnership relates to crime prevention and diversionary schemes, or to 'added value' services to offenders supervised by probation, or to voluntary help to ex-offenders. New partnerships will also require changes with those sections of the voluntary sector more used to being grant-aided, with few questions being asked. In one case known to us, a voluntary organisation was used to receiving its three-year block grant and being simply told to 'get on with it' until their next grant was due in three years' time! Those days have now gone.

Advantages and disadvantages of partnerships

There have been several conferences and seminars exploring issues concerning partnerships. Table 10.1 lists key points raised by voluntary and statutory sector participants at those events, as well as from independent research (see Vass, 1990: 73–6). Interestingly many of these listed advantages and disadvantages are similar to those given in answer to questions reported elsewhere by the author (Broad, 1991: 38–45) about the perceived advantages of community involvement. There again, hopes were expressed for greater choice for users, as well as worries about a cultural shift for probation. The experiences reported to date about partnerships are too limited to generalise from, but they do tend to point towards the creation of more formal agreements and expectations and a measure of tension.

Table 10.1 *Perceived advantages and disadvantages of partnerships*

Advantages	Disadvantages
Meeting users' needs better by combining skills	Exploitation of junior partners
Increased choice for users	Hidden agendas of senior partners
Opportunity to learn from each other	Clash of cultures
Greater coordination of services	Lack of clear accountability
Protecting services through joint funding	The creation of unfair monopolies
The voice of the user being heard more	Lack of respect towards voluntary organisations (equating voluntary with amateur)
More coordinated and better informed crime prevention strategies could be introduced	The more independent voice of the voluntary sector may be stifled
Local partnerships should respond better to local need	Competing perspectives and difficulty in establishing long-lasting coalitions

Some experiences of partnerships

Elsewhere Smith et al. (1993: 25–38) provide illustrations of partnership 'successes rather than failures', pointing to long-standing and traditional work (both pre-dating the harsher pruning back of the welfare state) involving community service volunteers, accommodation work and supervision of juvenile offenders. It is important to note here that these experiences pre-date the sorts of new partnerships described in the partnership decision document (Home Office, 1992a). Further it is of some considerable significance that each of the three examples is based on a national initiative with relatively secure funding. But what are the experiences of medium-sized voluntary organisations concerning partnerships? The author's previous employing organisation, the Royal Philanthropic Society, has operated in the contract climate in both county and metro-politan areas over a period of seven years. The Society works in partnership with others to provide a number of after-care projects for young people leaving care as well as bail support projects and other work concerning teenagers at risk. The Society has had, and continues to have, a series of partnership arrangements with a variety of statutory (including probation) and voluntary organis-ations. Its experience is that the process of negotiating with partners establishing or renewing agreements is valued and as important as the outcome.

The service agency agreement is the mechanism for enabling

voluntary organisations to receive the necessary funding to provide good quality services. These agreements usually cover three main areas: definition of service, accountability (including monitoring) and administration (including staffing and financial arrangements). A model service agency agreement is contained in the Society's comprehensive resource guide entitled *Partnership in Action* (Smith, 1994). The four areas which have involved protracted negotiations and frustrations with a number of partners have been funding (for what service level? how much? who? when?), the related issue of project security, service continuity for users, and, lastly, monitoring (who is monitoring what? how? why?).

The Society prefers a project service agreement lasting at least three years with some funding being provided by itself to take to negotiations. It is fair to say that where the Society, and, we suspect, other voluntary organisations, in partnership with the statutory sector, makes a financial contribution to a service it seeks and expects to have an influential voice in negotiations and service design. Exceptionally (and this did not involve probation) there have been instances of negotiations , where one of the partners has displayed brinkmanship to the extent of holding back agreed funding contributions to encourage a greater contribution from the voluntary sector side, within weeks of contracts being renewed, or not. This reveals an unacceptable underside to partnerships which it is hoped will not surface again, but perhaps in the current economic climate such brinkmanship should be expected. In smaller local voluntary organisations than the Society, such attitudes could well lead to closure, similar to a business going bankrupt. A national survey into leaving care work indicated that in the majority of cases the contract culture had adversely impacted on services in the sense that 'it had made it more difficult for providers of leaving care services to obtain resources from purchasing teams' (Broad, 1994: 17). It is hoped the same will not be true for these new partnerships with probation.

In a number of service areas (for example, youth counselling or leaving care services) there is not a queue of quality prospective service providers waiting to form partnerships with statutory authorities. From the user's point of view, continuity of relevant quality service is vital. Once established, at least a year's notice, preferably two, is necessary if service agency agreements are not to be renewed. However, in the contract culture, with its administrative imperatives and business plans, longer-term notice is very difficult to provide. The monitoring issue can be a complex one and it is one where the negotiations are most important. In one of the Society's negotiations it took some two years to agree with a partner what was being monitored, by whom and how. Whilst it was probably worth the wait, the delay illustrates the sensitivity of the issue. It is now virtually agreed that all the Society's partnership projects and monitoring requirements will not only be contained in the service agreement but will also contain a strong element of users' views. One way this has been achieved is for there to be an ongoing survey for the young people and the social services receiving a service from the organisation.

The Society's experience, and this is probably not unique, is that negotiations with prospective as well as actual partners are time-consuming, demanding and cost money, especially in relation to new partners. A strong element of trust underpins any formal agreement. Quite rightly statutory organisations and others, for example housing associations, expect a certain level and quality of service from voluntary or private organisations, but it should be recognised that some developmental costs will accompany protracted agreements. In our view priority should be given to simplifying and streamlining procedures, otherwise a paperchase ensues, in effect siphoning off energies and funds which should go to direct services for users. Another issue is that unless voluntary organisations help to set local strategic probation plans, or at least are represented at meetings where such plans are set, voluntary agencies will enter the partnership process at the very end with probation priorities and budgets already committed. On the other hand, it is relatively early days concerning these new national partnerships and the Society has found probation services and others very open to being approached for exploratory discussions about needs and services without, as it were, either side making any commitment or promise at that stage or even necessarily later.

New suppliers or new services?

There is a danger that the lobbying and campaigning role of voluntary organisations will be discouraged or even curtailed when partnerships within the 5 per cent framework are formed. Other government initiatives within the charity sector about separating service provider functions (eligible for block grants) from campaigning and lobbying functions (and therefore not eligible for block grants) may, if followed through, further silence the voice of constructive criticism. An associated point is whether this new partnership framework in criminal justice work will change the role of the voluntary sector to becoming more one of another routine mainstream service provider and less one of complementing statutory services with innovative approaches and ideas (on this point see Gutch et al., 1990).

A more adventurous approach, reflective of a localised understanding of working with offenders and crime prevention, would be
for various agencies, including probation, the voluntary sector and
other interest groups, to be established, jointly meet and set and
manage probation area plans. Elsewhere the author has written
about the struggles that faced probation, as well as the achievements, in working with a variety of voluntary groups in inner-city
areas in the early 1980s (Broad, 1991). The research revealed that
there was a tendency for probation to colonise local groups and
contain or ignore dissenting views, especially about poverty or police
racism. At the time of the inner-city disturbances a number of
voluntary organisations, including black groups, were most dis-
appointed by the probation services' silence about social injustices,
poverty and discrimination (Broad, 1991: 46–9, 184–93). There is a
history of probation services primarily funding projects which,
understandably, are in accord with statutory imperatives, currently
and for some time now focusing on more punitive measures. As
implied earlier in this chapter, already the framework for new
partnerships is becoming excessively formal in terms of administration. It is most important that this tendency is restrained now if
the independent sectors and probation services of the future are not
to spend endless hours drawing up cumbersome service agency
agreements or contracts.

Conclusion

Since the dawn of these new 5 per cent partnerships following the
Criminal Justice Act 1991 and with the three years' partnership
plans having only just begun, there is to our knowledge no independent research available yet on the effectiveness, purpose and
durability of partnership schemes in England and Wales. However,
in Northern Ireland the Northern Ireland Order of 1982 empowered
the probation boards (committees) to purchase or to grant aid to the
private or voluntary sector. Gadd, the Chief Probation Officer of
Northern Ireland, as at 1991, has written about partnerships there.
She states that 10 years after that legislation was introduced
approximately 17 per cent of the annual budget is paid to community voluntary organisations (Gadd, 1992). Although this figure
might well alarm NAPO and others in England and Wales, the
starting level for funding the voluntary or private sector there is not
known. Additionally, to our knowledge, there is generally a higher
level of voluntary and community activity in Northern Ireland than
in England and Wales. Gadd (1992: 161) makes a further important
point that 'a scheme evolving from the community which tackles a

local problem of crime is likely to be much more successful than one imposed from outside by a statutory agency'. Although this view, and the potentially explosive implications of it, is not expounded upon in her article, it again raises a crucial debate, now surprisingly muted. This debate centres on the extent to which the imposition of additional external formal social control measures and initiatives (for example, probation partnership initiatives) weakens or strengthens the existing formal social control networks (whether informal carers or families or others).

The second important and associated outstanding question centres not on the effectiveness or funding of partnerships but on their capacity for local democratic accountability. In the increasingly centralised probation world, in terms of the Home Office's role and training, funding or management, partnership is yet another phenomenon where the nature of the relationship between the state, its agencies and citizens reflects the broader social and political arrangements. Then there is the further question of who monitors and researches the working partnerships between the statutory and independent sectors. The accountability element of that particular discussion brings us back to issues about the three levels of partnerships: at a situational (or case) level, a systematic service provision level and at the strategic level. This strategic level involves not only others influencing a particular organisational strategy (probably the probation services), but also the development of inter-organisational strategies.

Kay (1993: 5) has suggested in one of the National Partnership Forum papers that the final performance indicator for partnerships at the strategic level is 'how far the probation services have progressed in the implementation of the target figure of a minimum of 5 per cent of their annual revenue being "allocated to partnership schemes within the independent sector" by 1997'. At this stage it remains to be seen whether in England and Wales the partnerships will build up to the sorts of levels reported in Northern Ireland within 10 years of their introduction, or whether the existing controls and resistances will in practice have exactly the reverse effect of limiting the size and scope of partnership schemes. In these early days with arguments being proposed (Home Office, 1994b) for seconded probation staff (accounting for 23 of 59 partnership projects as reported in the ACOP [1993] paper) to count towards this figure of 5 per cent, it would seem that the more creative aspects of partnerships will take some considerable time and further changes to surface. The most pressing concern is that partnerships benefit service users and communities alike and help to reduce crime. These are difficult aims to achieve. It is also essential that they are delivered by staff with proper conditions of service. It is a cause for regret, however, that so far emerging partnership work is relatively small scale when it could be something greater and better.

Notes

1. On this point see the detailed discussion by Nellis (1989).
2. The new requirements, that is to say, the review of the DipSW referred to earlier in the present volume (CCETSW, 1995), does not address the issue in any more detail than the original Paper 30. It merely states that a competent social worker should be working with organisations.

References

ACOP (1993) *Partnership: Purpose, Principles and Contractual Arrangements.* London: Association of Chief Officers of Probation.

Audit Commission (1989) *The Probation Service: Promoting Value for Money.* London: HMSO.

Broad, B. (1991) *Punishment under Pressure: The Probation Service in the Inner City.* London: Jessica Kingsley.

Broad, B. (1994) *Leaving Care in the 1990s.* Kent: Royal Philanthropic Society.

CCETSW (1991) *DipSw: Rules and Requirements for the Diploma in Social Work.* Paper 30 (2nd edn). London: Central Council for Education and Training in Social Work.

CCETSW (1995) *DipSw: Rules and Requirements for the Diploma in Social Work.* Paper 30 (rev. edn). London: Central Council for Education and Training in Social Work.

Department of Health (1990) *Caring for People.* Cmnd 849. London: HMSO.

Department of Health (1991) *The Children Act 1989: Guidance and Regulations, Vols 1–6.* London: HMSO.

Gadd, B. (1992) 'Partnerships: the Northern Ireland dimension', in R. Statham and P. Whitehead (eds), *Managing the Probation Service: Issues for the 1990s.* Harlow: Longman. pp. 154–62.

Gutch, R. et al. (1990) *Partners or Agents? Local Government and the Voluntary Sector – Changing Relationships in the 1990s.* London: National Council for Voluntary Organisations in conjunction with Birmingham Settlement and the University of Birmingham.

Haxby, D. (1978) *Probation: A Changing Service.* London: Constable.

Home Office (1984) *Probation Service in England and Wales: Statement of National Objectives and Priorities.* London: Home Office.

Home Office (1986) *Criminal Justice: A Working Paper* (2nd edn). London: Home Office.

Home Office (1990a) *Crime, Justice and Protecting the Public: The Government's Proposals for Legislation.* Cmnd 965. London: HMSO.

Home Office (1990b) *Supervision and Punishment in the Community: A Framework for Action.* Cmnd 966. London HMSO.

Home Office (1990c) *Partnership in Dealing with Offenders in the Community: A Discussion Paper.* London: Home Office.

Home Office (1992a) *Partnership in Dealing with Offenders in the Community. A Decision Document*. London: Home Office.

Home Office (1992b) *The Probation Service: Three Year Plan for the Probation Service, 1993–1996*. London: Home Office.

Home Office (1992c) *Regional Criminal Justice Conference: A Conference Report*. London: Home Office.

Home Office (1993a) *Probation Services and the Management of Voluntary Sector Organizations*. Probation Circular, PC 6/1993. London: Home Office.

Home Office (1993b) *Probation Service Partnership Policy: Submission of Partnership Plans 1993–1994*. Letter to chief probation officers, CP 23/1993. London: Home Office.

Home Office (1993c) *Probation Supervision Grants Scheme: Arrangements for Grants to Local Projects 1994–5*. Probation Circular, PC 16/1993. London: Home Office.

Home Office (1993d) *Partnership in Dealing with Offenders in the Community: Submission of Partnership Plans, 1994–1997*. Probation Circular, PC 17/1993. London: Home Office.

Home Office (1993e) *Partnership Monitoring*. Discussion paper to National Partnership Forum. London: Home Office.

Home Office (1993f) *Partnership in Dealing with Offenders in the Community: National Guidance*. London: Home Office.

Home Office (1994a) *The Probation (Amendment) (No. 2) Rules 1994 (draft) Statutory Instrument*. London: Home Office.

Home Office (1994b) *Minutes of National Partnership Forum, 14 January, 1994*. Mimeo. London: Home Office.

Kay, R. (1993) *Secondary Performance Indicators – Partnership*. Discussion document. London: Rainer Foundation.

NAPO (1993) *Partnership between the Statutory and Voluntary Sector Statement from Professional Committee*. London: National Association of Probation Officers.

Nellis, M. (1989) 'Probation, the state and the independent sector', in P. Senior and D. Woodhill (eds), *Criminal Justice in the 1990s*. Sheffield: Pavic. pp. 33–48.

Senior, P. and Woodhill, D. (eds) (1989) *Criminal Justice in the 1990s*. Sheffield: Pavic.

Smith, C. (ed.) (1994) *Partnership in Action: Developing Effective After-Care Projects. A Resource Guide*. Kent: Royal Philanthropic Society.

Smith, D., Paylor, I. and Mitchell, P. (1993) 'Partnerships between the independent sector and the probation service', *Howard Journal of Criminal Justice*, 32 (1): 25–39.

Statham, R. and Whitehead, P. (eds) (1992) *Managing the Probation Service: Issues for the 1990s*. Harlow: Longman.

Stern, V. and Weston, B. (1990) 'Partnership between the statutory and voluntary sectors in criminal justice', *Justice of the Peace*, 154: 607–9.

Vass, A.A. (1990) *Alternatives to Prison: Punishment, Custody and the Community*. London: Sage.

11

Crime Prevention

Daniel Gilling

In the previous chapter we concluded that partnerships have not as yet delivered their promised benefits. In this chapter we continue in the same vein by specifically concentrating on crime prevention.

Since 1984 the probation service has been asked – or required, depending on one's perspective – to become directly involved in crime prevention (Home Office, 1984). For a number of reasons, this has proved to be problematic. What exactly is meant by crime prevention? What is meant by involvement? What are the particular skills and values which probation officers are expected to contribute to crime prevention initiatives, and how do these complement or conflict with the skills and values of other agencies involved in such initiatives? These are some of the questions which this chapter seeks to consider. We begin with a description of the development of the probation service's crime preventive role from 1984 to the present. The next section will then explore this role in more detail through the discussion of a single case study – the Kirkholt Project, which is one of the most celebrated examples of success in crime prevention and one from which the probation service has derived much credit. A final section will then summarise the difficulties and dilemmas the probation service faces when participating in crime prevention, and discuss how, or whether, these might be resolved.

Overall, the aim is to demonstrate that whilst there are several practical considerations to the further development of crime prevention within the probation service, there are as many political ones which must first be negotiated. Crime prevention has both its supporters and its detractors within the service, and this chapter seeks to explore why this should be so.

The development of crime prevention and the probation service role

Prior to the 1980s, crime prevention as a nominally distinct activity – as opposed to a label which can be applied to virtually any activity conducted in the name of criminal justice or social policy – was a small and relatively insignificant part of the criminal justice whole. In the main it was confined and related to the publicity campaigns initiated by the Home Office and insurance industry from the 1950s (GLC, 1986), and to the specialist security advice-giving of police crime prevention departments which first appeared in the 1960s. Measures such as the establishment of a national Standing Conference on Crime Prevention and the institution of local Crime Prevention Panels (on which the service was and is often represented), both also originating in the 1960s, had been intended to raise the profile of, and institute a national infrastructure for, crime prevention. However, these remained relatively marginal to the dominant interests of professions and agencies operating within the criminal justice system, and there were far more important articles of faith than crime prevention at this time, such as welfarism.

This situation began to change in the mid-1970s largely as a result of the coincidence of two forces: a hardening of political attitudes towards measures reckoned to be 'soft' on the offender (shown most clearly in the retreat from the Children and Young Persons Act 1969: see Pitts, 1988); and the acquisition of research evidence which raised serious misgivings about the effectiveness of any of the main pillars of criminal justice policy – police, prisons and probation. Since research does not usually have such a significant influence on the policy process, one might say that the former acted as catalyst to the latter's importance.

More specifically, the probation treatment paradigm (Bottoms and McWilliams, 1979) fell into disrepute as a result of some very unflattering research (Brody, 1976); the reconviction rates of those sent to custodial institutions told their own story; and the police fared little better with regard to evidence about the effectiveness of their patrol and detective functions (Clarke and Hough, 1980). For a while, the system lapsed into a 'nothing works' complex. However, seeking to resolve this and driven forward by the perennial problems of rising crime rates, burgeoning prison populations and a growing cost-consciousness, the Home Office (1977) earnestly set in motion a Review of Criminal Justice Policy, out of which emerged a commitment to set up a working party to assess the future potential of crime prevention. By the end of the decade the working party had devised a very clear four-step problem-oriented methodology for crime prevention (Gladstone, 1980).

It began with a project-focused close scrutiny of a specific crime problem (a crime 'hot spot'), turned next to consideration of a range of preventive solutions, then to the selection of the most promising of these, and finally ended with implementation, monitoring and evaluation. Underpinning the methodology was a belief that it would be effective only if it entailed the collaboration of a number of agencies, since experience from the 1970s had made it clear that no agency possessed sufficient resources (including information) to successfully tackle crime by itself.

This methodology, where used, had demonstrably succeeded in reducing crime levels (Clarke and Mayhew, 1980). Moreover, when this methodology was followed closely, as it was in a school vandalism demonstration project in Manchester (Hope and Murphy, 1983), it invariably ended up with the selection of a range of measures which were focused on reducing criminal opportunities. Such measures tended to be of a traditional 'locks and bolts' type, and acquired the label of *situational* crime prevention.

At much the same time, in the late 1970s, a similar but subtly different crime prevention paradigm was emerging through the estate-based work of the National Association for the Care and Resettlement of Offenders (NACRO) (Stern, 1987). This combined situational methods of prevention, often in the shape of crime prevention through environmental design, with more social policy-type interventions, focusing particularly on youth and problems of deprivation. A similar problem-oriented methodology was employed, and the same importance was attached to inter-agency collaboration, but the nature of the crime prevention was clearly different, with the social policy-type interventions later attracting the label of *social* crime prevention. The probation service was a collaborative partner in these ventures, with such collaboration fitting in not only with the long-standing tradition of officer autonomy (Fielding, 1984) which justified such 'sidelines', but also with Bottoms and McWilliams's (1979) emphasis upon crime reduction as one of the four primary aims of the non-treatment paradigm.

Moving into the 1980s, the optimism surrounding the potential and actual effectiveness of crime prevention stood in stark contrast to the pessimism surrounding its alternatives, and particularly in the light of the crisis of confidence following the 1981 urban riots, the Home Office sought ways of bringing crime prevention more into the mainstream. The logic of crime prevention was becoming irresistible, not least because of the first British Crime Survey's (Hough and Mayhew, 1984) revelation about the extent of unreported crime, which, together with knowledge of low police clear-up rates, led to the obvious conclusion that the problem of controlling crime in society is to a large extent distinct from the problem of how to deal with individual offenders (Laycock and Pease, 1985: 43).

Consequently, following the establishment of an inter-departmental working group on crime reduction in 1982, and the working group's report in 1983, an inter-departmental circular was issued to a multi-agency audience in 1984. Known to the Home Office as Circular 8/84, this urged local agencies, including the probation service, to develop a coordinated approach to crime prevention, although more of an emphasis was placed upon situational crime prevention:

> . . . whilst there is a need to address the social factors associated with criminal behaviour, and policies are continually being devised to tackle this aspect of the problem, these are essentially long-term measures. For the short-term, the best way forward is to reduce through management, design, or changes in the environment the opportunities that exist for crime to occur. (Home Office, 1984: 2)

Focusing specifically upon the probation service's position, further 'encouragement' for it to participate in this coordinated approach came in the shape of the 1984 *Statement of National Objectives and Priorities* (SNOP), which suggested that one of the service's objectives might entail

> . . . encouraging the local community in the widest practicable approach to offending and offenders, taking account of the influences of family, schools, and other social factors and of the other potential contributions of other agencies; developing the service to the wider public by contributing to initiatives concerned with the prevention of crime and the support of victims, and playing a part in the activities of local statutory and voluntary organisations. (Home Office, 1984: objective D, paras (viii) and (ix))

Similarly, Rule 37 of the 1984 *Probation Rules* required the service 'to take part in crime prevention projects, reparation schemes, victim support and other work in the wider community' (quoted in Harding, 1987: 10).

The combined effect of Circular 8/84, SNOP and the 1984 *Probation Rules* is confusing. SNOP defines the service's role socially, in a form which has many parallels with Henderson's (1986) conception of community probation work. However, Circular 8/84 prioritises situational prevention, because this is seen as 'the best way forward' in the short term. Since crime prevention *projects* are by their very nature short-term affairs – of which there were growing numbers in the mid-1980s – then this logically implies that the service should become involved in projects where its 'brand' of crime prevention is not prioritised, because its focus is long term.

In view of this state of affairs, it is not surprising that the service experienced some difficulty. As Lloyd (1986) points out in his survey of local responses to SNOP, areas were unclear as to whether they were meant to commit resources to crime prevention projects, or whether their role might be wholly representational.

In early 1985 the Home Office sponsored a conference at Bournemouth entitled 'Crime Prevention and the Probation Service', intended to clarify the probation role and to establish some sort of coherent strategy. From the conference it became clear that the service was unwilling to see crime prevention in narrow situational terms: it had a much wider perspective, principally as a consequence of its detailed knowledge of offender motivations.

Meanwhile, also in 1985, the Association of Chief Officers of Probation (ACOP) produced a document (ACOP, 1985) which in tone was welcoming of the service's increased role in crime prevention, clearly conceived of in social terms. It also conducted a hurried survey of each probation area to determine precisely what was currently being done in the name of crime prevention. The results of that survey, produced in early 1986, demonstrate the definitional elasticity of the term 'crime prevention', since it was used to cover a number of traditional probation 'sidelines' such as juvenile liaison or mediation. In addition, the crime preventive potential of more mainstream activities, such as community service and community probation, was noted.

The Central Council of Probation Committees (CCPC) did not miss out on the act either. In 1984 it established a working party to consider the implications of SNOP's crime prevention objective. This working party provided a final report in 1987 in which it made a number of recommendations about the future development of crime prevention within the service. It was supportive of a crime preventive role for the service and justified it thus: 'The probation service has always been concerned with crime prevention. A widening of its boundary to participate in community-focused prevention projects and activities would be a legitimate development' (CCPC, 1987: 4).

It is suggested that this role could be taken forward by probation committees (see Chapter 6 here) drawing up policy statements; by local services nominating a member of headquarters management with special responsibility for crime prevention; by improving links between probation committees and local authority and police equivalents with whom they share boundaries; and by giving consideration to resourcing issues. Needless to say, resourcing was regarded as the most problematic of these, and without much money for expansion in this area, the CCPC proposed some solutions to this dilemma. Whilst the appointment of specialist staff might be the ideal, it was conceivable that crime prevention could be pursued by bending mainstream activities such as community service, day centres and links with voluntary agencies. Moreover, expertise on offender motivations could give the service an advisory role with other agencies engaged in crime prevention initiatives.

Whilst resourcing difficulties were regarded as a potentially significant barrier to the further development of crime prevention, the CCPC did, however, concede that 'there was much ambivalence in the service' and that '[w]e were not so sure that this was entirely related to the issue of resources' (CCPC, 1987: 9).

One possible source of this ambivalence was the National Association of Probation Officers (NAPO). Its policy document said that whilst in general NAPO supported situational crime prevention, it foresaw 'few direct opportunities for probation officers to become directly involved' (NAPO, 1984: 3), and was keen to point out the potential limitations of this form of crime prevention in terms of its disregard of the broader social causes of crime. It was more positive about social crime prevention, but even here made the point that 'it is important in this context to make links with other groups who may be in a better position to develop particular initiatives and that involves probation officers knowing the limits of working within a statutory agency' (NAPO, 1984: 3).

Clarifying this latter point, the document goes on to say that 'our particular contribution is based on our work with offenders' (NAPO, 1984: 4). Evidently, this is where NAPO saw its crime preventive role, with other agencies having the responsibility for other forms of crime prevention. But NAPO was swimming against a realist tide fed mainly by the goal of organisational self-preservation. As the CCPC (1987: 5) noted: 'We were also sensitive to the implications for the service in not participating in crime prevention initiatives at a time when the subject was featuring significantly on the political and criminal justice agendas.'

One can see here, then, the divisions that existed between organisational management and main grade workers over the subject of crime prevention. In practice it has been the former's view which has prevailed, not least because in resourcing terms it holds the balance of power, and because it has been assisted in the development of crime prevention by a few enthusiastic converts at all levels within the service. Perhaps more fundamentally, the service's internal politics has proved largely irrelevant in the face of policy developments outside: since 1984 the wheels of crime pre-vention have moved inexorably forward under the steam of Home Office exhortation (the promotional activities of the Home Office Crime Prevention Unit, established in 1983, and Circular 44/90 to back up the message of 8/84), and financial incentives (including

Home Office money for demonstration projects, the Five Towns Initiative [Home Office, 1988] and the Safer Cities Programme; and employment opportunities under the now defunct Community Programme scheme [Home Office Crime Prevention Unit, 1985]). There is a certain irony here: crime prevention offers more resources to the service in the short term but, if successful, threatens to reduce the number of traditional cases on which the service depends for its longer-term survival.

ACOP has continued to be the most enthusiastic of the probation representational triumvirate with regard to crime prevention. It established a Crime Prevention Committee in mid-1987 to act in a promotional capacity both within and outside of the service. Speaking at a crime prevention conference in 1989 the Chair of this committee, Malcolm Bryant, presented the maturation of the service's views on crime prevention. Although Laycock and Pease (1985) had put forward the provocative proposal that the service did have something to contribute to situational crime prevention, because it was in an advantageous position to obtain information about offenders' modus operandi and to teach their clients opportunity-reducing behaviours, the service in the shape of the ACOP committee continues to resist any such notion, thus supporting the authors' prediction that this would prove 'too narrow a definition to be acceptable as the sole basis for probation involvement in preventive activity' (Laycock and Pease, 1985: 44).

Rather, Bryant (1989) outlines a wider vision which accepts the legitimacy of situational crime prevention but cleverly envisages the service's role lying not so much in criminal opportunity reduction, as legitimate opportunity creation, incorporating mainstream components of both traditional probation work and social policies. Put in these terms, crime prevention becomes less of a sideline, and more 'a major opportunity to present some traditional probation service objectives in a way which commands widespread public support' (Bryant, 1989: 15).

This emphasis on public support, or perhaps public relations, takes on a significant position as a motive for probation involvement in crime prevention. If the service can present itself as an agency whose major focus is crime prevention, and whose 'client' is therefore the whole community, then the longer-term beneficiary is the traditional client, the offender. As Bryant (1989: 13) suggests: '[t]he more we are seen to support local communities in understanding and dealing with crime and supporting victims, the greater the support we receive in return for dealing with the offender in the community wherever possible'.

Consequently, studying the sub-text, crime prevention could be regarded as a significant element of a rearguard action in which the service prepared to fight the threats to its future implicit in the Green Paper of 1988 and the White Paper of 1990. Evidently, if the service won public support in this way it would have been of benefit both to itself and to its traditionally conceived client.

Involvement in crime prevention, however, is certainly not conceived of at any cost. As noted above, it is seen in its social context, similar to the term 'community safety' which was promoted first by NACRO and the Morgan Report (Home Office, 1991), and is now increasingly regarded within the service as a preferred term to the oppositional and conceptually awkward distinction made between situational and social crime prevention. In addition, it is envisaged that probation involvement in crime prevention can ensure the pursuit of anti-discriminatory values whereby, as Bryant (1989: 6) puts it: 'every crime prevention project should ask specific questions about the relevance of its activity to black people and women, and . . . local community groups should make a special effort to include women and representatives of ethnic minorities.'

Even when the service is not directly involved in the delivery of crime prevention, it is envisaged by Bryant, and later by Wilson-Croome (1990), that it might make a useful contribution in informing other agencies about the motivational causes of crime which might then inform broader social strategies. Again, this echoes an earlier point made by the CCPC and noted above.

As ACOP sought to develop what was by 1990 a quite coherent policy towards crime prevention, one of the members of its Crime Prevention Committee – Jane Geraghty – was seconded to the Home Office Crime Prevention Unit with the purpose of discovering to what extent existing practice within the service was in harmony with this policy. This she did by means of an audit survey of four representative probation areas. Although from her account (Geraghty, 1991) it is evident that she had a certain amount of difficulty defining categories of crime prevention, she eventually excluded those categories which represented traditional offender-centred work (tertiary prevention). Instead, she looked for activities focused either on the general population (primary prevention) or a population 'at risk' (secondary prevention), and counted those where crime prevention was either a central, additional or incidental concern of the activity.

With this very broad focus it is not altogether surprising that she discovered a considerable amount of crime preventive activity, much of which took in traditional probation 'sidelines' such as work on homelessness or addictive problems. In addition to these issue-focused activities, she identified three other main categories of activity: crime-focused; area-focused; and probation representation on some general forum, such as a Crime Prevention Panel.

Whilst Geraghty found a great deal of activity in her audit, she also found a few points of concern. She writes thus:

> In summary, there is clearly much variation in the nature and extent of probation representation in local crime prevention initiatives. There are differences in commitment and understanding of the service's role and potential that suggest the need for an identified policy, strategy and system in order to promote consistent and high quality practice that is closely linked to service objectives. What is also revealed, however, is the need for guidance on, for example, level of representation, time commitment, use of information, and training. (Geraghty, 1991: 13)

She particularly highlights the differential levels of commitment of headquarters staff and main grade officers, the latter being noticeably less committed to crime prevention. Further, she notes a lack of clarity about the specific purpose of crime preventive activity; the lack of attention paid to implementation and impact evaluation; and the potential marginalisation of crime prevention when pursued as a specialism. This latter point relates to concerns about the whole service's 'ownership' of crime prevention, noted also by Bryant (1989) and Wilson-Croome (1990). We will return to these issues below.

Since 1991, crime prevention within the probation service has tended not to receive such a high profile. This may be partly because the government's rejection of the Morgan Report's (Home Office, 1991) recommendation that local authorities be given the lead responsibility for crime prevention has halted, until recently, further national policy developments beyond the expansion of the Safer Cities Programme to another 20 cities. ACOP had been strongly supportive of the Report (ACOP, 1991). It may also have something to do with the focus of attention switching to the Criminal Justice Act 1991, which by placing the service 'centre-stage' (but see Chapters 7 and 8 in this volume for shifts in policy and practice) has obviated the need for crime prevention to be used as a legitimation tool for traditional offender-centred work.

In summary, this section has sought to introduce the reader to the background, development and institutionalisation of crime prevention within the probation service, raising along the way some of the issues with which the service must wrestle. In particular, although little reference has been made to it thus far, it must be remembered that whilst the service can pursue crime prevention by itself, it more frequently does so or attempts to do so, as was pointed out in Chapter 10, in collaboration with other agencies, and the inter-agency dimension has now become an established prerequisite of effective crime prevention. Consequently, many of the issues confronting the service must be addressed and resolved within the constraints imposed by an inter-agency context. The next section seeks to describe what some of these issues and constraints are through a discussion of a single case study of collaborative crime prevention.

Probation and crime prevention: the case of Kirkholt

The purpose of discussing the Kirkholt Project is essentially twofold. First, it raises a number of issues which are pertinent both to the service's resolution of what crime prevention means, and to the difficulties it can encounter when collaborating with other agencies. Secondly, it may be a single case study, but it is a highly influential one, receiving a good deal of publicity, and being the source of many replications, not least the Safer Cities Programme (Tilley, 1993).

The present author researched Kirkholt for 21 months, from January 1988 through to September 1989, employing a qualitative methodology which took in observations of the numerous inter-agency fora linked to the Project, interviews with key participants and documentary analysis. The Project started life in late 1985, and continued through to the 1990s under the stewardship of the probation service in concert with Rochdale Safer Cities.

The Kirkholt Project began as a Home Office-funded burglary prevention demonstration project, which followed the problem-focused methodology already discussed above. The initial idea was that an inter-agency structure would be established, from which a police secondee would devise a package of situational methods of prevention whilst the probation side would work on the social side, 'mopping up' the frustrated motivations of offenders now thwarted by a successful situational strategy, and thereby preventing displacement. University researchers would help with the data collection and, crucially, the evaluation.

As events transpired, however, the social side did not materialise, and instead only the situational measures (the removal of pre-payment fuel meters, the target-hardening of victims' dwellings and the establishment of a massive Neighbourhood Watch scheme) were implemented from March 1987 in what became known as Phase One of the Project. These proved to be phenomenally successful: by 1990 the chances of becoming a burglary victim in one of the 2,280 households on the estate had diminished from 23 per cent to 6 per cent – a fall in annual numbers from 526 to 132.

The early success of the Project encouraged the Home Office to extend funding both to see the continuation of Phase One and to see the probation side develop its social strategies, in what became known as Phase Two, beginning in late 1987. Whilst the concurrent Phase One built upon its early success, however, Phase Two experienced significant problems in getting off the ground, and it was only a short while before the end of the Home Office funding period that its core elements – structured groupwork for Kirkholt offenders and a Schools Project to challenge the 'negative ingenuity' of Kirkholt children – began to take shape. Consequently, the second of two official reports on the Project (Forrester et al., 1988, 1990) contained little more than a description of these measures, and there was no indication as to their crime preventive effectiveness. So, whilst Kirkholt was a politically important success story, from which the probation service derived credit by association, in practice its role was problematic.

The initial difficulty was that the blueprint for the Project was never communicated to the area team: they simply did not know they were supposed to develop a social crime prevention strategy to complement the one put in place by the police. Instead, their Assistant Chief Probation Officer (ACPO) negotiated with the researchers for them to assist in the administration of a burglar survey to run concurrently with victim and victim's neighbour surveys, and to be used as the data on which to base preventive solutions. The ACPO had an alternative agenda, believing that the experience of administering questionnaires would serve to enhance his officers' awareness of the community, thereby improving the quality of their social inquiry reports.

As events transpired, the burglar survey did not proceed as smoothly as the others, which were completed within a few months. The difficulty arose because burglars could only be interviewed after conviction, which often meant a substantial delay awaiting the court process, and sometimes a substantial journey to interview convicted burglars dispersed to prisons around the region. It did not help that the questionnaires took longer to administer than permitted visiting times. Full probation representation at this stage might have anticipated such problems.

The other collaborative partners were ignorant of the reasons for the delay, and, at an inter-agency seminar called for the purpose of discussing research findings and deciding upon a preventive strategy, an insinuation was made that the probation side had not been pulling its weight, and that a possible reason was resistance (when the researchers presented the local area probation team with the questionnaires concern had been expressed about the potential compromising of client confidentiality, and hence such an insinuation appeared to make sense). This had been made in the presence of the Chief Probation Officer (CPO), and subsequent to the seminar changes were made. Two part-time officers were brought in to complete the survey as quickly as possible, and a main grade officer was attached to the Project for a day per week, joining the regular research meetings between researchers and the seconded inspector, and thereby establishing an inter-agency Management Team. However, whilst this improved communications, it was all a bit late: the shape of the crime prevention initiatives had been agreed at the inter-agency seminar; pressures of time meant that the offender survey could play no meaningful part in the shaping of these initiatives, and the service had no significant role to play in them. Consequently, whilst the main grade continued his involvement, he was never clear what he was supposed to be doing – he too was unaware of the original blueprint.

Meanwhile, the Deputy Chief Probation Officer (DCPO) who had been given a special responsibility for overseeing crime prevention developments within the service had noted the limited impact the service had made, and the great potential which remained. Together with one of the researchers, he composed a bid for the continuation of the project, this time with the full secondment of a main grade officer to work on a social strategy. The Home Office approved the bid and Phase Two began, with the same main grade taking on the full secondment. Unfortunately, however, he carried the same sense of uncertainty with him, and he awaited the assistance of the researchers – in much the same way as they had assisted the seconded inspector with Phase One.

Research assistance was slow in coming, and when it arrived it proved to be of less assistance than imagined. The researchers, adopting the same problem-focused methodology and the same requirement for 'hard' data, proved to be highly critical of the seconded main grade's proposals for failing to approximate such requirements. The original burglar survey was rejected for being out of date and not wholly relevant since its sample included burglars other than from Kirkholt. The main grade turned instead to past social inquiry reports (SIRs) of Kirkholt offenders, but these data were rejected as being too 'soft' and impressionistic. Moreover, some of his ideas – such as safe houses for Kirkholt children, or a litter tidy-up campaign using offenders on community service orders (CSOs) – were rejected as having little to do with crime prevention. The seconded main grade, and his senior who also attended Management Team meetings, grew increasingly exasperated, especially following an attempt to seek help from an expert on community probation work, whose ideas were given similar short shrift from the researchers. The project lingered in an impasse for several months.

Meanwhile, the impasse with the Management Team stood in contrast to contemporaneous developments on the estate itself, where the seconded main grade established a Youth Forum in which ideas about crime prevention involving young people took shape. In the absence of researchers, there was no complaint about the lack of hard data backing up proposals, and on the Forum a number of like-minded liberal professionals, from schools and the Youth Service, considered a range of imaginative proposals which might address such problems as drug misuse, vandalism, domestic violence, racial harassment and what was seen by many as the underlying cause, the 'cult of masculinity'. However, they lacked the resources and influence to translate these ideas into action, and eventually settled on the idea of a schools project where children would be involved in a number of activities – notably drama – with a crime prevention theme. The Education Authority provided the resources for this.

The Management Team accepted the legitimacy of this venture, and also the seconded officer's ideas for an estate-based Credit Union and regular weekly advice centre. Acceptance, however, was only a consequence of an effective parting of the ways between researchers and the probation side: the relationship changed from coordination to cooperation – probation became the 'doers', and the researchers the 'evaluators', since they had failed to work more closely together. At the same time, the seconded officer's plans to establish a regular 'Kirkholt Team' of probation officers supervising Kirkholt offenders had to be dropped because, in the course of the impasse, the number of Kirkholt clients had fallen into single figures. Therefore, such a team could not be justified on resource grounds. In its place, a single officer was given the responsibility for taking all Kirkholt clients and, together with a colleague, establishing a groupwork programme exclusively for them, grounded in the particular circumstances of the Kirkholt estate. This idea, however, could not be sustained, because there was a lack of supervised offenders from the estate, and so the groupwork had to be integrated within the area-wide scheme. This demonstrates a tension between resource considerations and the legitimacy afforded to crime prevention work.

That, in essence, was the Kirkholt Project from the perspective of the probation service's involvement. One other point is worth noting. When the seconded main grade began work with the project on a full-time basis, he spent a good deal of his time overseeing the local infrastructure of the Project: regular meetings with various community groups, including Neighbourhood Watch coordinators; meetings with other agencies, notably the local police; and supervision of the Community Programme workers (up to eight), employed to recruit and support the Neighbourhood Watch schemes, and to carry out security surveys for burglary victims. This took up as much of his time as the more substantive elements of Phase Two, when the probation service was supposed to be the lead agency.

Lessons from Kirkholt

Given the impact and importance of the Kirkholt Project on the crime prevention world, the probation contribution seems unimpressive. What, then, can this teach us about the wider probation contribution to crime prevention?

The experience of Kirkholt tells us a good deal about the importance of communications in inter-agency collaboration and also within the probation organisation. As has been argued earlier, the area team were ignorant of the blueprint for its potential involvement. The probation contribution to the burglar survey was wrongly interpreted as resistance because the other collaborative partners had nothing else to go on beside the witnessing of what one participant described as 'a domestic' within the area team when the researchers met with them to discuss the survey. This explanation seemed 'good enough'. Improved communications might also have prevented the problem from arising in the first place, as a probation representative would probably have been able to identify the unrealistic timescale for the survey in view of the practicalities of court delays. In Phase Two communications were better because of a tighter inter-agency structure, but there were still difficulties arising from the physical secondment of the main grade from the probation area team: closer links might have prevented the waste of time incurred by the failed 'Kirkholt Team' idea. There are wider issues regarding secondment which will be returned to below.

A more substantive issue is that of the meaning of crime prevention itself. The term is characterised by definitional elasticity which means that it can be used to serve different sets of interests and value bases. For example, the ACPO defined it – quite legitimately, since there is no absolute definition – in terms of the improved quality of SIRs. The seconded main grade, however, struggled for a clear vision. In the early days, he conceived of himself as an innovator, and this created its own pressure to come up with something new and distinctive – in other words, something which was not tertiary prevention (traditional offender-focused work). Only later did he begin to realise that such work could legitimately be called 'crime prevention'.

There were also disputes with the researchers and Home Office officials over what was to be regarded as legitimate crime prevention. The seconded officer took up a position similar to community probation, looking for things which might improve the cohesiveness of the local community, thereby stimulating local informal social controls and preventing crime. The problem with such a vision is that it can sometimes appear only tangentially related to crime: how, for example, does a litter tidy-up campaign prevent burglary? It might do, in a long-drawn-out process, but it lacks the conceptual immediacy of fixing stronger locks to doors and windows – something which is far more attractive under the paradigm of short-termism which currently drives much public policy.

The Schools Project is equally vague here, although it has rather more common-sense appeal insofar as all children are expected to be taught what law-abiding behaviour is. The fact, however, is that situational crime prevention makes much better sense, because it can be visualised, it is already a 'proven' success, and because it is seen to protect the potential victim.

This latter issue points to the existence of a politics of crime prevention – certain forms are more influential than others because they have a greater resonance with dominant ideas of common sense, and with political trends, where the victim is considered much more deserving than the 'wicked' offender. If one places this politics within a collaborative framework, then, depending on the agency constitution of that framework, it is quite plausible that social crime prevention of this sort will find itself at a disadvantage. Evidently this did not happen in the contrasting case of the Youth Forum because of the ideological congruence of its constituent members.

A related issue concerns evaluation: the problem-oriented methodology of crime prevention projects requires a tight specification of what the problem is, so that the effect of the crime prevention initiatives can be measured using pre-test/post-test readings of the problem. But motivation-tackling initiatives cannot match this ideal, because they will always be based on vague impressions rather than hard data: if we do not know the offenders, we must guess why they might commit crimes; and if we know them, we can never prove we are right – you cannot see a motivation as you can an exploited opportunity. This aspect of evaluation helps to constitute what is regarded as 'real' crime prevention – a reality which is socially constructed around the contemporarily dominant and complementary discourses of rational managerialism and rational choice criminology (Cornish and Clarke, 1986). This was perhaps the major issue for Kirkholt, where, ultimately, the seconded officer could not provide any hard data to back up his ideas, relying instead on the notion that his ideas sought to improve the quality of life of the estate. This is a fundamental problem given that one of the values of social work is the enhancement of the quality of life of individuals, families and groups within the community (CCETSW, 1991: para. 2.2.1; see also CCETSW, 1995).

Paragraph 2.2.1 of CCETSW Paper 30 (1991) highlights the importance of anti-discrimination, and yet this sort of crime prevention raises another dilemma here. In Kirkholt, ideas about tackling racial harassment and domestic violence were dismissed by the police on the basis that they were not statistically significant problems on the estate, despite anecdotal evidence to the contrary. In this case, the statistics are discriminatory since they overlook chronically underreported crime problems, but the problem-oriented methodology as currently construed clearly dismisses them, and as such has serious limitations.

There are two further difficulties with crime prevention projects worth noting at this stage. First, they tend to be short term, whereas permanent agencies by their nature have a longer-term vision. On Kirkholt, this is a reason why the probation side lacked the sense of urgency displayed by its researcher partners: again, we can therefore conceive of another potential source of conflict in inter-agency fora. Where these concern 'projects' rather than long-term programmes, there is a pressure to select situational methods of prevention which are more likely to show short-term results.

Secondly, we must be mindful of the costs of secondments to inter-agency products. If they are full-time, as with Kirkholt, there is an obvious danger of marginalisation from the parent organisation. This may be personally uncomfortable, but, perhaps of greater significance, it can deprive the secondee of a sounding board and a reminder of his or her occupational roots and value base. At times the present author witnessed the seconded main grade losing sight of this, risking the compromising of client confidentiality and an over-identification with other agencies – going native, in effect. A further weakness of secondments is that individuals risk blame for when things go wrong, when the causes of both successes and failures generally have more to do with barriers and opportunities beyond their direct control. On Kirkholt, the seconded main grade was frequently unfairly and unfavourably compared with the seconded police inspector, who seemed, on the face of it, much more skilled at putting together a crime prevention package.

Finally, we return to a more straightforward, but no less important point. In Kirkholt the issue of inter-agency management responsibility was overlooked: who had responsibility for the local project infrastructure? As events transpired, the seconded main grade took on this role, but the cost was high insofar as he was less able to devote time to the more important aspects of his role – by his own admission, he found too many little things getting in his way. Ironically, this helped keep the momentum of Phase One's success, whilst simultaneously helping to confine Phase Two to ignominy. Such managerial issues, it seems, are simply overlooked by agencies which remain steadfastly within 'intra-agency mode'. This strengthens the case for having specially appointed independent project coordinators, something the Safer Cities Programme has done, although questions about managerial authority are not necessarily resolved, and might usefully be answered by further research in this area.

Conclusions: Beyond Kirkholt

Some of the difficulties encountered on Kirkholt were no doubt peculiar to that site, but others have a wider applicability and are of a nature which makes it difficult to establish clear pointers to good practice. The focus of this book is mainly on practice-related issues, contexts and outcomes, but, as we have pointed out throughout, the probation experience of crime prevention is as much political and crime prevention still presents the service with substantial problems.

In the collaborative arenas of crime prevention projects, social crime prevention finds itself at a disadvantage, although the extent of the disadvantage depends upon the constitution of the projects (meaning both the agencies involved and the form of collaboration) and the extent to which they follow a strict problem-oriented methodology. Situational crime prevention tends to predominate, and with displacement not proving to be the Achilles' heel once predicted, one must question whether there is a need for social crime prevention as currently construed: as both Kirkholt and the first half of this chapter show, the service remains far from clear about what its crime preventive role should be.

There seems a belief, partly driven by the requirements specified in SNOP, that crime prevention should mean something different from tertiary prevention – something which Geraghty (1991) excluded altogether from her audit. But, in its place, primary and secondary prevention are both spurious grounds for probation involvement. They are vague and nebulous and not based on hard data – though these have their own limitations – thereby making it unclear precisely how they are to contribute to the ultimate goal, the reduction of crime. The quality of life is undoubtedly an important value, but it is not a performance indicator or a sharp measure of effectiveness. This is not the only objection.

Primary and secondary crime prevention seek to tackle the social problems which are alleged to form criminal motivations, but they are focused on groups who are not known offenders, nor ever may be. Surely this is not a sound base on which to build probation practice. Its origins lie in community probation and traditional 'sidelines' such as work with homeless people, each of which has serious limitations when brought on to the crime prevention playing field, where, like carpet-bombing, they too often miss their target. More importantly, these areas more appropriately belong in the social policy domain, where they can be justified primarily in terms of social justice, not criminal justice. They certainly have a causal link with crime, but to emphasise this above all else is to risk undermining the rationale for social intervention when, in the hard-nosed reality of crime prevention projects, they may be ineffective. The fact that the probation service has become more engaged in social policy bears testimony to the current deficiencies of the welfare state and the positive social justice values of the service (see Vass, 1996), but it is ultimately an inappropriate role. Moreover, the lack of evaluation of these measures, already documented above, is understandable given that it is unclear what to evaluate (and how to do it), but it demonstrates further that there is as yet no strong case for them in the current construction of crime prevention.

This brings us to the matter of appropriate skills. Trained in social work, probation officers may well be equipped for what in the cases of primary and secondary prevention are effectively community work, but we need to ask whether this is making the best use of their talents, for there are other agencies capable of performing such a task. The core skills of probation officers lie in work with offenders, and it is here that their effectiveness is ultimately tested in terms of reconviction rates. The case for offender-focused crime prevention remains strong, and the Kirkholt model of structured groupwork, based on a close understanding of the crimogenic profile of the neighbourhood, and the neighbourhood organisation of probation work in high crime areas, is a good one. If this works, what better example of crime preventive success could there be, and what better rationale for probation work? The service should not run scared of working with offenders, as it currently seems to be doing in crime prevention, in part courtesy of SNOP's misleading approach.

Moreover, whilst offender-centred work should be the mainstay of the service's crime preventive role, there are two other contributions it could make. First, rather than conduct primary and secondary crime prevention itself, it should pass on its wealth of knowledge about offending motivations to other social agencies, who could take it into account when devising social policies, where crime levels correlate with other social indicators. Secondly, and more controversially, it should pass on its knowledge of offending techniques to agencies engaged in situational crime prevention. These data can be aggregated and made anonymous to protect client confidentiality. Furthermore, since crime is partly opportunistic, it is in no way inconsistent with the value of helping offenders not only to explore how opportunities are taken (and therefore to discuss how they may be avoided), but also to contribute to initiatives which seek to reduce them. At the same time, this approximates the wider notion of client that the service is being encouraged to adopt, for the assistance to society and to the victim is more tangible in this form.

In conclusion, although crime prevention remains the focus of probation work and, given the social-political context, it ought to remain so, there are serious concerns about the ability of probation officers to prevent crime. As the probation service may not be the correct agency to engage in crime prevention schemes for the reasons given earlier, this engagement may lead the service down a pathway which can only enhance its insecurity in the long term, once questions of effectiveness are seriously addressed. It is better to take a realistic appraisal of the disadvantaged position the service frequently encounters in collaboration, and to establish principles and working practices which counter this whilst staying truer to core values and purposes. The alternative may look good for political and public relations, but it is not one which secures the long-term interests of the service.

References

ACOP (1985) *ACOP Response to Safer Communities*. Wakefield, North Yorkshire: Association of Chief Officers of Probation.

ACOP (1991) *Crime Control: The Community and the Probation Service – Future Directions*. Wakefield, North Yorkshire: Association of Chief Officers of Probation.

Bottoms, A.E. and McWilliams, W. (1979) 'A non-treatment paradigm for probation practice', *British Journal of Social Work*, 9 (2): 159–202.

Brody, S. (1976) *The Effectiveness of Sentencing*. London: HMSO.

Bryant, M. (1989) *The Contribution of ACOP and Probation Services to Crime Prevention*. Wakefield, North Yorkshire: Association of Chief Officers of Probation.

CCETSW (1991) *DipSW: Rules and Requirements for the Diploma in Social Work*. Paper 30 (2nd edn). London: Central Council for Education and Training in Social Work.

CCETSW (1995) *DipSW: Rules and Requirements for the Diploma in Social Work*. Paper 30 (rev. edn). Central Council for Education and Training in Social Work.

CCPC (1987) *Crime Prevention: A Role for Probation Committees.* London: Central Council of Probation Committees.

Clarke, R. and Hough, J. (eds) (1980) *The Effectiveness of Policing.* Farnborough: Gower.

Clarke, R. and Mayhew, P. (eds) (1980) *Designing Out Crime.* London: HMSO.

Cornish, D. and Clarke, R. (1986) *The Reasoning Criminal.* New York: Springer-Verlag.

Fielding, N. (1984) *Probation Practice: Client Support under Social Control.* Aldershot: Gower.

Forrester, D., Chatterton, M. and Pease, K. (1988) *The Kirkholt Burglary Prevention Project.* London: Home Office Crime Prevention Unit.

Forrester, D., Frenz, S., O'Connell, M. and Pease, K. (1990) *The Kirkholt Burglary Prevention Project: Phase II.* London: Home Office Crime Prevention Unit.

Geraghty, J. (1991) *Probation Practice in Crime Prevention.* Crime Prevention Unit Paper 24. London: Home Office Crime Prevention Unit.

Gladstone, F. (1980) *Coordinating Crime Prevention Efforts.* London: HMSO.

GLC (1986) *Policing London: Collected Reports.* London: Greater London Council.

Harding, J. (ed.) (1987) *Probation and the Community.* London: Tavistock.

Henderson, P. (1986) *Community Work and the Probation Service.* London: National Institute of Social Work.

Home Office (1977) *Review of Criminal Justice Policy 1976.* London: HMSO.

Home Office (1984) *Probation Service in England and Wales: Statement of National Objectives and Priorities.* London: Home Office.

Home Office (1988) *The Five Towns Initiative.* London: Home Office Crime Prevention Unit.

Home Office (1991) *Safer Communities* (The Morgan Report). London: Home Office.

Home Office Crime Prevention Unit (1985) *Crime Prevention and the Community Programme.* London: Home Office Crime Prevention Unit.

Hope, T. and Murphy, D. (1983) 'Problems of implementing crime prevention', *Howard Journal of Criminal Justice*, 22: 38–50.

Hough, J. and Mayhew, P. (1984) *The British Crime Survey. First Report.* London: HMSO.

Laycock, G. and Pease, K. (1985) 'Crime prevention within the probation service', *Probation Journal*, 32: 43–7.

Lloyd, C. (1986) *Response to SNOP.* Cambridge: Institute of Criminology.

NAPO (1984) *Draft Policy Statement: Crime Prevention and Reduction Strategies.* London: National Association of Probation Officers.

Pitts, J. (1988) *The Politics of Juvenile Crime.* London: Sage.

Stern, V. (1987) 'Crime prevention: the inter-organisational approach', in J. Harding (ed.), *Probation and the Community.* London: Tavistock. pp. 209–25.

Tilley, N. (1993) *After Kirkholt: Theory, Method and Results of Replication Evaluations.* London: Home Office Crime Prevention Unit.

Vass, A.A. (1996) 'Crime, probation and social work with offenders', in A.A. Vass (ed.), *Social Work Competences: Core Knowledge, Values and Skills.* London: Sage. pp. 132–89.

Wilson-Croome, L. (1990) *Report to the Working Group on Partnership in Crime Prevention.* Wakefield, North Yorkshire: Association of Chief Officers of Probation.

12

Evaluating Probation: The Rehabilitation of Effectiveness

Peter Raynor

In the preceding chapters we have referred, on many occasions, to matters of rehabilitation, punishment and effectiveness. For example Chapter 8 on community penalties and Chapters 10 and 11 on partnerships and crime prevention have discussed the debates, the problems and successes or failures of those policies and practices. In this chapter we conclude by taking a fresh look at the issue of outcomes, and by reconsidering the 'rehabilitation of effectiveness'.

Ten years ago, observers of the probation scene could not be blamed for arguing that supervision in the community had to be justified by its greater humanity or economy compared with imprisonment, rather than by its greater effectiveness in reducing future offending. The consensus of weighty authorities was that different sentences did not result in different levels of recidivism. Several decades of searching for scientific 'treatments' which would reduce offending had finally come to grief in highly publicised research reviews: in the United States Martinson had announced that 'nothing works' (Martinson, 1974), and this simple but overstated conclusion stuck in the minds of those without time or reason to look at the more measured and ambiguous findings of the research from which it sprang (Lipton et al., 1975). Martinson's (1974: 49) comment that 'we have very little reason to hope that we have in fact found a sure way of reducing recidivism through rehabilitation' was echoed by a Home Office research review in Britain: 'Any assumption that different sentences, institutions or "treatments" are affecting offenders in significantly different ways needs to be carefully reappraised' (Brody, 1976: 66).

Attempts to measure the effectiveness of social casework and counselling services had been conveying a similar message for some time: widely read studies such as the Cambridge Somerville Youth Study (Powers and Witmer, 1951) and the 'Vocational High' school-based experiment (Meyer et al., 1965) showed no readily identifiable beneficial results for those who received social work attention when compared to those who did not, and an influential research review by Fischer (1976: 140) argued that 'the bulk of practitioners in an entire profession appear, at worst, to be practising in ways that are not helpful or even detrimental to their clients, and, at best, operating without a shred of empirical evidence validating their efforts'. The Home Office Research Unit had meanwhile carried out a number of studies of probation, often setting high standards of design and quantification, such as Davies (1974); these efforts culminated in the IMPACT study, a carefully controlled experiment to ascertain whether more probation input on lower caseloads would lead to lower reoffending, with generally discouraging results (Folkard et al., 1976). Two years later the Director of Research in the Home Office summed up the official consensus:

> Penal 'treatments', as we significantly describe them, do not have any reformative effect. . . . The dilemma is that a considerable investment has been made in various measures and services. . . . Are these services simply to be abandoned on the basis of the accumulated research evidence? Will this challenge evoke a response . . . by the invention of new services and new methods? (Croft, 1978: 4)

Understandably, perhaps, the Home Office researchers had by this time virtually abandoned the topic of probation's effectiveness, and left the search for 'new services and new methods' largely to others until the late 1980s.

Reactions to this situation at the levels of theory, policy and practice were diverse and complex, involving both a shift in goals and a rather selective approach to available evidence. For the probation service itself, this was paradoxically a period of steady expansion both in resources and in the range of tasks undertaken. Many practitioners remained consistently optimistic, committed and creative in their approach, and continued to believe in their own effectiveness; but to the extent that morale was maintained by indifference to research or by a belief that it was irrelevant to the 'real world' of practice, this may have contributed to a practice culture in the probation service which is based more on shared values or beliefs than on an empirical approach to the results of practice. A healthy scepticism about negative research findings may sometimes be a practical necessity, but if this becomes a hostility to empirical appraisal and a lack of curiosity about outcomes, or leads to a preference for a purely subjective or intuitive approach to practice, there is a danger of stagnation and it becomes difficult to develop well-founded models of good practice.

At a policy level, the most obvious trend in the late 1970s and early 1980s was a shift from the goal of rehabilitating offenders towards the provision of alternatives to custody. The community service experiments of the mid-1970s were evaluated by the Home Office primarily in relation to their effectiveness in avoiding custodial sentences, and the decision to make them available to all courts was taken before their impact on further offending had been fully assessed (Pease and McWilliams, 1980; Vanstone and Raynor, 1981). Work with juvenile offenders came to be informed primarily by principles of diversion, aiming to do less harm rather than to effect positive changes in behaviour (Thorpe et al., 1980), and the government's first attempt to spell out national objectives and priorities for probation services was clearly aimed at reductions in imprisonment through persuading sentencers to use more community-based supervision (Home Office, 1984). Home Office performance indicators for probation services came to include indirect measures of diversion from custody and the use of probation for 'low-tariff' offenders not at risk of a custodial sentence was discouraged.

At the level of theory, the most striking development of this period was the 'non-treatment paradigm', as expounded by Bottoms and McWilliams (1979). In their influential paper the ineffectiveness of 'treatment' was transformed from a crippling disadvantage into the basis for a rational and humane practice: supervision in the community, the authors argued, should be developed as an alternative to the waste, expense and equal ineffectiveness of imprisonment, and used as a vehicle for help. Unlike 'treatment', which saw offenders as objects of manipulation, 'help' was the outcome of negotiation and agreement in a spirit of 'respect for persons' which recognised offenders as people and as morally responsible. These arguments fitted well with other writers' advocacy of a humanistic and non-manipulative model of practice (for example, Harris, 1985; Raynor, 1978, 1985; Vass, 1982); they also provided a rationale for the development of practice which did not depend on specifying effective methods, and could be readily enlisted in support of the strategy of alternatives to custody. But these undoubtedly positive developments carried one disadvantage with them: by developing a strategy which did not depend on risky claims about reductions in offending, they continued to marginalise the issue of effectiveness and contributed to a situation in which practice could continue to develop without a routine commitment to its evaluation. The logic of the non-treatment paradigm did not actually depend on the incapacity of supervision to reduce offending, and it has recently been argued that the central principles of the paradigm, which are moral rather than empirical, are not contradicted by improvements in effectiveness (Raynor and Vanstone, 1994a); however, the very attractive idea that the probation service could manage without 'treatment', in combination with the trends in practice and policy already outlined, may have helped to divert attention from the search for effectiveness.

Several practice developments of the 1980s seem, with hindsight, to show this tendency at work. The major success of this period was community service, increasingly popular with sentencers but aiming to deliver punishment and reparation rather than the reduction of recidivism, and responsible for a major expansion, both absolutely and proportionally, of untrained staff within the probation service (Vass, 1988). Probation officer grade staff, with social work training and qualifications, continued to search for appropriate skills and methods to make their supervision of offenders something more than monitoring and control. This was particularly necessary in relation to those offenders who now found themselves under many hours of supervision in day training centres (later day centres), and these were to prove a fertile source of practice innovations, but almost invariably without adequate monitoring of their effects. Reduction of reoffending might still have been a recognised aim, but attempts to assess whether it was being achieved were few and far between. The systematic study of effectiveness was off the probation service's agenda; the main purpose of this chapter is to argue that in the harsher climate of the 1990s effectiveness can and must become a more central concern. Effective rehabilitation cannot be more reliably achieved until the issue of effectiveness itself is rehabilitated as a legitimate professional priority.

Was the news all bad?

One paradox of the retreat from effectiveness was that many promising innovations went untested and unassessed. When new projects depended on the enthusiasm of individual officers who progressed to other specialisms or into management, this often meant that they disappeared. Another paradox was that good news was neglected: the negative consensus was built on highly publicised conclusions rather than on the detail of the studies from which they were drawn. Martinson (1979) himself was later to blame the media for this exaggeration and to withdraw the conclusion that 'nothing works'. In fact, the early effectiveness studies were not uniformly negative, but contained some positive indicators of the directions in which more encouraging results might later be found.

For example, Martinson's own study had found that 'to the degree that casework and individual counselling provided to offenders in the community is directed towards their immediate problems, it may be associated with reductions in recidivism rates' (Lipton et al., 1975). The IMPACT study, despite its negative overall conclusion, also pointed to a sub-group of probationers who were assessed as having low 'criminal tendencies' but a high level of self-reported problems, and who performed better in the experimental (low caseload) group than in the 'normal' caseload control group. Although this successful sub-group was perhaps rather untypical of offenders in general, it did provide some indication that where probation officers' preferred methods happened to suit the offenders' self-identified needs, lower levels of reoffending could result. Two other studies with interesting implications had also been largely ignored by the 'nothing works' bandwagon. The 'Midlands experiment' in two prisons showed that additional welfare officer input into pre-release preparation was associated with lower recidivism than in a comparable group of prisoners who did not receive such input (Shaw, 1974); and a study of probation hostels showed a link between lower offending and absconding and the quality of regimes (Sinclair, 1971). Few implications of these studies were translated into practice, though Shaw's attracted enough attention to stimulate a kind of replication study which, in rather less favourable circumstances, did not produce a positive result (Fowles, 1978). In the latter case, policy-makers were probably relieved that substantial additional spending on welfare officers, which was clearly supported by Shaw's study, was apparently not supported by further research.

Other contributions to social work research were also moving in directions which could have conveyed some encouraging messages to probation officers. Fischer, for instance, despite the generally negative tone of his conclusions, identified three promising directions for development where the evidence suggested at least the probability of effective interventions. He pointed out that research on counselling tended to support approaches based on empathy, concern, 'genuineness' or an open and honest approach, and a concrete and specific approach to problems which are mutually recognized rather than imputed by one-sided diagnosis (Fischer, 1976, 1978; Truax and Carkhuff, 1967). He also pointed to evidence that structured and focused intervention, as advocated in the influential 'task-centred' model (Reid and Epstein, 1972), showed promising results, and that behavioural methods based on learning theory provided another encouraging avenue. An influential British textbook by Davies (1981) pointed to a broadly similar set of promising strategies, including also crisis intervention as a method with some empirical support, but discussion of this book tended to focus on its alleged conservative political stance rather than on its empirical observations. Such findings were in fact quite congruent with the more open and contract-based style of working with offenders which was developing from the 'non-treatment' paradigm. However, the links between research and practice remained tenuous, and few practitioners realised that the style of work which they found consistent with their values could also receive at least guarded support from research.

The incomplete and fragmented nature of connections between probation practice and research in the 1980s is illustrated by one of the most positive practice developments of the decade, namely the adoption by a large number of probation officers of cognitive and behavioural approaches to the learning of social and problem-solving skills. These reached the probation service primarily through the work of Priestley and McGuire, first as an approach to what could broadly be defined as 'life-skills' (Priestley et al., 1978) and later as a set of specific approaches to reducing offending (McGuire and Priestley, 1985). They had a particular market among workers in day centres who needed to devise useful programmes, but also had a wider appeal, and were significantly influenced by research on the effectiveness of the methods used. In an ideal world such methods, selected on the basis of their potential effectiveness, would be systematically tested by provisional implementation and ongoing evaluation; this would close the learning loop, and allow beliefs in potential effectiveness to be confirmed or modified by measurement of the results of implementation. Sadly this rational route was not usually followed, and the widespread use of these methods has produced little evidence about their results.

In these circumstances there is a greater risk of drift away from concentration on those features of a method which contribute to effectiveness. A later survey by Hudson (1988) suggested that in practice probation officers were often using 'social skills' methods in ways which did not meet psychological criteria for effective learning: for example, new skills were not being reinforced by repetition, and programmes were often too short to consolidate the intended learning. Again the potential gains of an empirically based approach to practice were being partly lost through lack of systematic implementation and evaluation. Meanwhile the Home Office Research Unit continued largely to neglect questions of the effectiveness of probation, or to redefine them as issues about diversion from custody. A planned Home Office evaluation of the day training centres was never completed.

Some probation researchers, however, remained interested in the impact of probation on offending or at least on reconviction. Like other researchers on the effectiveness of social work, they began to identify features of the old 'nothing works' studies which limited their usefulness as evidence to guide practice. These often included a failure to identify clearly the aims of a programme, its intended target group or the working methods actually used by practitioners. For example, early studies like Powers and Witmer's (1951) experiment had addressed problems as vaguely defined as 'pre-delinquency', and social work inputs were not defined or controlled even enough to ensure that effective practice by some workers might not be cancelled out, in eventual aggregate results, by other workers' ineffective or damaging practice. Even the later and better-designed IMPACT study had left officers largely to decide for themselves how to use the extra time created by lower caseloads, so that it remained unclear what actual practices were being evaluated. In this it resembled earlier reduced-caseload research such as the 'San Francisco parole experiment' in which lower caseloads produced higher violation rates, because parole officers given little guidance about how to use additional time simply increased the level of surveillance and detected more violations (Adams, 1967).

A similar failure to specify inputs was identified by reviewers of other social work research (Reid and Hanrahan, 1981; Sheldon, 1987). It became clear that studies of probation's effectiveness needed not only a sound design involving 'experimental' and comparison groups of similar offenders, but also a clearer specification of the aims of experimental programmes; of the type of supervision actually provided; and of the intended impact both on offending and on decision-making in local criminal justice systems, and if possible also on problems identified by probationers themselves. In Britain, two local studies of programmes for young adult offenders incorporated a number of these features (Raynor, 1988; Roberts, 1989), and both showed rates of reconviction after involvement in the programme which were significantly lower than those of comparable offenders who received custodial sentences. One (Raynor, 1988) also showed substantial diversion from custody resulting from the programme and signs of a positive impact on offenders' self-reported difficulties.

News from elsewhere: new evidence and new policies

These local studies in Britain attracted some attention through their novelty, but were on a tiny scale compared to efforts in other countries where research resources were more widely distributed and the dogma that 'nothing works' had been less universally accepted. In Canada, for example, psychologically oriented practitioners had continued to develop and test programmes intended to reduce offending. Their approach to identifying and specifying effective programme components produced the influential 'Reasoning and Rehabilitation' programmes based on the use of cognitive and behavioural methods to develop thinking and problem-solving skills (Ross et al., 1988). Other researchers re-examined large numbers of published studies using the new statistical technique of meta-analysis to aggregate and identify common findings about effectiveness (for example, Andrews et al., 1990; Lipsey, 1992). Carefully evaluated experiments with intensive supervision in the United States also produced interesting material, though with mixed findings on effectiveness (for example, Clear et al., 1987; Petersilia, 1990). This kind of material began to come to the attention of practitioners in Britain through McIvor's (1990) wide-ranging research review (undertaken not for the Home Office but for the Scottish Office) and through a series of 'What Works' conferences organised largely by probation services. By the early 1990s effectiveness was clearly back on the British probation agenda after a decade of relative neglect. The amount of effort and interest now devoted to the issue of effectiveness by practitioners as well as researchers marks a dramatic change, and one which is decidedly welcome to those who have observed the uneven progress of the last 20 years.

Partly this reflects considerable changes at the political and policy-making level. Preparations to implement the Criminal Justice Act 1991 were made at a time of rising public concern about levels of crime, and Home Office spokespersons emphasised that the Act's encouragement of community sentences was not simply intended as a strategy to reduce costly imprisonment (already on a downward trend through the late 1980s) but also as a strategy to reduce crime. Unable for political reasons to make explicit links between crime rates and economic factors such as poverty and unemployment (although the evidence exists, see Dickinson, 1993; Farrington et al., 1986; Field, 1990), they made bold claims about the adverse impact of imprisonment ('an expensive way of making bad people worse': Home Office, 1990) and, by implication, about the superior effectiveness of community sentences. Probation services felt a need to address again the impact of supervision on subsequent offending and to develop programmes which could deliver this. Crime reduction as an explicit aim of probation services required a commitment to effectiveness and this had implications for the targeting, content, management and evaluation of supervision programmes, as Chapter 11 in this book cogently argues.

Before attempting to summarise the main strands of emerging evidence about effective programmes, some preliminary observations are necessary. First, the search for effective ways of supervising offenders does not imply that crime has only individual causes, and does not deny the impact of social factors such as deprivation and discrimination, but it recognises that even in adverse circumstances some people offend more than others, and it aims to offer more options for persistent offenders to reduce the negative impact of crime on their own lives as well as other people's. Secondly, it is not simply a search for more effective control; instead it aims to help offenders to be more effectively responsible for their own lives and their own choices about further offending. Psychologically influenced programmes do not imply psychological reductionism if implemented in accordance with established probation service values as part of a wider strategy (see Raynor and Vanstone, 1994a); in particular, critics who emphasise their own commitment to social reform (for example, Neary, 1992) do not explain how this is promoted by an indifference to effectiveness. The evidence deserves an objective appraisal from practitioners, rather than the suspicion it has sometimes encountered: the ingrained scepticism of the 'nothing works' era can be a handicap.

What, then, are currently appearing as the promising directions of development for those in search of effective programmes? The following suggestions are necessarily provisional, like all empirically based generalisations, and they draw on the work of a number of researchers in a number of different areas (particularly Lipsey, 1992; McGuire, 1993; McIvor, 1990; Petersilia, 1990; Raynor, 1988; Raynor et al., 1994; Roberts, 1989). Broadly speaking, the emerging evidence tends to support the following approaches to targeting, programme content and delivery, and management:

Targeting. Programmes should be aimed at and designed for offenders who are high risk in the sense that they are otherwise likely to continue to offend, rather than at low-risk offenders who may gain little from them or be harmed. They should focus on those characteristics or circumstances of offenders which have contributed to their offending, that is, on criminogenic need, not simply on 'offending behaviour'.

Content and delivery. Effective programmes tend to be highly structured, following a logical sequence determined by their learning goals and designed to maximise and reinforce learning; they tend to use a directive working approach, so that expectations are explicit and people know what they are meant to be doing; they are likely to use broadly cognitive-behavioural methods, providing opportunities to learn new thinking and behaviour; and they are delivered in a consistent manner, with procedures to monitor and maintain programme integrity and reduce drift.

Management. Effective programmes require committed and effective management, appropriately trained staff who care about effectiveness, adequate resources for continuity, and are best located in the community. They also benefit from integral and ongoing evaluation with feedback to practitioners.

Whilst some of these characteristics of effective programmes may seem at first sight counter-intuitive in the light of traditional probation practice (for example, the emphasis on programme integrity), the majority appear consistent with many past developments, and particularly with the tradition of offender-centred practice which engages the active participation of probationers themselves in identifying and addressing their own needs and priorities. Clarity and structure in the supervision process and an explicit approach to expectations are also long-standing commitments based on the importance of clear agreements and respect for persons. This kind of convergence between ethical and empirical considerations is welcome and not wholly coincidental, since the ethical commitments of a profession are also products of experience. The prospect that widely shared ideas about good practice might both support and be reinforced by a commitment to effectiveness is encouraging, as it suggests that many officers may find it both fairly easy and congenial to orientate their work towards a greater awareness of results. However, the cultural shift involved for some practitioners and some managers should not be underestimated.

Effectiveness and the culture of curiosity

One example of what can happen when a probation service commits itself to the development of more effective methods is provided by the STOP programme ('Straight Thinking On Probation') in Mid Glamorgan, where an enhanced probation order based on the Canadian 'Reasoning and Rehabilitation' programmes has been implemented on a service-wide basis. The programme itself and the interim results of evaluation have been described elsewhere (Lucas et al., 1992; Raynor and Vanstone, 1992, 1994a, 1994b), but for the purposes of this chapter it is worth briefly reviewing those findings which are particularly relevant to the introduction and consequences of a focus on effectiveness. Similar issues will have arisen in other services which have made a corporate commitment to effectiveness and evaluation (for example, McGuire et al., 1992), but the STOP programme provides one of the clearest examples so far of an attempt to implement effective supervision on the principles outlined in the previous section. One of the first lessons learned was that an innovation of this kind on a service-wide basis needed to be management-led and adequately prepared over a considerable period. The initial planning, training of staff and designing of the evaluation study took about a year, including discussion by senior managers with all teams and inputs from researchers to staff conferences about effective practice and research design. The process was not like launching a project but like modifying the approach of a whole service, and this needed to be reflected in the evaluation design: one of the programme's explicit aims was a change in the working culture of the organisation to place greater emphasis on the issues of quality and effectiveness in practice.

As a result of this initial period of service-wide involvement and preparation, a pluralistic research design was adopted owing something to the ideas of Smith and Cantley (1984). Evaluation was to concern itself not simply with effects on reconviction but also with the implementation process; the views of practitioners and consumers; effects of the programme on attitudes to offending and on other problems identified by consumers; programme integrity; and, because of the need for appropriate comparison groups, the effects on reconviction of other community sentences and custodial sentences. In effect, the researchers would be evaluating not simply a 'project' but a broad slice of the activity of a probation service in a period of rapid change. Now that innovations are not always 'projects' owned by a few enthusiasts but may be part of an organisation's strategy for its own development, this kind of broad and pluralistic evaluative approach is increasingly necessary and contributes to the development of the 'learning organisation' in which services are systematically improved by learning from their results (see, for example, Raynor, 1990).

Readers interested in the detailed results of the study so far are referred to the interim evaluation reports (Lucas et al., 1992; Raynor and Vanstone, 1994b), but a few findings are worth summarising here. Briefly, the study of implementation during the first year showed appropriate targeting, with 133 STOP group members having an average of nine previous convictions and substantial previous custodial experience at an average age of 23, and showing a risk profile comparable to those receiving custodial sentences rather than those receiving other community sentences. Attendance and completion rates were broadly comparable with those recorded nationally for community service (though see some pitfalls in this in Vass, 1984, 1986), and the level of consistency and integrity in delivery of the programme was high. Feedback from consumers who were interviewed after completing the programme was predominantly positive, and in some cases illustrated changes in thinking such as greater awareness of victims or a less impulsive approach to problems. An independent survey of probation staff showed broadly positive (but not credulous) reactions to the programme, with some indications that methods developed in the programme were also being applied in other areas of work; many staff also reported more positive beliefs about the capacity of offenders to change their behaviour and a greater interest in issues of quality and effectiveness. (Some impressionistic confirmation of this last point may be offered by the fact that the trickiest questions about the research have so far been asked by the probation officers involved rather than by academic audiences at conferences.)

The reconviction evidence (Raynor and Vanstone, 1994b) so far covers a 12-month follow-up of those entering the STOP group and the various comparison groups in the first nine months of the experiment. Random allocation to 'experimental' and 'control' groups is not feasible in real-life studies when allocation is in practice carried out by sentencers rather than researchers, but there are other ways of resolving problems of comparability. In this study the actual reconviction rates calculated from Home Office records of standard list offences for each group are being compared with expected rates calculated by using the 'Risk of Reconviction Predictor' developed for the Home Office by Copas (1992). Readers interested in the full figures will find them in the original report, but it is interesting to note here that the predicted and actual 12-month reconviction rate for those sentenced to STOP was 44 per cent, while in the custodial comparison group, with a predicted rate of 43 per cent, the actual reconviction rate within 12 months of release was 49 per cent. A separate analysis of those who actually completed the STOP programme and had therefore been fully exposed to it showed a predicted rate of 42 per cent and an actual rate of 35 per cent. Members of this group also tended to be convicted of less serious offences, and to be sentenced less severely for them. In fact this was the only group in the study to receive no immediate custodial sentences for offences committed during the follow-up period, although three-quarters of STOP group members had served custodial sentences in the past.

These are interesting and broadly encouraging results; for the purposes of this chapter, it is also relevant to note that this kind of study could in principle be carried out by any probation service, since the technology and the methods are generally available. The 'Risk of Reconviction Predictor' seems destined for widespread use in the context of new performance indicators for probation services, and the resulting data will help to inform the new policy commitment to crime reduction in community sentences. On a local level, the Mid Glamorgan probation service now evaluates all programmes as a routine part of the process of development and implementation, and has established a Resource and Development

Unit to encourage and evaluate effective programmes, using research designs derived from the STOP experience. The aim is to develop a 'culture of curiosity' in which questions about effectiveness can be asked and answered, and officers are beginning to propose and implement their own quite sophisticated research designs to test local initiatives. These are perhaps some indications of the kind of change in probation services which can follow from a curiosity about effectiveness, and which can move us on from the individualised, private and intuitively evaluated practice of the 'nothing works' era.

The national context: reclaiming the initiative

Positive developments of this kind, however promising, have to be seen against a background of national criminal justice policy which is distinctly less favourable to probation than it was as recently as three years ago. This change has nothing to do with effectiveness, and everything to do with politics. An unpopular government has resorted to populist law-and-order policies; the positive intentions of the Criminal Justice Act 1991 have been undermined by two further Acts with little attempt at evaluation; and prison numbers are once again rising fast. While probation services begin to address the questions of effectiveness raised by the policy context of the 1991 Act, a changed regime in the Home Office seems to have virtually abandoned the earlier concern for objectivity and evidence in policy-making. Prejudice is presented as common sense, and even prisons for children are seen as effective. Pragmatic Home Office reformists seem to be in retreat before the onslaught of sound-bite politics and ministers' own party-political agendas, and the demand for more centralised, accountable and effective probation services sometimes sits uneasily with an almost wilful misunderstanding of what they are for and what they can do. Perhaps the only encouraging feature of current problems is that they may not last long: a policy of increasing imprisonment is likely to prove unacceptably expensive and dangerous as well as ineffective.

Meanwhile probation practice is regulated by national standards designed to increase consistency and accountability, but lacking a primary focus on effectiveness. In some respects they even contradict well-established research findings: for example, the 'risk principle' (Andrews et al., 1990) clearly indicates that levels of supervision which are appropriate for high-risk offenders are not appropriate for lower levels of risk, yet national standards set the same minimum contact levels for all probationers, regardless of risk assessment. It has been argued (most recently by Raynor et al., 1994) that probation services must have a dual focus: on the one hand, they seek to help offenders to avoid offending; on the other hand, they seek to influence the criminal justice system towards less coercive and more effective responses to the problems caused by offending. In the current climate, this argues for attempts to regain some initiative in the policy arena by articulating the probation service's own contribution to humane and effective criminal justice, and to the policies and methods which might help to achieve this. Ideological manifestos will not be persuasive, but evidence of effectiveness might. A collective effort to initiate, evaluate and publicise effective practice could be very timely, but a few domestic problems need to be resolved on the way.

The first, as has been argued throughout this chapter, concerns the need for a decisive shift towards a practice culture which questions effectiveness in order to increase it. It is one thing to publicise encouraging findings from a few high-profile projects, and quite another to subject the full range of probation activities to the same kind of appraisal. The second and perhaps more serious problem is one which may well arise as evaluation becomes more widespread: namely, the difference between the capacity to deliver some effective practice and the capacity to do so consistently and reliably. This involves not only celebrating good practice but actively identifying and challenging less good practice, and seeking to improve it. When the strategy of the 1991 Act was being developed, the best evidence for the effectiveness of community sentences came from evaluations of projects (such as Raynor, 1988; Roberts, 1989; Vass and Weston, 1990) which were effective, but were not necessarily representative of normal probation practice. The same could be said of STOP. However, the development of the Offender Index has now provided the Home Office with a powerful research tool which allows reconviction rates following all sentences to be compared on a national basis, and such exercises will reflect the impact of average practice rather than of selected projects.

Some early products of this material give cause for concern: for example, probation orders with requirements of attendance at day centres or on special programmes seem on average to have higher reconviction rates than are recorded for offenders with comparable previous convictions subject to other forms of supervision (Home Office, 1993). There are also indications from other index-based studies (such as Copas, 1992; see also Chapter 8 in this volume) that we cannot be altogether confident that community sentences routinely perform significantly better than imprisonment. A strategy of promoting effective community sentences requires the effectiveness to be demonstrated rather than simply claimed; the evidence so far shows that probation practice can be significantly effective in reducing offending, not that it routinely achieves this. Applying the lessons of effectiveness research requires the capacity and the will to apply its findings in a general strategy of improvement, and it is to be hoped that probation services will move into this next stage with the same enthusiasm they have shown in re-entering the effectiveness debate.

References

Adams, S. (1967) 'Some findings from correctional caseload research', *Federal Probation*, 31 (4): 48–57.

Andrews, D.A., Zinger, I., Hoge, R.D., Bonta, J., Gendreau, P. and Cullen, F.T. (1990) 'Does correctional treatment work? A clinically relevant and psychologically informed meta-analysis', *Criminology*, 28 (3): 369–404.

Bottoms, A.E. and McWilliams, W. (1979) 'A non-treatment paradigm for probation practice', *British Journal of Social Work*, 9 (2): 159–202.

Brody, S.R. (1976) *The Effectiveness of Sentencing*. London: HMSO.

Clear, T.R., Flynn, S. and Shapiro, C. (1987) 'Intensive supervision in probation: a comparison of three projects', in B.R. McCarthy (ed.), *Intermediate Punishment*. Monsey: Criminal Justice Press. pp. 31–50.

Copas, J.B. (1992) *Statistical Analysis for a National Risk of Reconviction Predictor*. Report to the Home Office. Warwick: University of Warwick.

Croft, J. (1978) *Research in Criminal Justice*. London: HMSO.

Davies, M. (1974) *Social Work in the Environment*. London: HMSO.

Davies, M. (1981) *The Essential Social Worker*. London: Heinemann.

Dickinson, D. (1993) *Crime and Unemployment*. Cambridge: Department of Applied Economics.

Farrington, D.P., Gallagher, B., Morley, L., St Ledger, R.J. and West, D.J. (1986) 'Unemployment, school leaving and crime', *British Journal of Criminology*, 26 (4): 335–6.

Field, S. (1990) *Trends in Crime and Their Interpretation*. London: HMSO.

Fischer, J. (1976) *The Effectiveness of Social Casework*. Springfield, IL: C.C. Thomas.

Fischer, J. (1978) *Effective Casework Practice*. New York: McGraw-Hill.

Folkard, M.S., Smith, D.E. and Smith, D.D. (1976) *IMPACT. Vol. II: The Results of the Experiment*. London: HMSO.

Fowles, A.J. (1978) *Prison Welfare*. London: HMSO.

Harris, R. (1985) 'Towards just welfare', *British Journal of Criminology*, 25 (1): 31–45.

Home Office (1984) *Probation Service in England and Wales: Statement of National Objectives and Priorities*. London: Home Office.

Home Office (1990) *Crime, Justice and Protecting the Public. The Government's Proposals for Legislation*. Cmnd 965. London: HMSO.

Home Office (1993) *Reconviction of Those Given Probation and Community Service Orders in 1987* (Statistical Bulletin 18/93). London: Home Office.

Hudson, B. (1988) 'Social skills training in practice', *Probation Journal*, 35 (3): 85–91.

Lipsey, M. (1992) 'Juvenile delinquency treatment: a meta-analytic enquiry into the variability of effects', in T. Cook, H. Cooper, D. Cordray, H. Hartmann, L.

Hedges, R. Light, T. Louis and F. Mosteller (eds), *Meta-analysis for Explanation: A Case-Book*. New York: Russell Sage. pp. 83–127.

Lipton, D., Martinson, R. and Wilks, J. (1975) *The Effectiveness of Correctional Treatment*. New York: Praeger.

Lucas, J., Raynor, P. and Vanstone, M. (1992) *Straight Thinking on Probation One Year On*. Mid Glamorgan Probation Service.

McGuire, J. (1993) 'What works: the evidence'. Paper presented to probation service conference on 'What Works: The Challenge for Managers', Loughborough, October.

McGuire, J. and Priestley, P. (1985) *Offending Behaviour: Skills and Stratagems for Going Straight*. London: Batsford.

McGuire, J., Broomfield, D., Robinson, C. and Rowson, B. (1992) *Probation Evaluation Project*. Department of Clinical Psychology, University of Liverpool.

McIvor, G. (1990) *Sanctions for Serious or Persistent Offenders*. Stirling: University of Stirling Social Work Research Centre.

Martinson, R. (1974) 'What works?', *The Public Interest*, March: 22–54.

Martinson, R. (1979) 'New findings, new views: a note of caution regarding sentencing reform', *Hofstra Law Review*, 7: 243–58.

Meyer, H.J., Borgatta, E.F. and Jones, W.C. (1965) *Girls at Vocational High*. New York: Russell Sage.

Neary, M. (1992) 'Some academic freedom', *Probation Journal*, 39 (4): 200–2.

Pease, K. and McWilliams, W. (1980) *Community Service by Order*. Edinburgh: Scottish Academic Press.

Petersilia, J. (1990) 'Conditions that permit intensive supervision programs to survive', *Crime and Delinquency*, 36: 126–45.

Powers, E. and Witmer, H. (1951) *An Experiment in the Treatment of Delinquency*. New York: Columbia University Press.

Priestley, P., McGuire, J., Flegg, D., Hemsley, V. and Welham, D. (1978) *Social Skills and Personal Problem-Solving*. London: Tavistock.

Raynor, P. (1978) 'Compulsory persuasion', *British Journal of Social Work*, 8 (4): 411–24.

Raynor, P. (1985) *Social Work, Justice and Control*. Oxford: Blackwell.

Raynor, P. (1988) *Probation as an Alternative to Custody*. Aldershot: Avebury.

Raynor, P. (1990) 'Measuring effectiveness in a principled probation service', in E. Sainsbury and R. Waters (eds), *Assessing the Effectiveness of Probation Practice* (Proceedings of the 1988 Probation Research and Information Exchange). Sheffield: University of Sheffield. pp. 11–16.

Raynor, P. and Vanstone, M. (1992) 'STOP start', *Social Work Today*, 16 February: 26–7.

Raynor, P. and Vanstone, M. (1994a) 'Probation practice, effectiveness and the non-treatment paradigm', *British Journal of Social Work*, 24 (4): 387–404.

Raynor, P. and Vanstone, M. (1994b) *Straight Thinking on Probation: Third Interim Evaluation Report: Reconvictions within 12 Months*. Bridgend: Mid Glamorgan Probation Service.

Raynor, P., Smith, D. and Vanstone, M. (1994) *Effective Probation Practice*. BASW Social Work Series. Basingstoke: Macmillan.

Reid, W.J. and Epstein, L. (1972) *Task-Centred Casework*. New York: Columbia University Press.

Reid, W.J. and Hanrahan, P. (1981) 'The effectiveness of social work: recent evidence', in E.M. Goldberg and N. Connolly (eds), *Evaluation Research in Social Care*. London: Heinemann. pp. 9–20.

Roberts, C.H. (1989) *Hereford and Worcester Probation Service Young Offender Project: First Evaluation Report*. Oxford: Department of Social and Administrative Studies.

Ross, R.R., Fabiano, E.A. and Ewles, C.D. (1988) 'Reasoning and rehabilitation', *International Journal of Offender Therapy and Comparative Criminology*, 32 (1): 29–35.

Shaw, M. (1974) *Social Work in Prison*. London: HMSO.

Sheldon, B. (1987) 'Implementing findings from social work effectiveness research', *British Journal of Social Work*, 17 (6): 573–86.

Sinclair, I. (1971) *Hostels for Probationers*. London: HMSO.

Smith, G. and Cantley, C. (1984) 'Pluralistic evaluation', in J. Lishman (ed.), *Evaluation*. Aberdeen: University of Aberdeen. pp. 140–62.

Thorpe, D.H., Smith, D., Green, C.J. and Paley, J. (1980) *Out of Care*. London: Allen and Unwin.

Truax, C. and Carkhuff, R.R. (1967) *Toward Effective Counselling and Psychotherapy*. Chicago: Aldine.

Vanstone, M. and Raynor, P. (1981) 'Diversion from prison: a partial success and a missed opportunity', *Probation Journal*, 28 (3): 85–9.

Vass, A.A. (1982) 'The probation service in a state of turmoil', *Justice of the Peace*, 146: 788–93.

Vass, A.A. (1984) *Sentenced to Labour: Close Encounters with a Prison Substitute*. St Ives: Venus Academica.

Vass, A.A. (1986) 'Community service: areas of concern and suggestions for change', *Howard Journal of Criminal Justice*. 25: 100-11.

Vass, A.A. (1988) 'The marginality of community service and the threat of privatisation', *Probation Journal*, 35: 48–51.

Vass, A.A. and Weston, A. (1990) 'Probation day centres as an alternative to custody: a "Trojan horse" examined', *British Journal of Criminology*, 30: 189–206.

Index